*Essential management accounting*

# *Essential Management Accounting*

Second Edition

M.W. Allen
D.R. Myddelton
*Cranfield School of Management*

**PRENTICE HALL**

NEW YORK   LONDON   TORONTO   SYDNEY   TOKYO   SINGAPORE

First published 1992 by
Prentice Hall Europe
Campus 400, Maylands Avenue, Hemel Hempstead
Hertfordshire HP2 7EZ
A division of
Simon & Schuster International Group

© Prentice Hall Europe, 1992

Text design by Sue Clarke

Typeset in 10/12 pt Palacio
by MHL Typesetting Ltd, Coventry

**Printed and bound in Great Britain by**
Redwood Books, Trowbridge, Wiltshire

British Library Cataloguing in Publication Data

Allen, M.W.
  Essential management accounting. — 2nd ed.
  I. Title  II. Myddelton, D.R.
  658.15

  ISBN 0-13-284647-0

7  8  9  10    00  99  98  97

# Contents

# Preface

This book aims to meet the essential needs of students of management by covering the key areas in management accounting in suitable depth, while keeping in mind the time constraints of busy students.

The book is mainly for students on full-time and part-time MBA programmes, and on other business management courses. It explains what management accounting can and cannot do. Business managers at large may also find the book helpful: it should enable them to make better use in their own organization of management accounting information, and indeed of management accountants.

In this second edition we have made a number of changes to reflect comments from users of the first edition. We have revised the entire text, and, as before, we have made a special effort to write clearly. Significant changes in contents include the following:

- Chapter 1 now contains a summary of financial accounting, which should make it easier to use the book as a stand-alone text on short courses.
- We have substantially extended the capital investment material in Chapter 7 to cover the payback and average accounting rate-of-return appraisal methods, and to deal with the main aspects of taxation, inflation, and working capital in the context of discounted cash-flow methods.
- There is a new chapter on the presentation and communication of management accounting reports (Chapter 10) that aims to provoke thinking about improving user understanding of such reports.
- Other new topics in this edition include: activity-based costing, joint costs, agency theory, and economies of scale; and we have included more on opportunity costs, pricing, learning curves, and international transactions.

To make way for the above additions, we have dropped the chapter on microcomputers, and we have switched some material to more suitable chapters. Chapters 5, 6, 7, and 8 in the old edition have become chapters 6 and 7, 8, 9, and 5 respectively in this new edition.

Most of the chapters include one or two problems for readers to work through as they read the text. We hope that students will find the interactive nature of the book an improvement over passive reading.

Each chapter contains a summary at the end, together with about fifteen review questions and answers. Some students may find that reading these first helps them to understand the scope of the chapter content. Others may prefer to use the chapter summaries and review questions to consolidate their knowledge after they have first read the text. For maximum benefit we do recommend writing out answers to the review questions before looking at the answers.

Chapters 2 to 9 each also contain about half a dozen quantitative problems at the end, more than half of which are new to this edition. We provide answers to the first two problems in each chapter, to enable the reader to self-test understanding. For instructors there is an Instructors' Manual which suggests how to use this book as an integral part of an MBA Management Accounting course. The Instructors' Manual also contains answers for those problems where the book itself does not provide them. These problems may be suitable for setting as separate assignments.

The glossary defines more than two hundred common words or phrases in management accounting. We strongly recommend readers to consult the glossary whenever they come across an expression they are not sure they fully understand.

We would like to thank everyone who has offered helpful comments on the first edition of this book, including our academic colleagues, recent students on full-time and part-time MBA programmes at Cranfield, and a number of constructively critical academic reviewers of the first edition. We have tried to take account of many of their suggestions. Finally, we are most grateful to our secretaries Sheila Hart and Aileen Treacy for working so hard and effectively in preparing this second edition.

M.W. Allen
D.R. Myddelton
*Cranfield 1992*

# *Accounting, planning and control*

## 1.1 **Financial accounting**

### 1.1.1 **Introduction**

Financial accounting classifies and records an entity's transactions, normally in money terms, in accordance with established concepts, principles, accounting standards and legal requirements. The profit and loss account, covering a period of time, and balance sheet at the end of the period aim to present a true and fair view of the overall results of those transactions. A company which has subsidiaries also prepares group accounts. The company's auditors report to shareholders on these financial statements. As Figure 1.1 shows, companies use financial accounts to inform many actual and potential outsider users.

Membership of the EC has influenced UK accounting practice in recent years. EC directives have required changes to company law, including rules on format and wording. These changes are now contained in the 1985 Companies Act, as amended by the 1989 Companies Act. Company accounts must also conform with financial reporting standards which are based upon generally accepted accounting practices. In the United Kingdom, twenty-two Statements of Standard Accounting Practice (SSAPs) are currently in force as at 31 July 1991 (see Appendix A, p. 223).

### 1.1.2 **Balance sheet**

The **balance sheet** shows a firm's financial position as at the end of an accounting period. It classifies items between the following:

- Assets owned     (= *uses* of funds).
- Liabilities     (= *sources* of funds which a business controls).

Table 1.1 sets out a simple example of a balance sheet. Note that it deducts current liabilities from current assets, to show a sub-total for **working capital** (or **net current assets**).

An **asset** is a valuable resource controlled by a business, normally stated at original cost.

**Fixed assets** are long-term resources of a business, used to provide goods or services, rather than to be sold in the normal course of business. They include land, buildings, machinery, vehicles and equipment. Fixed assets are normally stated at original cost less cumulative depreciation

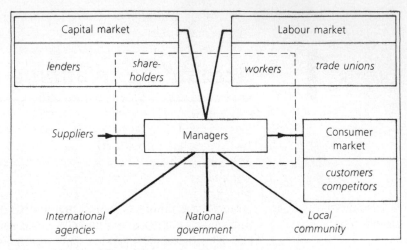

Figure 1.1 *Users of financial accounts*

Table 1.1 *Balance sheet for Simpson Engineering Ltd as at 31 March 1992*

|  | £'000 | £'000 |
|---|---|---|
| *Uses of funds* |  |  |
| *Fixed assets* |  | 850 |
| *Current assets* |  |  |
| Stocks | 451 |  |
| Debtors | 404 |  |
| Cash | 152 |  |
|  | 1 007 |  |
| Less: *Current liabilities* | 357 |  |
| = working capital |  | 650 |
| Net assets (= total assets less current liabilities) |  | 1 500 |
| *Sources of funds* |  |  |
| *Shareholders' funds* |  |  |
| Called-up ordinary £1 shares |  | 800 |
| Retained profits |  | 400 |
|  |  | 1 200 |
| *Long-term liabilities* |  | 300 |
| Capital employed |  | 1 500 |

to date, though some companies revalue land and buildings from time to time. Chapter 7 discusses decisions about investment in long-term assets.

**Current assets** are short-term resources, either cash or expected to become cash within twelve months from the balance sheet date. The three main current assets appear in reverse order of liquidity: first stocks, then debtors, then cash.

A *liability* is money which a business owes to others. **Current liabilities** are due for payment within twelve months from the balance sheet date and often much sooner; the main items are trade creditors, taxation and bank overdrafts. They are deducted from current assets, to produce a total for working capital (or net current assets).

The total of fixed assets plus working capital is called **net assets** (or total assets less current liabilities). This means the net long-term uses of funds which must be financed by long-term sources of funds.

*Shareholders' funds* are amounts which the owners of a company have provided directly or indirectly. Companies issue ordinary share capital directly to shareholders in exchange for cash. Investors can then buy or sell issued shares in quoted companies on the Stock Exchange. Companies *retain* profits when they do not pay out all of their profits to shareholders in dividends. In effect, the shareholders provide retained profits indirectly. One may regard shareholders' funds as a company's ultimate liability to its shareholders; but (apart from dividends) no amounts are legally payable to shareholders as long as the company continues in business.

*Long-term liabilities* are amounts a company has borrowed and which it must repay more than twelve months after the balance sheet date. Regular interest payments are due on the amounts owing.

*Capital employed* is the total of shareholders' funds and long-term liabilities. The amount of capital employed ( = long-term sources of funds) must equal net assets ( = long-term net uses of funds), hence balance sheets always balance. This is the famous principle of *double-entry accounting* which Goethe called: 'The finest invention of the human mind'.

| 1.1.3 **Profit and loss account** | The **profit and loss account** (P & L account) lists the income and expenses of a business for an accounting period (usually a year). It shows how much profit a company has paid out to shareholders in dividends, the balance being retained in the business. Table 1.2 shows an example of a profit and loss account. |

The **profit and loss account** (P & L account) lists the income and expenses of a business for an accounting period (usually a year). It shows how much profit a company has paid out to shareholders in dividends, the balance being retained in the business. Table 1.2 shows an example of a profit and loss account.

**Profit** is **sales turnover** less total **expenses** for a period; while a **loss** is simply a negative profit. Much of the detail in a profit and loss account consists of a classified list of the various expenses. The published profit and loss account would not normally show the details of cost of goods sold, contained in the box in Table 1.2.

### 1.1.4 Return on net assets

A common measure of operating performance is **return on net assets** (or return on capital employed). This ratio expresses the operating profit (profit before interest and tax) as a percentage of the business's long-term net assets and can also measure the performance of separate parts

Table 1.2 *Profit and loss account for Simpson Engineering Ltd for the year ended 31 March 1992*

|  | £'000 | £'000 |
|---|---|---|
| Sales turnover |  | 2 400 |
| Cost of goods sold |  | 1 700 |
|     Raw materials | 500 |  |
|     Production labour | 600 |  |
|     Production overheads | 600 |  |
| Gross profit |  | 700 |
| Selling and administrative overheads |  | 460 |
| Operating profit |  | 240 |
| Interest payable |  | 40 |
| Profit before tax |  | 200 |
| Corporation tax |  | 70 |
| Profit after tax |  | 130 |
| Ordinary dividends |  | 60 |
| Retained profit for the year |  | 70 |

of a business (see Chapter 5). A company can compare how well it employs its assets against the returns available from other possible uses of scarce capital funds.

For Simpson Engineering Limited, the return on net assets for the year ended 31 March 1992 is 16.0%.

$$\frac{\text{Operating profit}}{\text{Net assets}} = \frac{240}{1500} = 16.0\%$$

This can also be expressed as profit margin times asset turnover:

$$\frac{\text{Profit}}{\text{Sales}} = \frac{240}{2400} \qquad \frac{\text{Sales}}{\text{Net assets}} = \frac{2400}{1500}$$

Profit margin 10.0% × Asset turnover 1.6 times = 16.0%.

Another useful way to analyse a company's rate of return on net assets is to set out the various items of profit and loss and of net assets in the form of a diagram, as Table 1.3 shows.

To improve its return on net assets, a company can either increase its profit, for a given amount of net assets, or maintain its operating profit while reducing the net assets employed. It can invest any surplus capital to earn a return (for example, with a bank), and thus increase the total profits of the business.

Table 1.3 *Analysis of return on net assets*

```
                        Return on net assets
              ┌──────────────────┴──────────────────┐
           Profit                               Net assets
     ┌────────┼────────┐              ┌───────────┼───────────┐
   Sales   Materials,  Overheads    Fixed      Current     (Current
            labour                  assets      assets     liabilities)
```

The three main components of operating profit (sales revenue, cost of materials, cost of labour) can each be analysed between volume and price (as can variable overheads). While the details will vary for different businesses, this general approach will often give useful clues to possible improvements.

1.1.5 **Accounting concepts**

Four basic accounting concepts underlie the figures in any set of accounts, as follows:

1 *The going concern concept* assumes that an enterprise will continue in business in the foreseeable future. This normally means showing assets in accounts at *cost* — on the assumption that they are worth at least this much. An alternative assumption might be that the business would soon be wound up (liquidated): it would then be prudent to value assets at the amount they would realize on immediate sale (which might be much *less than cost*).

2 *The accruals concept* where possible matches expenses against revenues: businesses recognize revenues as they earn them and expenses as they incur them in transactions. An alternative approach would be to recognize transactions only when the business received or paid cash: this would normally be less realistic (though some government agencies, for example, still use cash accounting).

3 *The consistency concept* requires the same accounting treatment for similar items from one period to another. Otherwise comparing business results between periods would be meaningless. For example, it would not be good accounting practice to change the method of valuing stock from one year to another.

4 *The prudence concept* means that accounts include revenues or profits only when they are realized, either in cash or in the form of assets whose ultimate cash proceeds are fairly certain. In contrast, accounts provide in full for all losses and expenses, even where their amount has to be guessed.

The basic purpose of accounts is to show a **true and fair view** of the business's financial position and profit or loss for the period. The balance sheet makes no attempt, however, to disclose the true worth of a business (so the American expression 'net worth' to refer in balance sheets to the interests of shareholders is misleading). Many major assets are excluded, especially internally generated **intangible assets**, such as business 'know-how'.

## 1.2 Management accounting

### 1.2.1 Scope

**Management accounting** aims to help managers to run their firms. Of course, accounting alone is not nearly enough: managers also need data about production technology and raw materials, market research on customers' wants and competitors' actions, information about the labour market, and much else.

Management accounting deals with two different matters, as follows:

- The use of scarce resources.
- How people behave.

It contributes to the following four main purposes, emphasizing different time periods:

- Score-keeping      Past
- Problem-solving   Present
- Controlling          Present
- Planning              Future

Planning involves co-ordinating the different parts of a business, gaining the agreement of various responsible managers to their part in the plan, and projecting possible outcomes of future events. Control involves monitoring actual outcomes against the agreed budget, and where necessary taking corrective action.

The distinction between the various purposes may not always be clear. For example, many internal report forms are designed to help control as well as keep score, by both reporting *actual* performance and comparing it with a *standard* (budget). But as Table 1.4 shows, various kinds of management accounting information may be better suited for specific purposes. The numbers in brackets refer to the chapter numbers in this book which deal with the various topics.

### 1.2.2 Contrasts with financial accounting

**Financial accounting**, like management accounting, summarizes data, mainly from operating information such as the following:

- purchases of materials
- production records
- labour payrolls
- fixed asset (plant) registers
- sales and debtors
- cash.

Table 1.4 *Uses for different kinds of accounting information*

| Basis of costs and revenues | Past facts | Future estimates |
|---|---|---|
| 1. Total | Financial accounting (1) | Long-range plans |
| | Cost-plus contracts (3) | Normal pricing decisions (4) |
| | Reporting and analysing business unit performance (5) | |
| 2. Marginal | | Special pricing and alternative choice decisions (6) |
| | | Capital investment decisions (7) |
| 3. Controllable | Variance analysis (9) | Budgeting (8) |

Table 1.5 *Differences between financial accounting and management accounting*

| | *Financial accounting* | *Management accounting* |
|---|---|---|
| Governed by | Company law, SSAPs giving 'true and fair view' | Needs of managers |
| Users | External | Internal |
| Time | Past and present | Present and future |
| Period | Usually one year | As appropriate |
| Coverage | Whole company or group | Divisions and sub-groups |
| Emphasis | Accuracy | Speed |
| Criteria | Objective, verifiable, consistent | Relevant, useful, understandable |
| Unit of account | Money | Money, or physical units |
| Nature of data | Somewhat technical | For use by non-accountants |

There are several differences between financial accounting and management accounting, as set out in Table 1.5.

There is a legal requirement to publish financial accounts, but management accounting is used only to the extent that its value outweighs the cost. However, many companies fail because of inadequate internal costing systems and budgets. Managers cannot afford to wait three or four months for precise details of past financial performance: instead, they want prompt reports that are accurate enough not to be misleading. These may be expressed in physical units as well as in money terms: for example, units of output (product) or units of input (quantity of materials, man-hours, etc.). In practice, only a few experts fully understand financial accounts, but ordinary managers must be able to follow management accounts.

## 1.3 **Kinds of organization**

### 1.3.1 **Profit-seeking**

Most profit-seeking organizations aim to provide an adequate long-term financial return for their owners. If they fail to provide this, the owners may either change the top management team or sell out to new owners who will. So directors and managers must be alert for opportunities to improve their firm's long-term financial return. They must either improve or curtail those parts of the business that fail to meet the profit test, and put to better use their related fixed assets and working capital. This is the pervasive economic principle of opportunity cost. (See section 2.5.)

Every business is likely to have other aims which may not link directly with financial returns, such as the following:

- high market share
- product (or service) leadership
- very good company image
- highly skilled, trained and motivated employees
- use of the latest technology.

It can be difficult to measure the financial return from achieving these non-financial aims, yet to disregard them may prevent the achievement of financial aims. (See section 5.3.5.)

In addition to their (chosen) aims, most businesses are subject to constraints. Extensive legislation now relates to safety, environmental protection, minimum wages and redundancy terms.

Where top management are also the owners of the business, they may serve aims other than financial; for example, the desire to run their own business. Profits might be forgone in some cases in order to achieve greater personal freedom. Where the owners of the business are not part of the management team, however, overemphasis of managers' personal aims at the expense of financial returns is likely to lead to changes in management, ownership or both.

### 1.3.2 **Non-profit-seeking**

Many organizations have primary aims which are non-financial in nature, as Table 1.6 shows. Non-profit seeking organizations do not have finan-

Table 1.6 *Organizational aims*

| Organization | Primary aim |
| --- | --- |
| Charities | Improving the welfare of those in special need. |
| Hospitals | Preventing and curing illness. |
| Schools | Helping students learn useful knowledge, skills and attitudes. |
| The police | Preventing and detecting crime. |
| Local authorities | Satisfactory performance of obligatory and discretionary functions, within a limited budget. |

cial considerations at the top of their list. They are none the worse for that! Adam Smith said: 'Defence is more important than opulence.' Still, effective use of management accounting techniques can enable such entities to achieve greater success in meeting their primary aims; for example, by achieving better value for money. Charities, for instance, should plan how to raise the desired amounts with the minimum input of time and cost, and how best to satisfy the needy with the sum available.

## 1.4 **Planning and control**

The process of management control involves two related activities: planning and control. 'Planning' means deciding what to do, when and how. 'Control' is seeing that desired results are achieved. Management accounting is vital for running any but the smallest business. Its various techniques provide a framework for solving problems, making decisions, planning and controlling the business. Table 1.7 illustrates important aspects of the planning and control process.

## 1.4.1 **Long-term planning**

Many bigger businesses make some attempt at long-term (corporate) planning. It may start with basic questions such as 'What business should we be in?'. It will include a review of the firm's Strengths and Weaknesses and of the Opportunities and Threats (a SWOT analysis) arising from the environment in which the business operates. The long-term plan will identify the products (or services) and the markets in which the business chooses to compete.

A long-term plan needs to take account of marketing, production (or

Table 1.7 *The planning and control process*

|  | *Important aspects* |
| --- | --- |
| Long-term planning | Company objectives<br>Business definition — current and future<br>Analysis of company strengths and weaknesses<br>Assessment of external opportunities and threats<br>Competitive position<br>Strategic market and product decisions<br>Identifying resource needs — financial, physical and people |
| Short-term planning | Operating plans and programmes<br>Budgets<br>Reactions to market changes |
| Controlling | Reports<br>Evaluation<br>Problem-solving<br>Decision making<br>Effective action |

provision of services), purchasing, personnel, and administrative sides of the business in addition to its financial aspects. Expressing the company-wide long-term plan in financial terms should comprise profit and loss accounts, balance sheets and cash-flow statements, year by year for the whole period. How long is 'long-term'? Five years might be typical: but this time-span may not be right for certain types of business. The Ministry of Defence needs to plan at least twenty years ahead, whereas for a fashion retailer the 'long-term' might be only two years.

## 1.4.2 Short-term planning

Most organizations accept the need for budgeting as a disciplined approach to planning and control. Typically, they set annual budgets for the coming twelve months, including details of production and sales volumes, sales revenue, cost of sales, marketing costs, administrative costs and finance costs. Detailed budgeted profit and loss accounts, together with cash flows and balance sheets, are often subdivided into monthly (or four-weekly) periods. This allows frequent comparison of actual results with budget.

At the lower level, the budgeting process is often a negotiated short-term plan for a manager of a responsibility centre, agreed with his organizational superior. For many managers, it may involve only costs, not revenues. Achievement of budgets is important, but if conditions change it may be desirable to deviate from previously agreed budgets in order to achieve better results. The budget should not needlessly restrain managers from making worthwhile changes, although they may require approval if they want to spend more money.

## 1.4.3 Control

Control, in the context of management accounting, is the process by which managers seek to ensure that firms obtain and use resources effectively and efficiently in the achievement of their goals. The goals of an organization are actually those of top management: other employees have their own personal goals.

Effectiveness means how well a unit contributes to the organization's objectives, whereas efficiency means optimizing the ratio of outputs to inputs. An organization can be efficient in producing outputs which are not valuable, or it can inefficiently produce outputs that are valuable.

A management control system will normally include at least four stages, as follows:

1 *Programming* Choosing in broad terms which activities a company will undertake and what resources it will assign to each programme. Depending on a company's precise organization, a product line or a whole plant may represent a programme.
2 *Budgeting* Preparing plans expressed in detailed quantitative terms covering a specific period (often one year). Budgeting translates plans

from approximate numbers relating to programmes into precise money amounts relating to responsibilities of particular managers.

3 *Reporting* Incorporating both broad programmes and specific responsibility centres. Accounting reports on the latter need not be only in terms of money.

4 *Appraisal* A primary purpose of management control. Data on programmes form part of the input to future budgeting decisions; while data on responsibility centres are used to evaluate managers' performance (usually by comparing *actual* performance with *budget*).

One important distinction in evaluation is between a business unit as an economic entity and the performance of its manager. A loss-making division may be assigned a good manager, who may still be performing well even if the unit for which he is responsible is not. Equally important, it can be expensive for a business unit not to 'cash in' when conditions are favourable. This implies that a manager's performance may be reckoned poor even if his unit makes large profits.

Top management is concerned not merely with how good or bad the results actually were, but with how good or bad they *ought* to have been; in other words, with suitable standards of performance. Actual performance may be compared with the following criteria:

- pre-determined standards (budgets);
- historical standards (past actual performance); or
- external standards (e.g. competitors' performance).

Managers being evaluated need to accept the standards as reasonable. Many internal accounting reports (like external ones) may tend to over-emphasize short-term results; but nearly all managers in practice have to balance short-term against longer-term performance. Internal reports may also serve other functions, such as keeping managers informed about what is happening and helping to co-ordinate activities.

1.4.4 **Motivation**

A management control system should lead individuals to take actions which are not only in accordance with their own perceived self-interests, but are also in accordance with the goals of the organization, as perceived by top management. This is sometimes called **goal congruence**.

It is people, not systems, that take action. Reports should, therefore, focus on the specific responsibility of individual managers; for example, in distinguishing between **controllable** and **non-controllable** items. But even controllable items may not be completely under any one person's control: all that is required is significant influence.

An individual whose personal goals conflict with those of the organization might find more personal satisfaction (fulfilment) by moving to another organization whose goals are more in line with his own. Similarly,

Table 1.8 *Incentives*

- 'Carrots' motivate people more strongly than 'sticks'.
- Time-lags dilute incentives, hence rewards should follow action promptly.
- Motivation may flag where a goal is either too easy or too hard.
- Money may be less important than non-monetary rewards; but often reflects (and measures) status.
- People tend more readily to accept and use reports of their performance which they regard as objective and unbiased.
- People's needs differ, hence management control systems and incentives need to be adapted to the personalities and attitudes of the people to whom they apply.

an organization, in setting recruitment policy, might well concern itself with the personal goals of the people it proposes to employ. For instance, the Church of England would not expect to recruit many people who were ambitious for worldly goods.

There are two basic aspects to inducing individuals to act in accordance with organizational goals, crudely summarized as 'carrots' and 'sticks'. Absence of a carrot may sometimes be more or less equivalent to a stick, but not always. Table 1.8 summarizes generalizations about incentives.

## 1.5 Chapter summary

External financial accounts report a true and fair view of companies' profit or loss for a period, and of their financial position at the end. Balance sheets normally show assets at cost or less, and do not even include some assets (e.g. internally generated intangible assets). Statements of Standard Accounting Practice employ conventions, and even financial statements which accord with them do not fully reflect economic reality.

Management accounting involves the provision, analysis and use of financial and other information in order to help managers run businesses better. The benefits need to outweigh the costs. In contrast, laws require external financial accounting in order to satisfy shareholders, lenders and other outside users. Management accounting deals with the use of scarce resources, and how people behave in business.

Effective use of management accounting techniques can help even non-profit-seeking entities to achieve better value for money.

Many firms accept the need for annual financial budgeting as well as for longer-term planning. Annual budgets can help to co-ordinate the actions of different managers and advance agreement can help secure commitment to achieving results, and standards against which to judge performance.

## 1.6 **Review questions**

1 What are the principal differences between the two main branches of accounting?

2 What is the formula for return on net assets?

3 How can return on net assets be expressed by two other key financial ratios?

4 What are the four fundamental accounting concepts that underlie financial accounts?

5 What is the primary aim for profit-seeking organizations?

6 If that aim is not achieved, what is likely to happen (in the end)?

7 What other aims might profit-seeking organizations have?

8 What legal constraints are profit-seeking organizations subject to?

9 Identify three non-profit-seeking organizations and their likely primary aims.

10 Why is management accounting relevant to non-profit-seeking organizations?

11 What important aspects need to be considered in the long-term planning process?

12 What does 'long-term' mean?

13 What is the major management tool for short-term planning?

14 List four stages in a management control system.

15 Identify four common generalizations about incentives.

To maximize learning, please *write out* your answers on a separate sheet of paper. *Then* check with the answers in Appendix C, pp. 226–7.

## CHAPTER 2

# *The nature of costs*

## 2.1 Introduction

The cost of acquiring something is what must be given up to get it. This is often money, but may be goods, time or something else of value. Cost, however, is not the same as value (see 2.5). Someone who buys a book for £16 is valuing it, not at £16, but at *more than* £16. He might have been willing to pay as much as £30 for the book. (The hypothetical difference of £14 is sometimes called 'consumer surplus'.)

Table 2.1 lists the main reasons why a business wishes to measure its costs. There are four major headings — planning, controlling, decision making and reporting — which are interrelated. For example, regular reports may help control costs, and one must make some decisions in order to plan.

When dealing with costs, one should beware of spurious accuracy. It is more important to get a rough idea than to calculate costs to the nearest penny. Most costs can at best only be estimates. And different costs may be relevant for different purposes (see Chapter 6). Indeed, some accountants are reluctant to provide any cost figures at all unless they know what managers are going to use them for!

### Example 2.1

Economy Hire Cars Ltd owns a one-year-old car which, when not out on hire, shares a garage with three other cars. The annual garage rent is £2,400, insurance costs £300 a year, and the annual licence fee is £100. The car does 7 miles per litre, petrol costs 52.5p per litre, and maintenance is reckoned to cost 2.5p per mile. Depreciation is £2,000 a year, and the car is expected to travel 20,000 miles next year. Table 2.2 classifies expected operating costs for next year between fixed (see section 2.2.1) and variable (2.2.2), and between direct (2.3.1) and indirect (2.3.2).

## 2.2 Fixed and variable costs

A fixed cost remains the same, for a given period, even when the volume of output changes. Thus, the cost of rent and rates for a retail shop will be the same whether business is booming or slack. However, this is true

Table 2.1 *Purposes of costing*

1. *Forecasting, planning and budgeting*
   (a) Next year.
   (b) Longer-term.

2. *Cost control*
   (a) Comparing actual costs with planned/budgeted/standard costs; or with competitors.
   (b) Implementing cost reduction schemes.

3. *Decision making*
   (a) Make or buy (products and/or services).
   (b) Set levels of output and stocks (and production mix).
   (c) Help set selling prices (internal or external).
   (d) Capital investment (and disinvestment).
   (e) Assess product or process changes.

4. *Accounting reports*
   (a) Monthly management accounts.
   (b) Stock valuation (raw materials, bought-in items, work-in-progress, finished goods, consumables).
   (c) Profitability of product/service/contract/customer/project.
   (d) Published financial accounts.

Table 2.2 *Expected car operating costs for next year*

|  | Direct (£) | Indirect (£) | Total (£) |
|---|---|---|---|
| *Fixed costs:* |  |  |  |
| Insurance | 300 |  | ⎫ |
| Licence fee | 100 |  | ⎬ 3 000 |
| Depreciation | 2 000 |  | ⎪ |
| Garage rent |  | 600 | ⎭ |
| *Variable costs:* |  |  |  |
| Petrol (7.5p/mile) | 1 500 |  | ⎫ 2 000 |
| Maintenance (2.5p/mile) | 500 |  | ⎭ |
| *Total costs* | 4 400 | 600 | 5 000 |

**2.2.1 Fixed costs**

only within a given range of activity; for example, if the volume of business were to triple, larger premises might be needed which would increase rent and rates. Such major changes in scale are infrequent, so the fixed cost concept is of practical use for short-term business planning such as annual budgeting.

As Figure 2.1 shows, Economy Hire Cars Ltd's total fixed costs remain

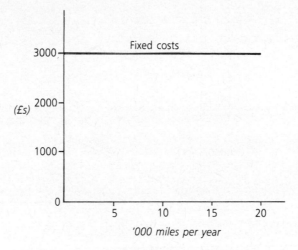

Figure 2.1 *Fixed costs for Economy Hire Cars Ltd*

at £3,000 per year, regardless of the number of miles travelled. Of course, this means that the amount of fixed costs per mile (the unit cost) falls as volume increases.

Total fixed costs do not vary with output volume changes, but due to inflation the money amounts are likely to increase over time. For instance, the cost of insurance, licence fee and garage rent will probably go up almost every year. The annual straight-line depreciation charge, if based on actual historical vehicle cost, will remain constant until the total cost has been written off or until the car is sold. A business needs to review fixed costs regularly and allow for any changes.

## 2.2.2 **Variable costs**

A **variable cost** is a constant amount per unit of output, hence total variable costs change in proportion to the volume of output. In a manufacturing business, the higher the level of production, the higher the cost of materials used. The relationship between output and material costs would probably be directly proportional, unless the volume changed enough to provide **economies of scale**, e.g. bulk purchase discounts.

In order to classify costs as fixed or variable, we may need to identify whose viewpoint is being taken. For instance, a firm's computer department would probably regard **depreciation** and personnel costs as fixed. But if it charges other departments in proportion to usage, *they* will view computer services as variable costs (see section 5.5.2).

Economy's variable costs (petrol and maintenance) are 10.0p per mile, or £2,000 for the 20,000 miles forecast (see Figure 2.2). Economy Hire Cars Ltd might hire out the car at 30p per mile (petrol included). The difference between the hiring out fee (or selling price) of 30p per mile

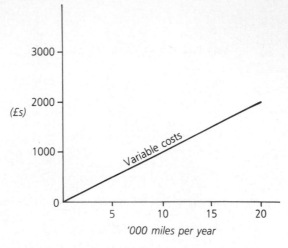

Figure 2.2 *Variable costs for Economy Hire Cars Ltd*

and the variable cost of 10p per mile is called the **contribution** (to fixed costs and profit). Contribution may be expressed per unit (here, 20p per mile) or in total (e.g. for 1000 miles the contribution would be £200).

2.2.3 **Semi-variable costs**

The distinction between fixed and variable costs may not be clear-cut. For example, some expenses may be semi-variable: utility charges often consist of a basic fixed charge plus a variable charge depending on usage (a two-part tariff — see section 5.5.2).

Direct labour costs may, in fact, be partly or wholly fixed, though they are still commonly treated as if they were wholly variable. Even if a recession or supplier strike reduces the workload, the workforce may still be retained on full pay for a specified period. Some firms even agree to pay employees something without requiring them to attend the workplace. And most employees, apart from the higher levels of management, expect overtime pay when they work more than the normal number of hours. The wage rate per hour of overtime is often higher than the basic rate: perhaps 1½ times basic for evening work and Saturdays and double for Sundays. Figure 2.3 illustrates how changes in output may affect a firm's production wages.

We have shown depreciation of the car as a fixed cost, assuming it to be calculated by the straight-line method (an equal percentage of original cost each year). But depreciation of certain assets might be calculated by the **usage** method. For the car, this might involve assuming a life, not of three years, but of 60,000 miles. Under the usage method, depreciation would be a constant amount per mile; the change of method would actually mean reclassifying depreciation itself as a variable cost.

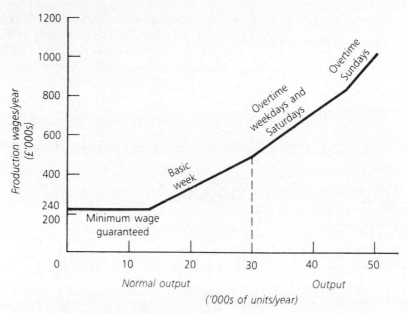

Figure 2.3 *Production wages and output*

## 2.2.4 **Discretionary costs**

Some costs are neither fixed nor variable nor in-between. Spending on advertising, training or research, for example, may change, not in line with changes in volume, but as a result of management's discretionary decisions. For instance, if sales volume fell, advertising might well increase. Such **discretionary costs** need not be committed for the long term like rent and rates: management can decide to reduce training costs by cancelling future programmes at short notice.

Spending on advertising, training or research is usually determined by management's subjective assessment of the (often long-term) benefits to the business compared with the (immediate) measurable cost. (Because these benefits may be highly uncertain, financial accounts normally write off such discretionary costs as expenses when incurred. The argument is that it would be imprudent to carry them forward on the balance sheet as deferred expenditure in order to match them against hoped for future benefits.)

Now examine Case study 2.1.

### Case study 2.1

*Problem*

Pio Sarno opened a pizza parlour in Hertfordshire, which he operated on his own. He leased the premises for two years at an annual cost of £6000, paid in monthly instalments. Rates and the standing charges for electricity and gas amounted to £150 per month. Pizzas were sold to customers at three times their (uncooked) cost from the supplier. Pio reckoned the usage charge for electricity and gas for last month was about £100. His pizza sales for the month were £4800.

*Question*
Analyse Pio's costs between fixed and variable. What were his total contribution and profit for the month?

**Solution**
Cost analysis:

| Fixed | | Variable | |
|---|---|---|---|
| Item | Amount (per month) | Item | Amount (per month) |
| Lease | £500 | Pizzas — uncooked | £1600 |
| Rates and standing charges | £150 | Gas and electricity usage | £100 |
| Total fixed = | £650 | Total variable = | £1700 |

Contribution (to fixed costs and profits):
      = sales revenue − variable costs
      = £4800 − £1700
      = £3100

Profit:
      = contribution − fixed costs
      = £3100 − £650
      = £2450

## 2.2.5 The importance of time

So far we have been discussing costs without much reference to time. We have defined fixed and variable costs by reference to their short-run behaviour. The **short run** is a period of time during which the inputs of *some* factors of production cannot be changed. The factor which is fixed is often capital equipment, but it might be land or labour or materials. The calendar length of the short run may vary widely: it will be much shorter for a computer software business than for an aircraft manufacturer. But in the **long run**, a firm can change the scale of its operations or the way it operates. A producer can alter plant capacity, a distributor can increase (or decrease) warehouse size, and so on. Thus, the long run corresponds to the outlook facing a firm planning to enter, or remain in business. It follows that, in the long run, inputs of all factors of production can be varied, including so-called fixed costs.

## 2.3 Direct and indirect costs

A further major classification of costs is between direct and indirect.

### 2.3.1 Direct costs

When a cost can easily be identified with a particular product, service or activity, it is known as a **direct cost**. An example would be the cost of material in making most products. With enough effort, it might be possible to relate nearly all costs to specific operations. But a management accountant must always ask: Is the resulting accuracy worth the cost of getting the information?

Table 2.2 shows that for Economy's car the direct costs are insurance, licence fee, depreciation, petrol and maintenance.

### 2.3.2 Indirect costs (overheads)

**Indirect costs** (or **overheads**) are all those costs which cannot conveniently be identified with a particular product or service. For instance, in a firm that produces several different products, factory rent and rates are indirect product costs. In order to determine the total production costs of a particular product, the business could apportion the cost of rent and rates on some reasonable basis (see section 3.2.1).

In the Economy Hire Cars example (see Table 2.2) the garage rent is an indirect cost. The annual garage rent of £2400 has been apportioned (shared out) equally between the four cars occupying the garage.

A recent large-scale study of industrial companies located in Belgium examined the importance of automation on cost accounting. It noted that the ratio of fixed costs to variable costs has increased, and suggested that 'direct labour costs have often become insignificant, while overheads have become more important' (Kerremans et al., 1991). Table 2.3 sets

Table 2.3 *Classifying costs*

|          | Total | Direct                  | Indirect                  |
|----------|-------|-------------------------|---------------------------|
| Fixed    | 35%   | Fixed/direct 15%        | Fixed/indirect 20%        |
| Variable | 65%   | Variable/direct 55%     | Variable/indirect 10%     |
| Total    | 100%  | = 70%                   | = 30%                     |

out the study's average percentages for the two major ways in which costs can be classified. Examples of each quadrant in Table 2.3 are:

- Fixed/direct     — depreciation[1] of equipment used on a single product.
- Variable/direct     — raw materials.
- Fixed/indirect     — factory rent for a multi-product factory.
- Variable/indirect — energy costs for a multi-product organization.

[1]assumed to be based on time rather than on usage

## 2.4 Marginal and average costs

### 2.4.1 Marginal costs

**Marginal cost** is the extra cost incurred as a result of producing one more unit of output. Within existing capacity constraints, marginal costs equal variable costs, unless the extra output changes the variable cost per unit. (For Economy Hire Cars Ltd the marginal cost is 10.0p per mile.) If, for instance, overtime is needed to produce more output, then the marginal cost will exceed the previous variable labour cost per unit. Alternatively, marginal material cost would be lower if quantity discounts reduced the purchase price per unit.

When extra output requires additional fixed costs, the marginal cost may be extremely high.

### 2.4.2 Average costs

The **average cost** is total costs divided by the total number of units of output. All costs are included whether they are fixed, variable, semi-variable, discretionary, direct or indirect. So, Economy Hire Cars Ltd's average cost per mile is expected to be 25.0p per mile (£5000/20 000 miles).

### 2.4.3 Marginal versus average costs

For many short-term business decisions, it is marginal, rather than average, costs which are relevant.

**Example 2.2**

A nice example of the difference between average and marginal costs is given by the story of the office worker who went to have a haircut. When he returned, the boss asked him where he had been.

Worker: To have a haircut.
Boss: In office hours?
Worker: Well, it *grew* in office hours!
Boss: Not *all* of it, surely?
Worker: No, but then I didn't have it *all* cut off!

In practice, different firms have widely different cost patterns. Unlike economists, accountants usually presume that marginal per-unit costs are constant, at least throughout the **relevant range** of output. And business firms are trying to maximize profits, not to produce at minimum cost.

The distinction between marginal and average can be illustrated by reference to political arguments about British tax levels. Some people argue that British tax rates are still high (by comparison with other countries), others that they are not. You might think this is simply a question of fact, about which it would be hard to continue arguing for decades on end. But the argument is still not over — because the participants often confuse average with marginal.

In terms of *average* tax levels, British taxes in 1991 do not seem to be out of line with most other countries, certainly in the EC: somewhat higher than Spain, somewhat lower than France. But in terms of *marginal* rates of tax on incomes, for most of the post-war years British marginal rates of income tax have been considerably higher than most other countries. (Because those top marginal rates of tax actually yield very little revenue, they have not significantly affected the overall *average* weight of taxes.) More recently, top marginal rates of tax in the United Kingdom have been lower than in many other countries. They were reduced in 1979 and again in 1988. But average rates of total tax were higher at the end of Mrs Thatcher's time as Prime Minister than they had been when she started eleven and a half years earlier.

Which is more relevant? It partly depends on the time horizon. Someone thinking of emigrating (a long-term decision) will probably be concerned with average tax levels (among many other things, of course). But a man who is wondering whether to work overtime this weekend will presumably be concerned with the rate of tax on his marginal earnings.

### 2.4.4 Learning curves

As we all know, another thing that depends on time is learning. A firm's workers are likely to know better how to make a product after they have been doing so for some weeks than on their first day on the job. This may enable the firm to reduce its direct labour time (and hence cost) per unit produced. The learning relates more to the volume of output produced than merely to the lapse of time. Learning reduces labour hours (and hence labour-related costs) per unit, not material costs nor machine costs nor other fixed costs.

The firm with the largest market share, and therefore the largest output per unit of time, should be learning faster than its rivals. If this does result in lower costs, a firm which is further along the **learning curve** can either reduce its selling price, or make a higher margin on each unit sold. Indeed, a firm might even plan to sell at a loss the first units produced in order to get business at a price which would enable it to make a profit later when it could produce more cheaply. This tactic might be used to penetrate the market and win a high market share. An obvious question is how long a view management is taking or, in other words, what time horizon might be relevant for pricing policy.

Experience in the aircraft industry (and others) suggests the following kind of formula for the learning curve: average time per unit to produce cumulative output = L × average time per unit to produce half of the cumulative output (where L is a percentage, normally between 70% and 90%).

The 80% learning curve shown in Figure 2.4 shows, for the first 8 units of output, average direct labour hours per unit of 2560 (= 80% of the 3200 hours per unit average for the first 4 units). For the cumulative average to fall to 80% of the previous average, the latest output batch must have needed only 60% of the time required to produce (the first) half of the present cumulative output (i.e. 1920 hours = 60% × 3200 hours). This is shown below

12 800 hours total = first 4 units × 3200 hours average

20 480 hours total = first 8 units × 2560 hours average

7680 hours total = second 4 units × 1920 hours average

Figure 2.4 shows that eventually the learning curve tends to lose impetus, giving a nearly constant production time per unit. Increased labour efficiency stems both from individual workers learning and from organizational learning. Maximum benefit is likely to occur only when management positively expects learning to occur, and builds it into company plans and budgets.

Learning curves apply in labour-intensive manufacture where there is continuous production and a stable workforce. They do not apply to machine-controlled manufacture. Learning how to produce existing

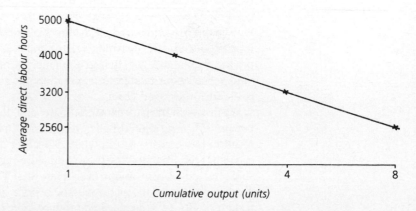

Figure 2.4 *The learning curve*

products faster is not, of course, the only way to reduce costs. Changes to design, materials and processes (see section 3.1.4 Value analysis) may well have even more effect. (But changes in design may interrupt learning, and push labour time some way back up the learning curve.)

2.4.5 **Economies of scale**

Increasing the volume of output may enable certain fixed costs to be spread over a larger number of units (books are a well-known example). More general examples might be initial design costs, or research and development costs. In the same way, doubling output may lead to a less than proportionate increase in the volume of stocks needing to be held (the new level of stocks should, in theory, be $\sqrt{2} \times$ the original level).

Some labour costs, too, may not increase in proportion, either because they are similar to fixed costs (like a night-watchman) or because an increase in scale of operations leads to a less than proportionate increase in certain labour costs (for example, internal auditors and many other office staff). Moreover, there may well be cost savings in employing highly specialized labour above a certain scale of output.

Specialization of equipment may also reduce unit costs where long enough production runs apply. Where capital equipment functions almost as a container (a crude-oil storage container, for example), output may rise in proportion to cubic capacity, while costs increase only in line with surface area.

Table 2.4 shows, for five selected industries, how unit costs for labour and capital may fall if output multiplies ten-fold (Jackson, 1982). Total

Table 2.4 Five examples of economy of scale

|  | Output multiple | | |
| --- | --- | --- | --- |
|  | 1 | 5 | 10 |
| *Beer brewing* | | | |
| Brewery capacity, thousand barrels p.a. | 100 | 500 | 1 000 |
| Index of unit labour and capital costs | 100 | 43 | 28 |
| *Oil refining* | | | |
| Refinery capacity, million tons crude oil p.a. | 1 | 5 | 10 |
| Index of refinery costs per ton (exc. crude oil) | 100 | 56 | 44 |
| *Machine tools* | | | |
| Factory output, number of m/tools p.a. | 10 | 50 | 100 |
| Index of ex-factory cost per unit | 100 | 55 | 49 |
| *Motor vehicles* | | | |
| Factory output, thousands of cars p.a. | 100 | 500 | 1 000 |
| Index of labour and capital costs per vehicle | 100 | 61 | 54 |
| *Cement works* | | | |
| Works capacity, thousand tons cement p.a. | 100 | 500 | 1 000 |
| Index of unit labour and capital costs | 100 | 69 | 58 |

average costs per unit will normally fall much less than this, since the cost of materials will often fall by little, if anything. (But increased output may well provide greater opportunities for suppliers of materials, too, to gain from economies of scale, and to pass on at least some of these gains in lower prices.)

## 2.5 Opportunity costs

Section 2.1 stated that: the cost of acquiring something is what must be given up to get it. This is often money but may be ... something else of value.

Suppose a business owns equipment, currently not in use, which a manager wants to employ on a marginal project. He argues that no cost should be charged for its use because the asset is idle. Is this reasonable?

To answer this question we need to consider what else, if anything, the business could do with the idle equipment. Use it on a different project? Sell it? If so, for how much? When we have determined the various alternative possible uses for the equipment, we estimate their values. The opportunity cost of the course actually taken is the value of the next-best alternative.

We estimate the value of a given event by comparing its expected good and bad consequences; but we still need to value the next-best forsaken option in order to determine the cost. Where it is not simply a cash payment, this is often difficult to measure.

Opportunity cost can be quite visible. For example, in the old days you joined one of four separate queues in a post office or bank, and could see at once how much faster or slower the other queues were moving. On the other hand, suppose a taxi-driver prefers to take you across town by one route rather than another which he thinks may be congested. You normally never know whether he was right or not (whether, in terms of time, you made a profit), since you did not take the other route. The taxi-driver analogy is probably more typical. The hypothetical and forward-looking nature of opportunity costs makes them somewhat unsuitable for use in routine management reports: they may be subjective and are often very hard to quantify.

Thus, most of the costs we have looked at so far have been similar to cash payments. Apportioning fixed overhead costs to activities is sometimes defended as a practical and measurable proxy for opportunity costs. Table 2.5 sets out a number of important differences between opportunity costs and ordinary costs as represented by cash payments.

## 2.6 Costs for comparison

To estimate future costs, one can either take past actual amounts as the basis, or else use other specific external or internal data. The first method uses historical costs, the second current or standard costs.

Table 2.5 *Differences between ordinary costs and opportunity costs*

|  | Ordinary costs | Opportunity costs |
| --- | --- | --- |
| Existence | Actual | Hypothetical |
| Timing | Past or future | Future |
| Measurability | Often objective and straightforward | Involves subjective 'valuation' |
| Consists of | Payment | Forgone value |

2.6.1 **Historical costs**

Costs that a firm has actually incurred are often readily accessible and easy to verify. External financial accounts normally use them. But the obvious danger is that past costs may no longer be relevant. They may not represent present, let alone future conditions. Using past costs as a basis for estimating future costs implicitly assumes that the past period was fairly typical, which it may not have been. And what if specific prices have changed since then?

2.6.2 **Current costs**

Current costs may be more relevant than historical costs, especially (but not only) in times of inflation. They use current prices of specific goods and services, rather than actual past prices. There can be problems in estimating current prices, but we have already seen that cost estimates are often not precisely correct. When it was proposed to substitute current costs for historical costs in external financial accounting, the subjective nature of current cost estimates did cause problems. But that should not matter, or not nearly so much, in internal management accounting.

Perhaps a more important objection to current costs is that they don't go far enough. They use current rather than past prices; but they don't use *future* prices. And they apply current price estimates to past *quantities*, without attempting to estimate current quantities. Standard costs can overcome both these problems, as Table 2.6 outlines.

2.6.3 **Standard costs**

**Standard costs** are estimates of costs that should be attainable in future, based on standards both for prices and for quantities. In both respects, the standards may depart from actual past experience.

Computing a standard (full) cost involves estimating the following:

- quantities and prices of *materials*
- *direct labour* times and wage rates
- an *overhead* charge, based on normal volume.

These estimates should allow for any (normal) wastage of materials, and for non-productive labour time. The standard is meant to be realistic not utopian. Overheads need to be based on normal volume; otherwise, the

Table 2.6 *Historical, current and standard costs*

| | | Quantity | |
| --- | --- | --- | --- |
| | | Past actual | Future estimate |
| | Past actual | Historical cost | |
| Price | Estimated current | Current cost | |
| | Estimated future | | Standard cost |

per unit overhead charge could be extremely high with below-normal volumes, and very low when the volume of activity was above normal. (And if standard costs varied with volume, they would continually need recalculating.)

For a new job, estimates based on similar work might be suitable. When in production, actual data may be used, possibly supplemented by time and method study. One can also modify past performance figures to allow for hoped-for or expected changes. Then, standard costs may indeed become a useful standard against which to measure actual future performance. Standard costs can also serve other purposes, such as valuing stock or as the basis for setting selling prices.

### Example 2.3

A firm plans to sell 90 000 pressings in June next year, which it must produce in April. The firm works a 5-day 40-hour week, plus overtime. One press and one operator will be available for this work next April, which will contain 22 working days. The projected wage-rate for press operators next April is £4.50 per hour, or £6.00 per hour with overtime. The presses can, in theory, make up to 10 pressings per minute but, in practice, the average output is only $7\frac{1}{2}$ pieces per minute because of breakdowns, etc.

We know the presses can produce $7\frac{1}{2}$ per minute, or 450 per hour. Hence, the number of machine hours needed to produce 90 000 pressings is 200 hours (90 000/450). 176 ordinary press hours are available in April (22 × 8); so there will be a need for 24 hours of overtime. The cost of the operator's wages will therefore be £792 (176 hours @ £4.50) plus £144 (24 hours overtime @ £6.00); making the total standard cost of direct labour on this job £936.

If the standard cost of materials is £11 448 and overhead is 600% of direct labour cost (= 6 × £936), then the total standard cost for the 90 000 pressings in June next year is: £936 direct labour plus £11 448 materials plus £5 616 overhead = £18 000 total (= 20p per pressing).

Using standard costs like this allows a firm to plan its use of financial resources. Budgets can predict production costs with fair accuracy; jobs can be quoted for (subject to market conditions); and so on. Standard costing does require a fairly complex arrangement for setting and monitoring standards, which may be beyond the scope of many smaller companies. Standard costs are more often used in high-volume manufacturing where the product life is several years. It may not be worth the effort to establish standards for low-volume short-life products.

| 2.7 **Chapter summary** | Cost estimates help in planning, controlling, decision making, and reporting. Three key distinctions are between: fixed and variable; direct and indirect; marginal and average. |
|---|---|
| | Fixed costs do not change with output (within the relevant range), whereas variable costs change in proportion to output (hence are constant per unit). Some costs contain elements of both; others are neither fixed nor variable, but depend on management discretion. The nature of costs depends partly on the time-scale: no costs are fixed for ever. |
| | Direct costs can be traced to a specific product, process or department, while indirect costs cannot (or not easily). In order to estimate total cost, one must apportion indirect costs between the various activities, on some suitable basis. |
| | Marginal cost is the change in total costs resulting from one more (or less) unit of output which may be relevant for some business decisions. Average cost per unit of output is total cost divided by output volume. Both marginal and average labour costs may fall rapidly in the early days of making a new product, due to the learning-curve effect. Increasing the volume of output may lead to economies of scale (lower unit costs), perhaps by spreading some fixed costs over more units. |
| | Opportunity cost is the benefit forgone by adopting one course of action instead of the next-best alternative. This hypothetical cost often involves subjective valuation, hence it is not normally used in routine management reports. |
| | One can base estimates of future costs on past actual, current or standard costs. In standard costing, both price and quantity estimates are forward-looking, taking into account realistic views of what should be attainable. |

## 2.8 **Review questions**

1 What are the main purposes of costing?
2 Define and give an example of each of the following types of cost:
   (a) variable  (b) fixed  (c) semi-variable
   (d) discretionary.
3 What is the distinction between a direct cost and an indirect cost?

4 Why are indirect costs apportioned to products (or services)? Explain the term 'basis of apportionment' and give two examples.
5 Give an example of each of the following types of cost:
   (a) fixed and direct cost  (b) fixed and

indirect cost   (c) variable and direct cost
(d) variable and indirect cost.
6 When, and why, can fixed costs change?
7 What is marginal cost?
8 What is the distinction between marginal
cost and variable cost?
9 'Since fixed costs are included in the
calculation of average cost per unit, but
not in the calculation of marginal cost per
unit, the latter must always be less than
unit average cost.' Do you agree?

10 Are the terms 'direct cost' and 'variable
cost' synonymous?
11 Are indirect costs the same as fixed costs?
12 What kind of cost may be subject to a
learning curve?
13 What are some of the implications of the
learning-curve phenomenon?
14 Why may economies of scale exist in some
industries?
15 What are opportunity costs? Why can they
be difficult to use in costing products?

To maximize learning, please *write out* your answers on a separate sheet of paper. *Then* check with
the answers in Appendix C, pp. 227–8.

## 2.9 **Problems**

1  Park's is a small family-owned fish-and-
chip shop selling fried fish and chips, fish
cakes, sausages and pasties, as well as wet
fish, vinegar, sauces, canned soft drinks and
other miscellaneous items.

During their most recent financial year,
Park's made a profit of £27 000, as detailed
below:

|  | £ | £ |
|---|---|---|
| Sales | | |
| Fried fish | 60 000 | |
| Chips | 30 000 | |
| Other fried products | 15 000 | |
| Wet fish | 15 000 | |
| Other items | 15 000 | |
| | | 135 000 |
| Expenses | | |
| Fish for frying | 42 000 | |
| Potatoes | 9 000 | |
| Other fried products | 9 000 | |
| Frying oil and batter | 3 600 | |
| Frying equipment: | | |
| depreciation | 6 000 | |
| Other equipment: | | |
| depreciation | 1 500 | |
| Fish sold uncooked | 15 000 | |

| Other items | 9 000 | |
|---|---|---|
| Advertising | 3 000 | |
| Rent, rates, gas and | | |
| electricity | 9 900 | |
| | | 108 000 |
| Profit (before | | |
| proprietor's | | |
| drawings) | | 27 000 |

The following costs are regarded as fixed:
(i) depreciation (which is calculated on the
straight-line basis); and (ii) rent, rates and the
standing charges for electricity and gas (£6000
in total).

*Questions*
(a) What was the total, respectively, of fixed
and variable costs?
(b) What was the contribution for the year?
How much is this (on average) per £1
sales?
(c) What is the variable cost of a piece of
fried fish sold for £1.60p? Assume that
the frying oil and batter costs, as well as
the variable electricity and gas costs, are
apportioned in the same ratio as the
expenses for fish for frying, potatoes and

other fried products. What is the contribution on this piece of fish?

(d) Which costs are direct and which are indirect?

(e) What is the average cost of each £1 of sales?

(See solution in Appendix C, pp. 228–30.)

**2**  Emilio De Camillo is a self-employed ice-cream salesman. The financial results of his first year in business are as follows:

|  | £ | £ |
|---|---|---|
| Sales of ice-cream and lollipops | | 42 000 |
| Expenses | | |
| Cost of goods sold ($\frac{1}{3}$ × sales price) | 14 000 | |
| Ice-cream van: | | |
| running costs | 3 900 | |
| depreciation | 3 000 | |
| | | 20 900 |
| Profit (before proprietor's drawings) | | 21 100 |

Running costs include £1100 for vehicle licence, insurance, garaging and routine maintenance. The remaining £2800 relates to fuel, oil and vehicle repairs. Depreciation has been calculated at 20% of vehicle cost.

*Question*
Determine the following:

(a) The fixed costs for the year.
(b) The variable costs for the year.
(c) Contribution, in total, and per £1 of sales.
(d) The direct cost of £6000 sales of lollipops.
(e) Total indirect costs for the year.
(f) Would Emilio have made even more profit if he had bought two ice-cream vans (same price) and also recruited a

driver-salesman at a cost of £12 000 per year if the latter made £31 500 of sales? Assume the fixed costs are the same for both vehicles and variable costs are linearly variable.

(See solution in Appendix C, pp. 230–1.)

**3**  A public utility operates at 100% of capacity for only four hours out of 24, at 50% of capacity for a further eight hours, and at only 25% of capacity for the remaining twelve hours each day. Total operating costs are £132 000 per day. How should costs be allocated? (Capacity actually used is shown in Figure 2.5.)

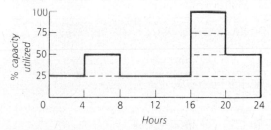

Figure 2.5 *Public utility: use of capacity*

**4**  In March 1993, Jim Fuller, a buyer for Nomad Aircraft, was trying to decide what price to offer Mayfield plc to make a further 100 metal passenger luggage containers. Mayfield had been making these metal containers for Nomad continuously since December 1990, when its bid of £1518 per unit* for the 120 containers had easily beaten the next lowest bid of £1632. Since then, Mayfield had met the demanding quality standards and all delivery schedules.

Based on his wide knowledge of the industry, Fuller believed that an 80% learning curve would apply for this sort of work. Breaking down Mayfield's £1518 bid, he took profit to be £138 (10% on cost), and materials

*All costs and prices are expressed in terms of March 1993 pounds.

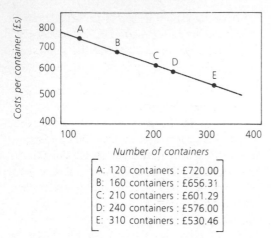

```
A: 120 containers : £720.00
B: 160 containers : £656.31
C: 210 containers : £601.29
D: 240 containers : £576.00
E: 310 containers : £530.46
```

Figure 2.6 *Learning curve of numbers and prices of containers*

to be £480 per unit. He assumed that Mayfield had amortized tooling cost of about £21 600 over the first 120 containers (= £180 per unit). Hence, he made no subsequent allowance for tooling. Fuller thus reckoned costs subject to the learning curve amounted to £720 per unit for 120 units. He was confident his estimates were fairly accurate.

Fuller plotted on log graph paper the original order for 120 units and the £720 costs subject to the learning curve. He then plotted double the quantity of the first order (i.e. 240 units) and 80% of the unit cost (£576), and drew a straight line between the two points. (See Figure 2.6.)

When Nomad required 40 more containers, the graph showed that, for the new total of 160 containers, the new cumulative average of cost elements subject to learning was £656.31 per unit. The relevant average cost for the latest 40 units was therefore £465.25.

Costs subject to the learning curve were as follows:

| | |
|---|---:|
| 160 units @ £656.31 | £105 010 |
| Less 120 units @ £720.00 | £86 400 |
| Latest 40 units [@ £465.25] | £18 610 |

To this amount of £465.25 Fuller added £480.00 for materials, and then added 10% of total costs for profit, making a total of £1039.77 per container. (Mayfield's profit allowance, being a fixed percentage on cost, thus declined with each new contract.) Mayfield accepted this price, and the price of £995.74 offered for a third batch of 50 containers (the current contract, due for completion in March 1993).

In February 1993, Nomad received aircraft orders that would require 100 more luggage containers. Fuller knew it was important for Nomad to continue dealing with Mayfield if at all possible. (Over the period from December 1990 to March 1993, Mayfield would have produced 210 container.) Fuller reckoned that for the 100 containers now required, any other contractor would charge at least £1650 per unit (including the cost of new tooling amortized over 100 units).

Faced with a further reduction in the price per unit for each new contract, a Mayfield spokesman doubted whether his company would take on any further contracts for containers unless the price were increased significantly.

*Questions*
(a) What price should Jim Fuller offer Mayfield per unit for 100 luggage containers, if he simply continues to apply the 80% learning curve?
(b) Should he actually offer Mayfield the price calculated in (a) above? Why? If not, what price should he offer? Why?

5 'It's enough to drive you off the rails for good! The costs below are based on British Rail second-class tickets. And on the energy-saving Sunderland Supersnarl (motor car) which averages 54.3 mpg at a steady 56 mph, with the cost of petrol at £1.59 per gallon. We appreciate you have to buy a Sunderland

Supersnarl in the first place; but at least you can run it when you want, and take four more adults at no extra cost. Just try that with British Rail.' (Advertisement in Sunday newspapers, 7 February 1982.)

There followed a list of 45 destinations from London, with cost figures under two columns headed BR and SS, and with mileage figures. A representative selection of four destinations is shown below:

|  | Mileage | BR £ | SS £ |
|---|---|---|---|
| Aberdeen | 503 | 39.00 | 14.73 |
| Birmingham | 105 | 11.30 | 3.07 |
| Bradford | 195 | 19.60 | 5.71 |
| Cambridge | 54 | 5.40 | 1.58 |

*Questions*

(a) How have the SS figures been calculated?

(b) Is the comparison being made a fair one? If not, why not?

(c) Roughly what would you reckon is a fair comparison for the Aberdeen to London journey? How have you calculated it?

(d) What would be a fair London–Aberdeen comparison for a husband and wife with their 17-year-old son?

(The solutions to Problems 3–5 will be provided in the *Instructors' Manual*.)

CHAPTER **3** *Product costing* _____

## 3.1 **Uses of product costs**

Business managers often want to know the cost of products they make or services they provide. In running a business, knowledge of costs can be helpful for a number of purposes (see Table 3.1).

### 3.1.1 **Planning financial resources**

Planning for future periods requires estimated costs to complete budgeted profit and loss accounts and balance sheets, and for cash-flow forecasts. As noted in Chapter 1, external financial accounts are largely based on historical costs; and (to a somewhat lesser extent) so are internal management accounts.

### 3.1.2 **Controlling costs**

Adequate business profits largely — though not entirely — depend upon continuing control of costs. There is a wide difference between the level of costs of the most efficient operator in an industry and the least efficient. Managers must regularly compare actual costs against budgeted costs (see Chapter 9) and, where necessary, take suitable action. The main classifications are: wages and salaries, purchases of materials, miscellaneous purchases of services and consumables.

### 3.1.3 **Stock valuation**

Published accounts of UK companies must conform with financial accounting standards (SSAPs). SSAP 9 requires balance sheets to state stocks at the *lower* of cost or net realizable value. 'Cost' comprises the following:

- direct materials (cost of purchase);
- direct labour;
- production overheads; and
- other attributable overheads.

### 3.1.4 **Value analysis**

To achieve satisfactory long-term profits, efficient use of resources is not enough. Resources must also be used effectively.

**Efficiency** implies either minimizing the use of inputs for a given level of outputs, or maximizing the level of outputs from a given level of inputs.

Table 3.1 *Uses of product costs*

(a)  Planning financial resources required.
(b)  Controlling costs — efficient use of resources.
(c)  Valuing stock 'at cost' for financial accounts.
(d)  Carrying out value analysis exercises (cost/benefit analysis).
(e)  Helping to set selling prices:
    (i)   internal ('transfer prices');
    (ii)  external.
(f)  Analysing distribution costs.

The ratio between the quantity of inputs and the quantity of outputs measures efficiency, which is essentially a production concept. It is possible to be highly efficient in producing useless products. In contrast, **effectiveness** relates to the value of outputs; for example, whether the customers want the product we make.

**Value analysis** is a technique which examines products in order to create ideas for cost reduction or increasing value. It may involve changing the materials, the design or the manufacturing process. The aim is to minimize product costs while retaining (or even enhancing) the product's functional performance and appearance. For example, plastic jug kettles have largely replaced aluminium kettles: they are easier and cheaper to produce, as well as having (arguably) an improved appearance.

Value analysis is likely to involve the following steps:

1  Determine precisely what customer needs must be satisfied.
2  Obtain detailed information on current product specification, supplies, production planning and methods, volumes, and detailed cost breakdown.
3  Analyse current practice and generate as many design, construction and assembly alternatives as possible.
4  Study each alternative for its viability and likely economic impact.

## 3.1.5 Setting selling prices

Private sector businesses need to sell their products at prices that exceed costs. It may therefore be tempting to use cost information to help set minimum selling prices. They may also need to justify internal (**transfer**) prices to government tax or currency officials by reference to costs which can be verified.

Many business people, however, are nervous about the idea of setting selling prices on a 'cost plus (profit margin)' basis. This is partly because in many competitive markets there is no guarantee that one will be able to recover costs in this way; and partly because reference to costs seems to ignore the important question of what price the traffic will bear. Even government contractors now tend to be reluctant to use 'cost plus' as the basis for pricing, since experience has shown it can easily lead to inefficiency and waste. It may not, therefore, be realistic to think of costs incurred as setting a 'floor' to the acceptable level of selling price.

It is true, of course, that sales revenues need, in total, to exceed costs in order for a business to make a profit over a period of time. But, with respect to any particular product, it is probably better to think of estimated achievable selling price as setting a 'ceiling' for permissible levels of cost to be incurred. Clearly, if the highest price that customers will pay does not even cover marginal costs, then the product in question should not be produced. More about pricing in Chapter 4.

### 3.1.6 Distribution costs

As well as manufacturing costs, many businesses also incur significant costs in distributing their products to customers. These could include costs of packaging, materials handling, warehousing, stock control, transport and administration. Firms may treat such costs as overheads and apportion them to products in some arbitrary way (see section 3.2) But if distribution costs differ widely for different products, customers or channels, a more detailed cost analysis may be useful. The results may well affect profit estimates for products, customers or distribution channels.

Distribution cost analysis is also relevant in the service sector, particularly where service products sell through more than one sales channel. (For example, an insurance company may sell policies directly itself or through a broker.) In the service sector, it may be important to identify profitability both by service product and by sales channel.

### 3.2 Full costing

**Full costing** aims to attribute all a business's costs (or all its manufacturing costs) to particular products. Unlike direct costs, however, indirect (overhead) costs, by definition, cannot be directly identified with particular products. Hence, there is a need first to apportion indirect costs to cost centres; and then to attribute the total costs of each cost centre to the various products which pass through it, on some more or less arbitrary basis.

Section 3.3 discusses an alternative system of costing, which allocates only variable costs to products (known as **marginal costing**). But many businesses prefer to use full costing, for reasons discussed in section 3.4.

### 3.2.1 Apportioning indirect costs to cost centres

A **cost centre** is a part of a business in respect of which costs can be identified and aggregated. It may be a whole factory, a part of a factory, or even single machines. Different cost centres may be appropriate for different levels of management decision. For example, possible cost centres are shown below for a company engaged in vehicle production:

Table 3.2 *Basis of apportionment of indirect costs*

| Cost | Basis of apportionment |
|------|------------------------|
| Rent and rates | Floor space |
| Heating and lighting | Floor space |
| Energy | Power rating of equipment and facilities |
| Depreciation of equipment | Machine minutes used |
| Production supervision | Direct labour minutes or cost |
| Indirect labour and expenses | Direct labour minutes or cost |

Table 3.3 *Apportionment of rent and rates to direct labour cost*

*Step 1* Apportioning rent and rates cost to departments

| Department | Floor space m$^2$ | Apportionment (£'000) |
|------------|-------------------|------------------------|
| A | 200 | 10 |
| B | 600 | 30 |
| C | 500 | 25 |
| D | 700 | 35 |
| Total rent and rates = | | 100 |

*Step 2* Applying departmental rent and rates cost to direct labour cost

| Department | Direct labour cost (£'000) | Rent and rates cost (£'000) | Rent and rates as a % of direct labour cost |
|------------|---------------------------|------------------------------|----------------------------------------------|
| A | 200 | 10 | 5 |
| B | 300 | 30 | 10 |
| C | 125 | 25 | 20 |
| D | 875 | 35 | 4 |

| Level of decisions | Possible cost centres |
|--------------------|------------------------|
| • Group directors | Operating divisions: cars, buses, trucks |
| • Truck division directors | Truck factories, A, B, C |
| • Factory director | Truck assembly lines, 1, 2, 3 |
| • Works manager | Welding machines, presses, lathes |
| • Press shop foreman | 100-ton presses, 50-ton presses, etc. |

The purpose of apportioning indirect costs is to estimate the total cost of a product or service. The basis of apportionment may be somewhat arbitrary, so excessive complication, time and expense should be avoided. Apportioned costs are not uniquely correct, and the resulting total product costs are only approximate. Table 3.2 shows some common bases of apportionment.

The apportionment of indirect costs usually involves two or more steps. For instance, rent and rates may firstly be apportioned on the basis of the floor space occupied by different departments, and then that proportion applied as a percentage of that department's direct labour costs. (See Table 3.3 for an illustration.)

In most businesses, indirect expenses may often most conveniently be allocated on some employee-related basis, such as number of personnel, direct labour hours worked, or total direct labour costs. Some businesses regard **direct labour** as including only gross wages paid for directly identifiable productive output. Many others also include employers' social security expenses and pension contributions, holiday pay, and possibly other **fringe benefits**. In total, these 'extras' can amount to a significant percentage of basic gross wages.

Now consider Case study 3.1.

---

### Case study 3.1

#### Problem

Pronto-Fix is a small garage dealing with motor car repairs and servicing. With the aid of three employees, the manager reckons that he could use a total of 6 000 hours per year effectively for repair and service work. Budgeted costs for the coming year are as follows:

|                                    | (£)    |
|------------------------------------|--------|
| Parts, materials, oils, etc.       | 90 000 |
| Total staff costs                  | 60 000 |
| Rent and rates                     | 10 000 |
| Depreciation of equipment          | 18 600 |
| Electricity, gas and telephone     | 3 000  |
| Advertising costs                  | 4 400  |

#### Questions

Determine the following:

1 The overhead cost per effective hour to cover the cost of rent, rates, depreciation, electricity, gas, telephone and advertising.
2 The gross labour cost per hour (for labour plus overhead).
3 The price paid by the customer for six hours of labour time and £40 worth (at cost) of parts. Assume that Pronto-Fix add 20% to total costs to provide for financial charges and profit.

#### Solution

1 Total overheads per year    = £36 000
  Annual effective hours      = 6000

$$\text{Overhead cost per effective hour} = \frac{£36\ 000}{6000} = £6.00 \text{ per hour}$$

**2** Gross labour cost per hour = labour cost per effective hour + overhead cost per hour

= £10.00 per hour + £6.00 per hour

= £16.00 per hour

**3** Total cost = (Labour hours × gross labour rate per hour) + cost of parts

= (6 hours × £16.00 per hour) + £40.00

= £96.00 + £40.00 = £136.00

Charge to customer = Total cost + 20% 'Profit' margin

= £136.00 + £27.20 = £163.20

## 3.2.2 Absorption of indirect costs by products

Once all overhead costs have been apportioned to cost centres, they can be charged out to individual products by sharing the overheads among all units passing through each cost centre. The accounting term for this is absorption (because the products absorb the overhead costs). It requires computing an **overhead absorption** (or recovery) rate, based on some notion of standard or normal volume. That predetermined rate of overhead absorption is then applied to actual volume in order to determine actual product costs. Common bases for overhead absorption are as follows:

- direct labour (either hours or costs);
- units of output; and
- machine hours.

Table 3.4 shows the general approach.

Table 3.4 *Absorption (full) costing*

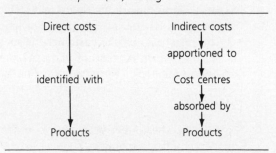

**Example 3.1**

Suppose a business expects total overheads applicable to a cost centre to be £480 000 next year; and the cost centre is expected to operate at 80% of capacity of 100 000 direct labour hours per year. Then overheads will be absorbed at the rate of £6.00 per direct labour hour (i.e. £480 000/80 000 hours) for the purpose of product costing. Then, for various purposes (such as quoting a price for a special job or valuing stock at the end of a period) one may estimate the direct costs (material and direct labour) separately and simply add on the standard overhead absorption rate. This is often expressed as a percentage of the direct labour cost. So if labour costs were £4.00 per hour, overheads (@ £6.00 per direct labour hour) would represent 150% of direct labour costs.

If costs for a particular job include £7000 for material and £4000 for direct labour, the standard overhead costs would be 150% of direct labour, i.e. £6000; and total factory costs for the job would be £17 000 (i.e. £7000 plus £4000 plus £6000).

Now examine Case study 3.2.

---

**Case study 3.2**

*Problem*

Easidig Garden Equipment Ltd make shovels, spades and garden forks which they sell to local retailers. During the last three months they made and sold 8000 forks, 7000 spades and 5000 shovels. The gross manufacturing labour cost (including holiday pay, sick pay, national insurance, etc.) is £6 per hour for each man. The manufacturing times and material costs are as follows:

|  | Fork | Spade | Shovel |
|---|---|---|---|
| Labour minutes per unit |  |  |  |
| Fabrication | 6 | 6 | 9 |
| Assembly | 3 | 3 | 3 |
| Materials cost per unit |  |  |  |
| Steel | £2.30 | £1.80 | £1.70 |
| Wood | £0.50 | £0.50 | £0.60 |
| Fasteners | £0.10 | £0.10 | £0.10 |

Total manufacturing overheads for the last three months were £39 000 and are recovered on direct labour minutes.

*Questions*

Determine for each product the following:

1 Labour cost per unit.
2 Manufacturing overhead cost per unit.
3 Total cost per unit.

*Solution*

1    Labour cost per unit:

|       | labour mins. per unit | × | labour rate | = | labour cost/ unit |
|-------|-----------------------|---|-------------|---|-------------------|
| Fork  | 9 mins.               | × | £6.00 per hour/60 | = | £0.90 |
| Spade | 9 mins.               | × | £6.00 per hour/60 | = | £0.90 |
| Shovel| 12 mins.              | × | £6.00 per hour/60 | = | £1.20 |

2    Manufacturing overhead costs per unit:

|       | labour mins. per unit | × | no. of units produced | = | labour mins. |
|-------|-----------------------|---|------------------------|---|--------------|
| Fork  | 9 mins.               | × | 8000                   | = | 72 000 |
| Spade | 9 mins.               | × | 7000                   | = | 63 000 |
| Shovel| 12 mins.              | × | 5000                   | = | 60 000 |

Total labour minutes    =    195 000

Manufacturing overhead cost per minute    $= \dfrac{£39\,000}{195\,000}$

= £0.20 per minute

Therefore, manufacturing overhead cost per unit = manufacturing overhead cost per minute × labour minutes per unit.

Manufacturing overhead:

|       | £/minute | × | minutes | = | £/unit mfg. overhead |
|-------|----------|---|---------|---|----------------------|
| Fork  | £0.20    | × | 9       | = | £1.80 |
| Spade | £0.20    | × | 9       | = | £1.80 |
| Shovel| £0.20    | × | 12      | = | £2.40 |

3    Total cost per unit:

|       | Labour | + | material | + | mfg. overhead | = | total |
|-------|--------|---|----------|---|---------------|---|-------|
| Fork  | £0.90  | + | £2.90    | + | £1.80         | = | £5.60 |
| Spade | £0.90  | + | £2.40    | + | £1.80         | = | £5.10 |
| Shovel| £1.20  | + | £2.40    | + | £2.40         | = | £6.00 |

### 3.2.3 Activity-based costing

Orthodox costing systems often relate overhead costs to products in proportion to direct labour time (or cost). Some people think this approach produces wrong numbers. They claim that the real cost of some low volume products may be up to ten times higher than such costing methods suggest.

**Activity-based costing (ABC)** relates overhead costs to products via **cost drivers**, i.e. causal links between products and overhead costs. ABC

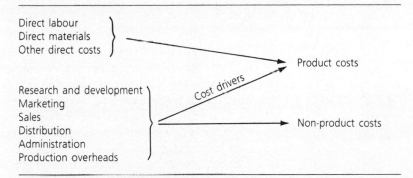

Figure 3.1 *Product costing using ABC*

Table 3.5 *Examples of cost drivers*

| Overhead cost | Activity | Cost driver |
|---|---|---|
| Product design | modelling, drawing, etc. | number of designs |
| Goods inwards | receipt of goods | number of orders |
| Scheduling<br>Set-up<br>Material handling<br>Inspection | production runs | number of production runs |
| Power | machine operation | number of machine hours |
| Sales commission | obtaining sales orders | amount of sales revenue |
| Despatch | shipping goods | number of shipping orders |

continues to attribute direct costs to products in the normal way, as Figure 3.1 shows.

Cost drivers are activities or transactions that significantly infuence the amount of specific overhead costs. Table 3.5 shows possible examples. Establishing cost drivers is often not easy. For instance, the goods inwards for different products may be very different in weight or bulk, requiring either a 'combination' cost driver or a different one (e.g. weight). The object is to establish a close link between the cost driver and the cause of overhead cost. Overhead costs are then apportioned to products in proportion to the number of cost driver transactions. ABC is not an exact science but aims to achieve less inaccurate costs than an orthodox costing system. To establish its own ABC system, a company must satisfy itself that the cost drivers it uses really are suitable for its particular business.

**Example 3.2**
Material handling costs for Hundy Products are £250 000 per year. The number of production runs (the cost driver) is 50 per year. If product XL is run seven

times per year, the material handling cost apportioned to it will be: 7/50 ×
£250 000 = £35 000 per year.

ABC may be useful when overheads are a major element of total cost,
as often happens in service businesses and non-profit seeking entities.
In recent years, advances in manufacturing technology have reduced
direct labour costs, often to as little as 10–15% of total product cost. At
the same time, they have led to increases in overheads. Costing systems
which recover overheads in proportion to direct labour costs may produce
even less accurate data as labour costs shrink in relative importance.

Product design, production planning, and some buying and selling
costs will not vary with the sales volume of a particular product. Product
range, design complexity, and number and type of distribution channels
and customers are more likely to affect them. Greater use of standard
components could mitigate the complexity costs (more parts, more
drawings, etc.) of a large product range.

For an ABC system to be cost effective, it should focus on expensive
overheads, consumption of which is not volume-related, and is likely
to differ between products. If ABC leads to more accurate costs, then
better decisions should result. These might include changes to prices,
product mix, or product range. ABC may also direct attention to reducing
costs by such measures as redesign, process changes, lower set-up times,
improved plant layout and material handling.

### 3.3 Marginal costing

#### 3.3.1 Contribution and profit

We saw in section 2.2 that variable costs are those which change in line
with output, while fixed costs remain unchanged. In relating costs to
revenues, it may be useful to attribute variable costs to products (see
Chapter 4). But any apportionment of fixed costs to products is likely
to be arbitrary and subject to a large margin of error.

The excess of sales revenue over variable costs is known as **contribution**, which means 'contribution towards covering fixed costs and profits'.
Of course, this is not the same as profit. In order to determine profit,
the total fixed costs have to be deducted from the total contribution of
all the firm's products.

Figure 3.2 illustrates with an example, the numbers for which are set
out in Table 3.6. In estimating each product's contribution, there are three
simple steps:

1 For each cost centre, allocate variable costs to the appropriate product.
2 For each product, total the variable costs from the various cost centres.
3 For each product, deduct total variable costs from sales revenue, to
  give the product's contribution.

and finally:

4 Add together all the products' contributions and deduct total fixed
  costs, in order to determine total profit.

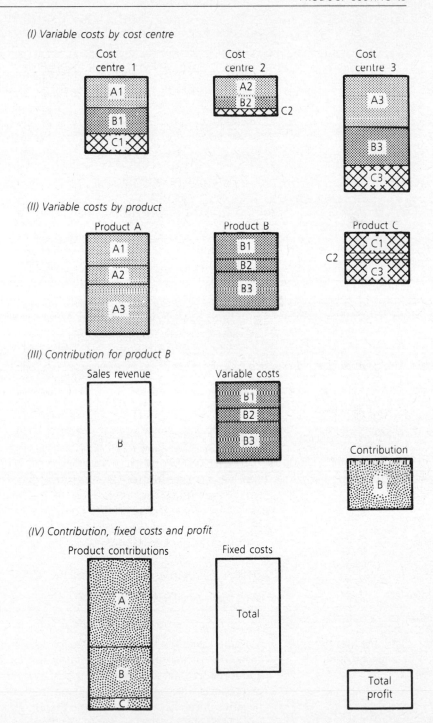

Figure 3.2 *Variable costs, contributions and profit*

Table 3.6 *Variable costs, contributions and profit*

|  | Cost centre 1 | Cost centre 2 (£'000) | Cost centre 3 |
|---|---|---|---|
| Product A | 5 | 3 | 8 |
| Product B | 4 | 2 | 6 |
| Product C | 3 | 1 | 4 |
| Total | 12 | 6 | 18 |

*(I) Variable costs by cost centre*

|  | Product A | Product B (£'000) | Product C | Total |
|---|---|---|---|---|
| Cost centre 1 | 5 | 4 | 3 | = 12 |
| Cost centre 2 | 3 | 2 | 1 | = 6 |
| Cost centre 3 | 8 | 6 | 4 | = 18 |
| Total | 16 | 12 | 8 | = 36 |

*(II) Variable costs by product*

|  | Product A | Product B (£'000) | Product C | Total |
|---|---|---|---|---|
| Sales revenue | 30 | 20 | 10 | = 60 |
| Variable costs | 16 | 12 | 8 | = 36 |
| Contribution | 14 | 8 | 2 | = 24 |

*(III) Contribution by product*

|  | Product A | Product B (£'000) | Product C | Total |
|---|---|---|---|---|
| Contribution | 14 | 8 | 2 | = 24 |
| Fixed costs |  | Not apportioned |  | = 18 |
|  |  |  |  | 6 |
| Profit |  |  |  | = 6 |

*(IV) Contribution, fixed costs and profit*

## 3.3.2 The uses of marginal costing

Marginal costing is objective, in that it does not try to apportion fixed costs to particular products. It is fairly simple. It can apply to current and future estimates, as well as for past evaluation. It focuses attention on products which appear to be making only small contributions (or even negative ones). Because it is simple the marginal costing approach can include changes in data as soon as they are known. This may be more difficult with more complex methods, which therefore tend to be out of date.

One of the main uses of marginal costing is in comparing actual current performance with the budgeted (planned) performance. (Chapter 9 discusses this kind of variance analysis.) It is helpful to be able to analyse a firm's planned total profit in order to know which aspects of the business need to be looked at further, and possibly corrective action taken. Managers who are not expert accountants will need to consider regular reports so the simpler the analysis is to understand, the better.

In interpreting the results, one will usually be comparing an actual outcome with a **standard**. Very often this will be the budget, prepared and agreed before the start of the accounting period. Marginal costing tends to look at short-term aspects of a business, where the scale of operations is already fixed. A good deal more information will be needed for decisions about *changing* the scale of the business. It is also more applicable where no major changes in stock levels are taking place.

There are certain drawbacks with marginal costing. Perhaps the most important is that some people may tend to confuse contribution with profit. They may regard even a small positive contribution as sufficient. It may not be disastrous for a product to show a small positive contribution (though a negative contribution would be unusual in most firms). A new product may take time for sales to develop. Or an old product may be on the way out because its costs have been growing more rapidly than selling prices. In order for a firm to make any profit, however, the positive contributions from all its products need in total to be at least large enough to cover the fixed costs.

In looking at operating results in the light of marginal costing, it may be difficult to know how much contribution any particular product should provide. But this should be resolved at the budgeting stage, difficult though it may be. The state of the markets for the various products is also critical. For example, if a product's costs increase (say because raw materials costs have increased more than expected), it may be impossible to raise selling prices, at least in the short term. It is true that some firms try to set their selling prices on the basis of variable costs plus a 'mark-up'. But (a) this mark-up percentage may not be the same for all products, and (b) it may not be possible to maintain the level of mark-up for a product if selling conditions change.

. Now examine Case study 3.3.

## Case study 3.3

### *Problem*
Continuing the study of Easidig Garden Equipment Ltd, results for the last quarter are as follows:

|  | Fork | Spade | Shovel |
|---|---|---|---|
| Sales (units) | 8000 | 7000 | 5000 |
| Price per unit | £8.50 | £7.50 | £6.50 |
| Variable costs: | | | |
| Labour cost | £0.90 | £0.90 | £1.20 |
| Materials cost | £2.90 | £2.40 | £2.40 |
| Fixed costs: | | | |
| Manufacturing overheads | £39 000 | | |
| Sales and admin. costs | £25 000 | | |

*Questions*

Determine the following:

1 Contribution per unit of each product.
2 Contribution in total for each product.
3 Total contribution.
4 Profit for the quarter.

***Solution***

1 Contribution to profit and overheads = selling price − variable costs

|  | price/unit | − | variable costs/unit | = | contribution/unit |
|---|---|---|---|---|---|
| Fork | £8.50 | − | £3.80 | = | £4.70 |
| Spade | £7.50 | − | £3.30 | = | £4.20 |
| Shovel | £6.50 | − | £3.60 | = | £2.90 |

2 Contribution in total for each product = contribution per unit × number of units sold

|  | contribution/unit | × | units sold | = | contribution |
|---|---|---|---|---|---|
| Fork | £4.70 | × | 8000 | = | £37 600 |
| Spade | £4.20 | × | 7000 | = | £29 400 |
| Shovel | £2.90 | × | 5000 | = | £14 500 |

3 Total contribution = £81 500

4 Profit = total contribution − total fixed costs
  = £81 500 − £64 000
  = £17 500

## 3.4 Full costing versus marginal costing

Both full costing and marginal costing are used in practice. Where indirect costs form a high proportion of total costs, management are more likely to make an effort to apportion them between products. But accuracy is often impossible. For example, indirect supervision may be split between products on the basis of direct labour hours worked on each product, although it may not follow that supervision is split in exactly the same proportions.

Full costing does arrive at a profit for each product, but only after more or less arbitrary apportionment of indirect costs. The accounting calculation, and resulting management reports, can be difficult to understand, especially since changes in stock levels can seriously distort the results. (See Problem 8 at the end of Chapter 4, pp. 77–8.)

Marginal costing is simpler to apply and easier to understand, but it does risk pressure to 'shave' margins as long as a product is showing any positive contribution at all. If this is not carefully watched, the result can be that the overall total contribution of all a firm's products added together is not large enough to cover the total fixed costs. There will then, of course, be a loss. Table 3.7 summarizes the advantages and disadvantages of full costing and marginal costing.

To show how the two approaches might differ, the fixed costs in Table 3.6 are apportioned below between products, on three different bases (see Table 3.8). Without knowing a good deal more about the business, we cannot tell which, if any, is most nearly correct. (Indeed, it may be that even people who have worked in the business for years cannot tell either.)

Table 3.7 *Full costing versus marginal costing: advantages and disadvantages*

| Full costing | Marginal costing |
|---|---|
| *Disadvantages* | *Advantages* |
| Difficult to understand | Easy to understand |
| Complicated and time-consuming to use | Simplifies budgeting and variance analysis |
| Tends to become out of date | Can quickly incorporate changes in cost |
| Full costs are subjective not uniquely correct | Avoids arbitrary apportionment of indirect costs |
| Potentially misleading when stock levels change | Identifies low contribution products |
| *Advantages* | *Disadvantages* |
| Indicates total cost of a product or service | Possible confusion of contribution with profit |
| Identifies product profitability | Overemphasis on short-term results |
| Useful to compare with selling price | May encourage selling at below full cost |

Table 3.8 *Three possible ways to apportion fixed costs*

|  | Product A | Product B | Product C | Total |
|---|---|---|---|---|
|  |  | (£'000) |  |  |
| (a) Fixed costs in proportion to sales revenue |  |  |  |  |
| Contribution | 14 | 8 | 2 | = 24 |
| Fixed costs | 9 | 6 | 3 | = 18 |
| Profit (loss) | 5 | 2 | (1) | 6 |
| (b) Fixed costs in proportion to variable costs |  |  |  |  |
| Contribution | 14 | 8 | 2 | = 24 |
| Fixed costs | 8 | 6 | 4 | = 18 |
| Profit (loss) | 6 | 2 | (2) | 6 |
| (c) Fixed costs apportioned equally |  |  |  |  |
| Contribution | 14 | 8 | 2 | = 24 |
| Fixed costs | 6 | 6 | 6 | = 18 |
| Profit (loss) | 8 | 2 | (4) | 6 |

The three ways to apportion fixed costs as in Table 3.8 might be justified as follows:

1 In proportion to sales revenue — if the fixed costs are salesmen's salaries.
2 In proportion to variable costs — if the fixed costs relate to supervision of manufacturing labour (assuming manufacturing labour is a large portion of variable costs).
3 Equally over each product line — where top management spends its time roughly equally over each of its products.

There are two basic approaches, as follows:

1 Use one common basis for apportioning all fixed costs to products.
2 Use the most appropriate basis for apportioning each category of fixed cost.

## 3.5 Joint costs

**Joint costs** arise when two or more (joint) products are made partly or wholly as a result of the same production process. Examples of joint products are crude oil derivatives (petrol, paraffin, oils), livestock (various cuts of meat, hides, petfood), and lumber products. Other products with relatively small resale value arising from the same process are called by-products (for example, animal hooves, fat, etc.). Before the **split-off point** costs cannot be traced to particular products; though for purposes of stock valuation (and hence profit determination) cost apportionments are required. Further processing costs may arise after the split-off point but before sale.

### Example 3.3

Table 3.9 shows costs and sales proceeds for joint products A and B, and for by-product C. Total profit is £56 000 (total sales revenue £144 000 less total costs £88 000). The question is how much profit is attributable to A and how much to B?

One approach to apportioning joint costs to products, and hence estimating their profitability, is as follows:

**1** Stage 1 deducts by-product C's sales proceeds of £6000 from the joint costs of £76 000, leaving net joint costs of £70 000 to be split between joint products A and B.

**2** Stage 2 deducts A's further processing costs of £12 000 from A's final sales revenue of £66 000, leaving net realizable value of £54 000 for A at the split-off point, and £72 000 for B.

**3** Stage 3 apportions net joint costs of £70 000 between A and B in proportion to the net realizable value at the split-off point, namely 3/7 [54/126] to A (= £30 000) and 4/7 [72/126] to B (= £40 000).

Overall profit is, thus, as follows:

| Joint product | Sales | Costs | | Profit |
|---|---|---|---|---|
| A | £66 000 | £42 000 | = | £24 000 |
| B | £72 000 | £40 000 | – | £32 000 |
| | | | | £56 000 |

Table 3.9 *Costs and sales revenue for joint products*

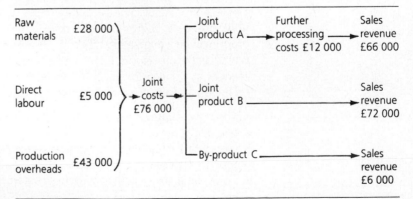

There may be other possible ways to apportion joint costs, based either on physical volume, or on the assumption that all joint products should make the same percentage gross profit on sales. As with apportioning of overheads to products, there is no single correct answer.

Because joint products cannot be produced independently, the firm must decide whether or not (i) to produce at all and (ii) to process further, based on the total profitability of all the joint products.

## 3.6 Costing services and projects

This chapter has explained the important principles of costing in a manufacturing context. Much of this chapter also applies to determining costs outside the manufacturing sector, and we now look briefly at two other major areas — services and projects.

### 3.6.1 Services

The cost of services may include little or no material costs, there may be no inventories, and most costs may be fixed in the short term.

**Example 3.4**

The Hotel Parkview has a restaurant and bar, both open to non-residents, as well as bedrooms. Direct materials for these three services comprise mostly variable costs. Staff costs are largely fixed, although the hotel employs extra staff at busier times. Most staff costs can be identified directly with the business area concerned.

The hotel can also probably identify other direct costs. It will capitalize, and depreciate over their expected useful life, those which involve substantial sums and are likely to last for a number of years; while it expenses other direct costs in the year in which it incurs the expenditure. There will also be some costs (rent, rates, financial charges, etc.) which the hotel cannot directly identify with any particular service. Table 3.10 summarizes the various kinds of costs.

In many service businesses profit is highly sensitive to volume. Thus, a hotel's profitability will be highly dependent on the occupancy rate. With most costs being fixed, the contribution (to cover fixed costs and profit) will be a large percentage of any additional sales revenue. That is why, in the off-season, hotels and airlines often combine to offer their services in a 'cut-price' package not very much above marginal cost.

The key aspects of service operations will tend to be the following:

- The initial strategy decision about the type of establishment and the size of the business.
- Generating a high level of capacity usage at selling prices which will produce profits.
- Controlling costs, while satisfying customers as to quality.

Table 3.10 *Hotel service costs: direct and indirect*

| Service | Direct costs | | | Indirect costs (mostly fixed) |
|---|---|---|---|---|
| | Materials (variable) | Labour (mostly fixed) | Other costs (mostly fixed) | |
| Bedrooms | Bed linen<br>Soap<br>Toilet paper<br>Tissues | Chambermaid | Furniture<br>Televisions<br>Telephones | Building rent<br>(or depreciation)<br>Rates<br>Electricity<br>Gas |
| Restaurant | Food<br>Cooking oil | Chef<br>Waiters<br>Washers-up | Furniture<br>Crockery<br>Cutlery<br>Cooking equipment<br>and utensils | Water<br>Laundry<br>Maintenance<br>Reception<br>General management |
| Bar | Drinks<br>Cigarettes<br>Cigars<br>Crisps<br>Nuts | Bar staff<br>Washers-up | Glasses<br>Bar equipment | Advertising<br>Financial charges |

## 3.6.2 Contracts and projects

Finally in this chapter, we need to consider costs for contracts and projects. Generally, the term 'contract' refers to standard products, and 'project' to non-repetitive work. Sections 3.1 to 3.4 also thus apply to contracts.

Job costing is used to estimate project costs. This requires cost estimates for material, labour and overheads. The greater the use of common component parts, the more accurate the estimated cost should be. For new types of businesses, the actual cost may differ widely from estimates. It is therefore usual to include in cost estimates a cost contingency allowance for unknown (but expected) problems.

Longer-term projects (5–15 years' duration) may encounter additional problems to those normal in a manufacturing business. For example:

- Great uncertainty due to unfamiliar non-repetitive work or untried new equipment.
- Construction or installation activities in foreign countries, perhaps under extremely adverse physical and political conditions.
- The cumulative effects of inflation over several years.
- Long-term exposure to currency fluctuations.

Technical problems may result in higher costs by having to carry out work for longer periods, and maybe a cost penalty for late completion.

Also, there may be liquidated damages if a completed project fails to perform adequately. Davy Corporation was reported to have lost over £100 million on the Ali Baba/Emerald oil rig, a £120 million fixed-price contract involving technology of which it had little experience.

Fixed price projects involve large financial risks. Delays or unexpectedly high inflation will increase contractors' costs, and therefore reduce profit. For this reason, contractors often seek a price which will be adjusted for inflation (by means of a cost escalation clause).

| | |
|---|---|
| 3.7 **Chapter summary** | Knowledge of product costs helps in planning financial resources, controlling costs, valuing stock, value analysis, and in setting selling prices. |

Full product costs include both direct and indirect costs. Full costing systems apportion indirect costs to cost centres whence products absorb them. Comparing full cost with the product selling prices indicates profit. The activity-based costing (ABC) approach apportions overheads to products via activity cost drivers.

Marginal costing takes account only of variable costs: it is simpler than full costing, in that it does not attempt to apportion fixed costs. Product selling price less variable cost gives the contribution to fixed costs and profit.

Joint costs arise from making joint products. They require cost apportionment in order to estimate (separate) product costs, and hence profits.

Either full costing or marginal costing techniques can apply to services. Many services involve few material costs, with a high proportion of fixed costs, hence a high contribution. Estimating and controlling long-term project costs can be difficult, due to the unique nature of the work, the problems of working abroad, inflation and currency movements.

## 3.8 **Review questions**

1 Why are cost centres needed for (traditional) full costing?
2 Suggest three different specific bases for apportioning indirect costs.
3 What is 'absorption'? Name three possible bases for overhead absorption by products.
4 What is activity-based costing?
5 What is the difference between contribution and profit?
6 What are the key steps in determining a product's contribution?

7 Name two advantages and two disadvantages of marginal costing.
8 Why may a small positive contribution be satisfactory?
9 Why may a small positive contribution be unsatisfactory?
10 Name three reasons why actual historical costs may be unsatisfactory as standards.
11 Name three different purposes for which standard costs can be used.
12 Name two advantages of full costing over marginal costing.

**13** In what major respects does costing for services differ from costing for manufacturing?

**14** What additional factors have to be considered when estimating long-term project costs?

**15** How do changes in stock levels affect profit in a company using a full costing system?

To maximize learning, please *write out* your answers on a separate piece of paper. *Then* check with the answers in Appendix C, pp. 231–2.

## 3.9 **Problems**

**1** Refer to Easidig Garden Equipment Ltd on pp. 41–2. What would be the cost of each product if manufacturing overheads were recovered on the basis of each product's labour plus material cost? (See solution in Appendix C, pp. 232–3.)

**2** Reynolds and Jukes Ltd, a light engineering firm, has received an inquiry for 10 000 components, which would need to be turned, milled and ground. Each 100 components will require 10 metres of 12 mm diameter steel bar, at a cost of £1.80p per metre. Turning output is 30 pieces per minute, milling 60 pieces per minute, and grinding 15 pieces per minute. Only one machine of each type is available, each staffed by a skilled machinist paid £6.00 per hour.

At the machine outputs above, works fixed overheads would correspond to 90p per 100 components. The variable overheads can be apportioned as 100% of direct labour costs. Company policy is to charge a selling price which is 10% above total standard costs.

*Questions*

(a) What is the standard cost for the order?
(b) What is the proposed selling price per 100 units?
(c) What are the main pros and cons of this system of calculating (i) product cost, and (ii) selling price?

(See solution in Appendix C, p. 232.)

**3** The managing director of Thompson Tailors is thinking of abandoning production of one of the company's four lines of trousers, on the basis of a costing statement (reproduced below) which shows style C as losing £5000 a year.

|  | Style | | | |
|---|---|---|---|---|
|  | A | B | C | D |
|  | (£'000s per year) | | | |
| Direct labour | 20 | 14 | 10 | 16 |
| Direct materials | 20 | 16 | 12 | 12 |
| Variable overheads | 20 | 20 | 8 | 12 |
|  | 60 | 50 | 30 | 40 |
| Fixed overheads | 30 | 25 | 15 | 20 |
| Total cost | 90 | 75 | 45 | 60 |
| Sales revenue | 94 | 110 | 40 | 76 |
| Profit (loss) | 4 | 35 | (5) | 16 |

*Questions*

(a) Does the information shown justify abandoning style C?
(b) Suggest an alternative presentation of the data. Does this new presentation suggest different recommendations for action?
(c) If Thompson Tailors abandons style C and re-allocates the fixed overheads between the remaining styles in the same proportions as now, what new decision is implied? What is the ultimate result of following this approach?

**4** The sales manager of Flexi-Lamp Ltd had just received a special order for 5000 adjustable reading lamps at a contract price of £26.00 each. He put this proposal to the managing director, who said: 'This really is the limit! A special order at less than the cost price of £29.20 per lamp, as well as an extra £4000 fixed overhead cost for a special design!' The company's latest profit and loss account for the first nine months of the current year is shown below:

Flexi-Lamp Ltd — Profit and Loss Account
January to September

|  | £ |
|---|---|
| Sales revenue | |
| (15 000 units @ £50 each) | 750 000 |
| Less costs: | |
| Materials | |
| (15 000 units @ £3.40) | 51 000 |
| Labour | |
| (15 000 units @ £15.00) | 225 000 |
| Manufacturing | |
| overheads: | |
| Variable | |
| (15 000 units @ £1.80) | 27 000 |
| Fixed (9/12ths of £360 000) | 270 000 |
| Admin., selling & distribution | |
| overhead @ £21 000 per | |
| month | 189 000 |
|  | 762 000 |
| Net profit (loss) | (12 000) |

A unit cost statement is set out below:

|  | £ per unit |
|---|---|
| Direct materials | 3.40 |
| Direct labour | 15.00 |
| Manufacturing | |
| overheads: | |
| variable | 1.80 |
| fixed (based on 40 000 | |
| units a year) | 9.00 |
| Total production cost | 29.20 |

*Questions*

(a) Should the firm make the special order? Give your reasons.
(b) Should the firm accept orders of this type in the future?

**5** The Roundabout Hotel has forty bedrooms, a sixty-seat restaurant and a bar which will accommodate up to eighty people. A recent cost analysis has identified the following cost structure:

| Fixed costs per year: | |
|---|---|
| Accommodation | £100 000 |
| Restaurant | £30 000 |
| Bar | £15 000 |
| General (i.e. indirect) | £40 000 |

| Variable cost per £1 revenue: | |
|---|---|
| Accommodation | 3p |
| Restaurant | 25p |
| Bar | 40p |
| General | 2p |

*Questions*

(a) What is the average fixed cost per day of: (i) a hotel bedroom; (ii) a restaurant table for four; (iii) a space in the bar?
(b) What is the hotel cost for: (i) one night in a £60 per night bedroom; (ii) a dinner party of four spending £60; (iii) a stag party of ten spending £50 in the bar?

**6** Izzard Products produce two joint products (J and K) and a by-product (L) in a single process. Ultimate selling prices are £1700 per tonne for J, £1325 per tonne for K, and £50 per tonne for L.

The costs for 100 tonnes of output are £68 000 up to the split-off point, resulting in 50 tonnes of J, 40 tonnes of K, and 10 tonnes of L. Products J and K incur further costs beyond the split-off point of £200 per tonne and £75 per tonne respectively.

*Question*

Determine the total costs and profits per tonne for products J and K assuming their costs to the split-off point are to be apportioned: (i) according to net realizable value; and (ii) to give the same percentage gross profit on sales.

(The solutions to Problems 3–6 will be provided in the *Instructors' Manual*.)

CHAPTER **4**    *Costs and revenues*

---

## 4.1 **Cost/profit/volume analysis**

Cost prediction and control are sometimes dealt with in isolation from sales revenue, and vice versa. At some level in the business, however, managers need to look at the interaction between them. For example, one fundamental problem with British Rail's regional organization had always been that those marketing the rail services had little idea of what it cost to provide them. According to John Welsby, BR's chief executive, speaking in his headquarters office: 'The lowest point in the organization at which the revenue side and the cost side of the equation came together was in this room' (Tomkins, 1991).

For a business to survive, revenues must exceed costs in the long run. Market forces, in the form of maximum attainable prices, often set a ceiling to long-term costs for a given volume of output. Very few firms can be confident of passing on whatever costs they incur in higher prices to customers. (Even monopolies are likely to be regulated if they go too far in this respect.)

Both costs and revenues usually vary with output; and a firm will want to know which level of output is likely to maximize profits. This chapter deals with short-term tactics, where existing facilities limit the scale of the business. Chapter 7 deals with longer-term capital investment.

A **breakeven chart** is a picture of costs and sales revenue for a firm (or a product), showing the volume of output at which sales revenue equals total costs. This is the breakeven volume when the firm (or product) is making neither profit nor loss. We shall first consider costs, then sales revenues, and then profit or loss, looking throughout at results for a whole firm. It can often be very difficult to apportion indirect costs between products (see section 3.2.1), hence breakeven analysis for individual products tends to be unreliable.

### 4.1.1 **Costs and volume**

In drawing breakeven charts, it is usual to make some simplifying assumptions. (We shall consider relaxing them later.) So we shall first assume that we can regard all a firm's costs either as variable or fixed. As we discussed in Chapter 2, these terms refer to how costs vary with

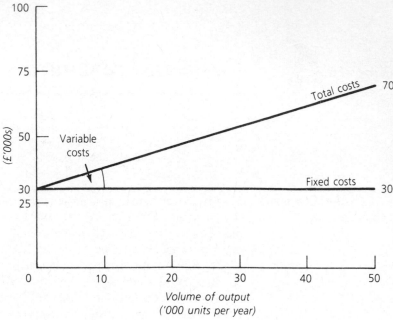

Figure 4.1 *Costs and outputs*

output. Variable costs vary linearly with output; fixed costs remain the same even if output changes.

For instance, suppose that a firm's variable costs amount to £0.80 per unit of output, and that fixed costs amount to £30 000 a year. Then we can draw a picture showing how total costs will vary with output (see Figure 4.1). Normal practice is to show volume of output on the horizontal axis, and money amounts on the vertical axis.

4.1.2 **Profit and volume**

To complete the breakeven chart, we must include sales revenue in the picture as well as costs. Let us assume there is only a single product, with a selling price of £2.00 per unit. Then, Figure 4.2 shows that the **breakeven point** occurs at 25 000 units of output. At that level, sales revenue of £50 000 exactly equals total costs of £30 000 fixed costs plus £20 000 variable costs. Above that level, sales revenue exceeds total costs and the firm makes a profit. At any level of output below 25 000 units a year, costs exceed sales revenue, and the firm makes a loss.

If the firm is planning to produce and sell, say, 40 000 units next year, the vertical line on the chart shows that the profit should be £18 000. We can check this in two ways. We know that total sales revenue will be £80 000 (= £2.00 × 40 000) and that total costs will be £62 000 (= fixed costs £30 000 + variable costs £32 000). Or we can say that the margin of safety is 15 000 units — this is the excess of planned output above

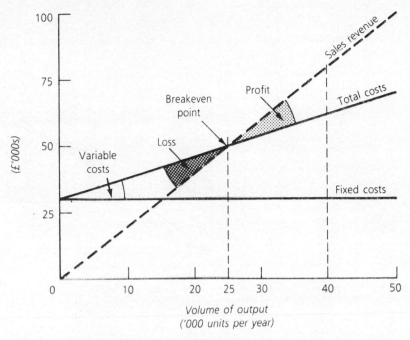

Figure 4.2 *The completed breakeven chart*

the breakeven level. On our assumptions, the extra profit (contribution) for every unit sold above the breakeven point is £1.20 (= £2.00 − £0.80). And £1.20 × 15 000 units is £18 000.

Another way to draw breakeven charts is to show the variable costs first and then add on the fixed costs (see Figure 4.3). The total cost line is, of course, the same as in Figure 4.2. This approach highlights the contribution to fixed costs and profit.

**4.1.3 Algebraic analysis**

The information we need to draw a breakeven chart also allows us to calculate the breakeven point by using simple algebra. We know that at the breakeven point total costs exactly equal sales revenue, and we can split total costs between fixed and variable costs. In order to calculate the breakeven point, therefore, we simply divide total fixed costs by the contribution per unit (in our example, £2.00 − £0.80 = £1.20).

At the breakeven point:

| | | |
|---|---|---|
| Sales revenue | = | total costs |
| Sales revenue (S) | = | variable costs (V) + fixed costs (F) |
| Sales revenue (S) − variable costs (V) | = | fixed costs (F) |

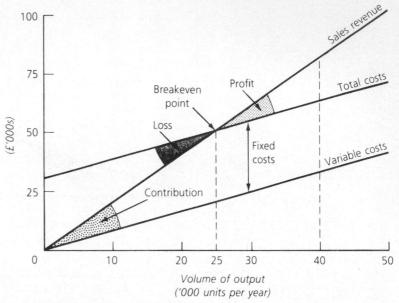

Figure 4.3 *Breakeven chart highlighting contribution*

Suppose we call breakeven output 'x' units, with 's' the selling price per unit; 'v' the variable cost per unit; and (s-v) the contribution per unit.

At breakeven, total sales revenue S = sx; and total variable costs V = vx. Then:

| | | | | | |
|---|---|---|---|---|---|
| £2.00x − £0.80x | = | £30 000 | sx − vx | = | F |
| £1.20x | = | £30 000 | x(s-v) | = | F |
| x | = | £30 000/£1.20 | | | |
| | = | 25 000 units | x | = | F/(s-v) |

Thus, to calculate the breakeven level of output, we simply divide the total fixed costs by the contribution per unit.

If the company planned to achieve a profit before tax of £12 000, we could establish the level of output needed by adding the profit before tax (P) to the fixed costs. The required level of output is then:

$$x = \frac{F + P}{s\text{-}v} \quad \text{which is} \quad \frac{£42\ 000}{£1.20} = 35\ 000 \text{ units.}$$

Using algebra to work out the breakeven point (and certain other aspects of the data) is usually quicker and more accurate than having to draw a breakeven chart and read off a rough estimate.

## 4.2 Changing the assumptions

One of the main uses of the breakeven chart is as an aid to profit planning. The chart, subject to its limitations, allows managers to see the effects on profit of varying cost/revenue/volume factors. One can, of course, read straight off the chart the effect of a change in assumptions about volume alone. For example, refer back to Figure 4.3: suppose that actual sales volume were 45 000 units next year, instead of the planned level of 40 000 units. The chart shows that profit would amount to just under £25 000 if other assumptions remained the same. (The calculated amount is: 20 000 × £1.20 = £24 000.)

Now suppose that the company cut the selling price per unit from £2.00 to £1.80 in an attempt to boost sales volume. What would happen to the breakeven point? It would rise from 25 000 units to 30 000 units (= £30 000 fixed costs divided by the new contribution per unit of £1.80 − £0.80 = £1.00).

Or suppose we keep the selling price at £2.00 per unit, but are able to reduce the variable costs from £0.80 per unit to £0.50. As a result, the contribution per unit increases from £1.20 to £1.50; and the breakeven point falls from 25 000 to 20 000 units.

Of course, it would be possible to combine the two changes, and other variations too. Thus, using very simple assumptions we can determine the profit or loss for any given level of output.

Now examine Case study 4.1.

## Case study 4.1

### Problem

Marion runs a small business that provides typing (using a PC) and photocopying services for other businesses, mostly small companies and sole traders. High-quality work and a rapid response allows her to charge a premium price of £15 per hour.

For next year, Marion estimates her fixed costs at £63 800 and her variable costs at 10% of sales revenue. The fixed costs include salaries, office building costs, equipment leasing costs and depreciation. The variable costs are mainly for consumables and electricity. The maximum number of productive hours is estimated at 4 people × 8 hours/day × 210 days per year = 6720 hours per year.

### Questions

1 How many hours of chargeable work need to be done next year in order to break even?
2 What is the breakeven sales revenue?
3 What percentage of capacity usage will provide a profit next year of £20 000?
4 What is the maximum profit potential of this business?

*Solution*

1 Breakeven number of hours:

$$= \frac{\text{fixed costs}}{\text{contribution per hour}}$$

$$= \frac{£63\ 800}{£15 - (£15 \times 0.10)} = 4726 \text{ hours}$$

2 Breakeven sales revenue:
$$= £15 \times 4726 = £70\ 890$$

3 Number of chargeable hours needed to give a profit of £20 000:

$$= \frac{\text{fixed costs \& profit}}{\text{contribution per hour}}$$

$$= \frac{£63\ 800 + £20\ 000}{£13.50} \text{ hours}$$

$$= 6207 \text{ hours}$$

Capacity utilization therefore:

$$= \frac{\text{chargeable productive hours}}{\text{maximum productive hours}} \times 100\%$$

$$= \frac{6207}{6720} \times 100 = 92.4\%$$

4 Maximum profit potential of this business:
$$= \text{sales revenue} - \text{fixed costs} - \text{variable costs}$$
(at full capacity)
$$= (6720 \times £15) - £63\ 800 - (6720 \times £1.50)$$
$$= £26\ 920$$

**4.2.1 The need for caution**

We have seen how to draw a breakeven chart and how to read off the breakeven point, and the amount of profit or loss at any given level of output. But we must remember the assumptions we have been making. Together they represent a highly simplified version of reality; hence, we need to interpret any conclusions with caution.

We have assumed the following:

- A single selling price per unit.
- An unchanging **sales mix** of products (if more than one).
- A single variable cost per unit (constant per unit, hence varying linearly with output).

- Fixed costs which remain the same at all levels of output.
- No changes in the level of stock (with output assumed to equal sales).

In practice, the mix of products may well change over time, and the selling price may need to vary with market conditions.

The variable cost may not remain exactly the same per unit throughout the entire range of output: at higher levels of output it may tend either to fall, because of quantity discounts and other economies of scale (see section 2.4.5), or to increase, because of overtime or other diseconomies of scale. (It would be an unlikely coincidence for these effects to cancel out across the whole range of output!)

Fixed costs may tend to increase in a 'step function' as output increases. As we shall see in section 4.3, they are fixed only for a limited range of output.

Finally, stock levels may change, which rather spoils our simple assumption that output equals sales. The financial accounting rules in SSAP 9 require firms to attribute some period (fixed) costs to the book value of end-of-period stocks held. Hence, the fixed costs incurred during a period may not equal the fixed costs charged as an expense in the profit and loss account; thus, any change in stock levels affects cost of goods sold, and hence profit.

In breakeven analysis, we are concerned with the behaviour of costs (and revenues) as output changes. The basic distinction is between variable and fixed costs. Variable costs would normally consist of direct labour, materials and some overheads.

Fixed costs would normally consist of the remaining overheads. It may not always be clear whether overheads are to be regarded as fixed or variable (see Chapter 2). All one can do is make (and state) what seems to be the most appropriate assumption. If fixed costs are stated separately, then any other item referred to as overheads is likely to be variable.

4.2.2 **More complex assumptions**

Figure 4.4 sets out a breakeven chart which includes more complex assumptions about three of the points just mentioned.

1 Sales revenue per unit falls slightly as volume increases, so that the sales revenue curve slopes down to the right.
2 Variable costs per unit fall to begin with, as quantity discounts begin to apply, but then increase as overtime costs outweigh this effect.
3 Fixed costs increase in a step function as output increases.

It is clear that these changes, taken together, result in a much more complex picture. As a matter of practice, it is quite common to draw breakeven charts using very simple assumptions; but they will then apply only for a rather limited range of output.

In Figure 4.4, one conclusion seems fairly obvious. The chart is worth

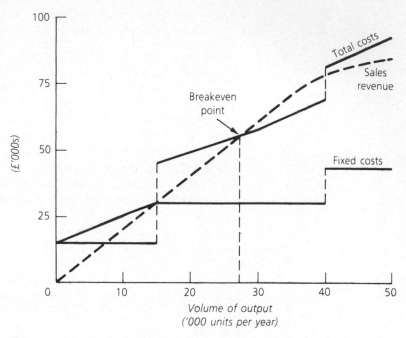

Figure 4.4 *Breakeven chart including more complex assumptions*

using only between output levels of 15 000 and 40 000 units a year; in other words, over the range for which fixed expenses are £30 000. Below an output of 15 000 units, no profit appears to be possible (the best outcome is breakeven, exactly zero profit, at 15 000 units); and above 40 000 units, because fixed costs jump by £12 500 to £42 500, total costs exceed sales revenue — and the position gets worse as output increases. Sales revenue per unit starts declining, and variable costs per unit start increasing.

Indeed, in Figure 4.4, there are no fewer than three breakeven points: at 15 000 units, at just under 28 000 units, and a transition from profit into loss at 40 000 units. This is perhaps more realistic than the charts we were looking at earlier, but evidently much harder to use and interpret.

### 4.2.3 Foreign currencies

So far we have calculated breakeven levels and profit in terms of a single currency. In practice, in international trade, costs and revenues will often arise in two or more currencies. When the currency exchange rates are not fixed but are free to vary, the effect on a firm's breakeven level and profit can be dramatic. For instance, between 1985 and 1991 the US dollar/£ exchange rate varied between $1.07 and $1.98 to the pound.

Now examine Case study 4.2.

## Case study 4.2

### Problem

Cheetah Bikes PLC makes motorcycles for the North American market. The current annual budget gives the following data:

Production output = sales = 20 000 units
Fixed costs = £6 million
Variable costs = £1500 per unit
Selling price = US $3000 per unit
Exchange rate: £1 = US $1.50

### Questions

1 What is the breakeven level of sales?
2 How much profit before tax is budgeted?
3 What would the budgeted profit be if the exchange rate was:
  (a) £1 = US $1.80?
  (b) £1 – US $1.20?
4 What would the new breakeven sales volumes be in 3(a) and 3(b) above?

### Solution

1 At breakeven:

| | |
|---|---|
| sales revenue | = total costs |
| $3000x | = £6 000 000 + £1500x |
| [1]£2000x | = £6 000 000 + £1500x |
| £500x | = £6 000 000 |
| x | = 12 000 motorcycles a year |

2 Budget:

| | | |
|---|---|---|
| Sales revenue 20 000 units @ £2000[1] | = | £40 million |
| Variable costs 20 000 units @ £1500 | = | £30 million |
| Fixed costs | = | £6 million |
| Profit | = | £4 million |

[1]$3000 @ $1.50 per £.

3 (a) Selling price $3000 @ $1.80 per £
    = £1666.67 per unit
  @ 20 000 units, total sales revenue
    = £33.3 million (a drop of £6.7 million from 2 above)
  Total costs = £36.0 million (= loss of £2.7 million)

  (b) Selling price $3000 @ $1.20 per £
    = £2500 per unit

@ 20 000 units, total sales revenue
$$= £50.0 \text{ million (an increase of } £10.0 \text{ million on}$$
2 above)
Total costs = £36.0 million (= profit of £14.0 million)

**4** (a) $£1667x$ = £6 000 000 + £1500x
$£167x$ = £6 000 000
$x$ = 36 000 motorcycles a year

(b) $£2500x$ = £6 000 000 + £1500x
$£1000x$ = £6 000 000
$x$ = 6000 motorcycles a year

## 4.3 Pricing

### 4.3.1 What affects price?

In setting prices, a business will be aiming for at least an adequate level of profit. Henry Ford I believed that motor vehicle prices were limited by what customers would be prepared to pay. To make a profit, therefore, Ford had to limit costs too. (Hence, perhaps, 'any colour you like, as long as it's black'?) In a well-informed competitive market there need be nothing unfair about charging whatever prices the market will bear. More broadly, prices may be affected by the following factors:

- The benefits which customers receive, and the value they attach to them.
- What it costs to make the product.
- The degree of competition in the marketplace.
- The prices of possible substitute products.

Monopolies such as British Gas have more discretion in pricing than, for example, textile companies (though there are political and regulatory restraints). But even British Gas would lose business, at least in the longer run, if it increased prices too much. Customers might then turn to electricity, oil or coal instead — in effect, putting some upper limit on feasible gas prices.

When firms introduce new products or enter new markets, they can adopt various pricing policies. Some firms may adopt a 'skimming' policy, pricing high for maximum short-term profits until fiercer competition arrives (which such a policy may attract!). They then cut prices to avoid losing too much market share (as with personal computers). Other firms may set prices much lower from the outset (like many Japanese companies) so as to achieve greater market penetration, and deter possible competitors from entering the market. They may also rely on costs falling due to the learning-curve effect (see section 2.4.4).

### 4.3.2 Costs and prices

In some types of business there is uncertainty about market prices. Competitors' prices may be unknown, product quality may vary widely, and nobody is really sure what the market will bear. As a result, many firms base the price of their goods and services on full cost plus a percentage mark-up. This approach is reasonably objective and aims to cover all a business's costs in the long run, even though apportionment of overheads cannot be precisely accurate (see section 3.2). Having computed what a 'full-cost plus' price would amount to, of course, a firm still has freedom to vary that amount depending on its view of market conditions.

### Example 4.1

For supplying and installing a gas central heating system for a large house, Robinson's Heating builds up its quoted price of £4608 as follows:

| | |
|---|---:|
| Cost of gas boiler, radiators, pipes, etc. | 2400 |
| Installation cost: 80 hours @ £9 per hour | 720 |
| Overheads @ 100% of labour cost | 720 |
| Total costs | 3840 |
| Plus: 20% mark-up | 768 |
| Quoted price | 4608 |

When the market is extremely competitive, some firms may be willing to quote prices only slightly above variable costs. They reason that, in hard times, any contribution towards fixed costs is better than none, and that when business improves they can move towards full-cost pricing. But of course, the danger is that times may remain 'hard', so that even in the long run, total contributions may fail to cover fixed costs.

### 4.3.3 Price elasticity

To help them set prices, firms may guess how much of their product they can sell at different prices. Table 4.1 sets out the estimated price/volume relationship (price-elasticity of demand) for Uni-Product Ltd's only product. Figure 4.5 shows the estimated price-elasticity of demand graphically (demand curve) and Figure 4.6 shows how total sales revenue varies with quantity sold. For most products, an increase in price (above general inflation) results in a fall in the quantity sold. But the total sales revenue may increase (see Figure 4.6).

### 4.3.4 Improving profit

Figure 4.6 shows which price will maximize total sales revenue (about £6). But maximizing sales revenue is less important than maximizing profit. Assuming no change in fixed costs, we can achieve maximum profit by maximizing contribution.

### Example 4.2

Uni-Product Ltd has fixed costs of £200 000 per year, and variable costs of £3 per unit. Given the price-elasticity estimates in Table 4.1, what selling price per unit

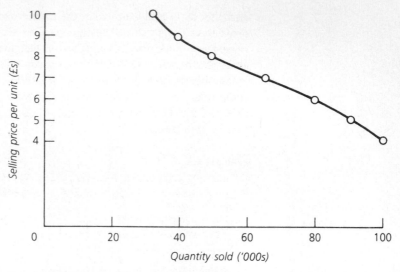

Figure 4.5 *Selling price versus quantity sold*

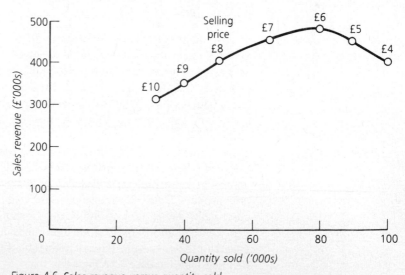

Figure 4.6 *Sales revenue versus quantity sold*

will maximize profit? To answer this question, Table 4.2 lists the total contribution at each price, and then deduct £200 000 to show total profit. Figure 4.7 charts the annual contribution and profit at each level of sales volume.

At the expected profit-maximizing selling price of £7.00, we can calculate the breakeven sales volume for Uni-Product to be 50 000 units. Thus, if sales are

Table 4.1 *Annual sales volume and total sales revenue for Uni-Product Ltd at various unit selling prices*

| Selling price (£ per unit) | Sales volume ('000 per year) | Sales revenue (£'000 per year) |
|---|---|---|
| 4 | 100 | 400 |
| 5 | 90 | 450 |
| 6 | 80 | 480 |
| 7 | 65 | 455 |
| 8 | 50 | 400 |
| 9 | 40 | 360 |
| 10 | 32 | 320 |

Table 4.2 *Contribution and profit versus sales volume*

| Selling price (£/unit) | Contribution per unit (£) | Sales × volume ('000 units/yr) | = | Contribution (£'000/yr) | Profit (£'000/yr) |
|---|---|---|---|---|---|
| 4 | 1 | 100 | = | 100 | − 100 |
| 5 | 2 | 90 | = | 180 | − 20 |
| 6 | 3 | 80 | = | 240 | 40 |
| 7 | 4 | 65 | = | 260 | 60 |
| 8 | 5 | 50 | = | 250 | 50 |
| 9 | 6 | 40 | = | 240 | 40 |
| 10 | 7 | 32 | = | 224 | 24 |

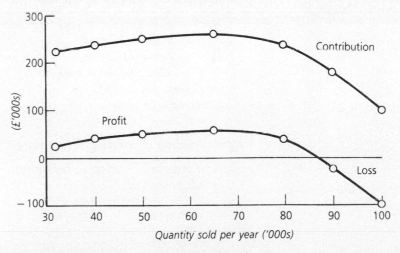

Figure 4.7 *Contribution and profit versus sales volume*

actually 65 000 units, as expected, profit is the contribution of £4.00 per unit × 15 000 (= £60 000).

A firm needs to consider the implications of changes in selling price, as follows:

- How will existing competitors react? Will new competitors enter the market?
- How will customers react? Will they all react in the same way?
- How long will selling price levels remain the same?
- How much will it cost to implement price changes?

Businesses whose costs are mostly fixed, such as cinemas, schools, hotels, airlines, may aim to maximize sales revenue as a proxy for maximizing profit. With low variable costs, sales revenue will be almost the same as contribution. Hence, maximizing sales revenue, an operating goal which is easy to understand, will result in almost optimum profits. But this will not be true where many costs vary with output.

Now consider Case study 4.3.

## Case study 4.3

### Problem

Ghudhaz New PCs Ltd is a small company which buys and sells second-hand personal computers (PCs). The company currently sells PCs at 70% of their original price, but believes that by reducing prices to 40% of the original price it can treble sales volume. The following data may assist with the final decision.

| | |
|---|---|
| Number of PCs sold per year (at present) | 1600 |
| Average original PC price | £1500 |
| Average cost to Ghudhaz New PCs Ltd | £525 |
| Average selling price (at present) | £1050 |
| Fixed costs per year | £600 000 |
| Other variable costs | 6% of sales revenue |

Estimated effect of reducing selling prices:

| % of original £1500 price | Average selling price | PCs sold per year |
|---|---|---|
| 70% | £1050 | 1600 |
| 60% | £900 | 2350 |
| 50% | £750 | 3400 |
| 40% | £600 | 4800 |

Table 4.3 *Estimated contribution and profit for Ghudhaz New PCs Ltd*

| Average selling price | Contribution per PC | PCs sold/year | Sales revenue (£'000) | Contribution per year |
|---|---|---|---|---|
| £1 050 | £1 050 − £525 − £63 = £462 | 1 600 | 1 680 | £462 × 1 600 = £739 200 |
| £900 | £321 | 2 350 | 2 115 | £754 350 |
| £750 | £180 | 3 400 | 2 550 | £612 000 |
| £600 | £39 | 4 800 | 2 880 | £187 200 |

*Question*
What pricing policy do you recommend?

**Solution**
Maximum contribution (and profit) occurs at an average selling price of £900, at which profit = £154 350 per year (see Table 4.3).

The company should consider reducing the selling price below £1050, but the estimated extra profit of £15 150 from cutting average selling prices by £150 to £900 is not very large. And we do not know what would happen at prices between £1050 and £900. For instance, it may be that a selling price of £1000 would yield sales of 1850, giving a contribution of £767 750 (£415 × 1850); or a selling price of £950 might yield sales of 2150, giving a contribution of £791 200 (£368 × 2150).

The estimates suggest that reducing average selling prices much below £900 per PC would result in a declining profit figure. Of course, the estimated prices versus volume relationship is only a guess. It is well known that many businesses have only a weak idea of demand curves for their products (which may anyway change over time). A cautious management of Ghudhaz New PCs might reduce the price by only £50 at a time and see what happened to sales.

## 4.4 Chapter summary

It is often useful for management to know how costs vary with output. A breakeven chart shows how changes in output affect total costs and sales revenues, hence profit. It also shows the breakeven level of output, at which total costs (fixed plus variable) exactly equal total sales revenue. One can also calculate the breakeven point by algebra: it is the output volume resulting from dividing total fixed costs for a period by the contribution per unit.

Breakeven analysis assumes the following:

- Sales price is constant.
- Sales mix is constant.
- Variable costs vary directly with output (are constant per unit).
- Fixed costs do not change over the forecast range of output.
- Output volume equals sales volume (stock levels do not change).

These rather restrictive assumptions make caution essential in using simple breakeven analysis; yet relaxing them in favour of realism can make breakeven analysis too complex.

Profit-seeking firms need to estimate how changing selling prices might affect sales volume, sales revenue and profit. In practice, this is often not easy. As selling prices increase, sales volume normally declines, but profit may increase as a result. For a given level of fixed costs, maximizing profits means maximizing contribution, not maximizing sales revenue.

## 4.5 Review questions

1 What is a breakeven chart?
2 What information is needed to construct a breakeven chart?
3 Name five simplifying assumptions usually made in breakeven analysis. Explain how each of them may be unrealistic.
4 What is the 'margin of safety'?
5 In drawing a breakeven chart, how would you determine a suitable scale: (a) for the vertical axis; and (b) for the horizontal axis?
6 What is the algebraic formula for calculating the breakeven point?
7 At breakeven, what do total variable costs equal?
8 What is the breakeven point for a firm whose costs are: (a) all fixed; and (b) all variable?
9 What will happen to the breakeven point:

(a) if variable costs per unit rise; (b) if fixed costs fall; (c) if sales volume increases; (d) if contribution per unit falls; and (e) if selling price per unit rises? Explain *why* in each case.
10 Why would changes in stock levels (i.e. output different from sales) affect profit?
11 Why might variable costs per unit: (a) rise; or (b) fall as output increases?
12 How can there be more than one breakeven point?
13 What factors affect prices?
14 What is price-elasticity of demand? Why is it useful to have an estimate of price-elasticity of demand?
15 In order to maximize profit with a given level of fixed costs, what needs to be maximized — sales revenue or contribution? Why?

To maximize learning, please *write out* your answers on a separate sheet of paper. *Then* check with the answers in Appendix C, pp. 233–5.

## 4.6 Problems

1 Simkins Pumps Ltd's fixed costs are £300 000 a year. Sales price per unit is £18.00. Variable costs are £240 000. Present output is 40 000 units a year.

*Questions*
(a) What is the breakeven level of output?
(b) What will the breakeven level of output be (all other information remaining in

each case as in (1) above) if (separately): (i) fixed costs increase to £400 000 a year; (ii) variable costs increase by £2.00 per unit; (iii) sales price per unit falls to £16.00; or (iv) all of (i) to (iii) occur together?

(See solution in Appendix C, pp. 235–6.)

**2** Scott Ltd makes and sells two products, A and B. Because of the nature of the production process, two As are made for each B, and all planning is done on the basis that the number of units sold will also be in the proportion 2 to 1. Costs are as follows: variable costs per unit are A £4, B £6; fixed costs £300 000 a year. Each A sells for £12, each B for £10.

*Questions*

(a) Counting two As + one B as one unit, on an aggregate basis, what is the breakeven number of units?
(b) If fixed costs are split, £160 000 to A and £140 000 to B, what is the breakeven number of units for A and for B?
(c) How would fixed costs have to be split between A and B in order for the breakeven number of units for A to be the same as for B?

(See solution in Appendix C, pp. 236–7.)

**3** Crookall Equipment Ltd is currently operating at 75% of capacity, and making an annual profit of £3 million, which is 10% of its total costs. The firm's fixed overheads are £5m per year. The production director has suggested modernizing the firm's production processes and buying new machinery. This would increase fixed overheads by £10m a year, but would reduce the variable costs in such a way that the profit at 75% of capacity would remain unchanged.

*Questions*

(a) Construct a breakeven chart to show the present situation and the proposed alternative.
(b) At what per cent of capacity is the new breakeven point?
(c) What is the effect of the new proposal on the firm's range of profitable operation?
(d) What other factors would you consider before deciding whether to modernize as proposed?

**4** Glasspool Gliders Ltd manufactures high-class gliders in the United Kingdom for sale in both the United Kingdom and France. The company comprises three divisions: the manufacturing division in the United Kingdom, the UK Sales Division and the French Sales Division.

The manufacturing division is budgeting to make 1000 gliders in 1993, with a standard manufacturing cost of £12 000 per glider. 60% of this standard cost is regarded as variable. In addition to the manufacturing costs there are other (non-manufacturing) costs of £300 000 in total, all of which are considered to be fixed costs.

The UK sales division has budgeted to sell 650 gliders in 1993 at £21 000 each. The budgeted costs to be incurred by this division are £1 900 000 of fixed costs plus £1500 per glider.

The French sales division has budgeted to sell 350 gliders in 1993 at FFr (French Francs) 224 640 each. Their budgeted costs are FFr 28 080 000 of fixed costs plus FFr 17 280 per glider.

*Questions*

(a) How much profit (or loss) before tax is budgeted for Glasspool Gliders Ltd in 1993, assuming FFr 10.8 = £1?
(b) What is Glasspool Gliders' breakeven level of sales if FFr 12 = £1?

(c) If the sales mix was rebudgeted to 800 glider sales in the United Kingdom and 200 glider sales in France, what would the UK price need to be to achieve a budgeted company profit before tax of £2 000 000? Assume the French selling price remains at FFr 224 640 per glider, and FFr 10.8 = £1.

5  Martin Simpson Ltd sells portable radios. Different price and marketing strategies are used in the three national sales territories (North, Midlands and South). The table below shows the results, together with transport costs, for each territory:

|  | North | Midlands | South |
|---|---|---|---|
| Number of sales p.a. | 40 000 | 50 000 | 30 000 |
| Price per radio (£) | 90 | 80 | 100 |
| Marketing expenditure (£'000s) | 800 | 1200 | 1000 |
| Transport cost (£'000s) | 200 | 100 | 200 |

The variable cost of production per radio (i.e. direct labour, direct materials and variable overheads) is £50. Fixed overheads are running at £1 200 000 per year.

*Questions*

(a) What is the present contribution of each sales territory?
(b) What is the firm's present profit?
(c) What would be the effect of raising the price by £10.00 in each area, assuming that this would not reduce the sales volume?

6  Home and Overseas Trolleys Limited (HOT) sold a heated food trolley (to serve 8 to 10 people). The HOT trolley had two important benefits: it kept food hot between cooking and serving, and it could be wheeled round the table, making the process of serving much easier.

In October 1992, home sales, at £100 per unit, were running at about 5000 units a year. When the company, two years earlier, had begun selling in the American market at $200 a unit, the trolley's success had surprised HOT's management. Export sales volume (nearly all to North America) amounted to 2000 units in the calendar year 1991, and would probably reach 3000 units in 1992. HOT decided to try to expand their American exports further in 1993.

Variable costs of manufacture amounted to £60 per unit, leaving a margin of £40 to cover fixed costs as well as provide a net profit.

In planning ahead, HOT decided to keep its price the same all through the year 1993. For various reasons, it was difficult to change the price in mid-year. Mr Andrew Rolls, the Finance Director, decided to begin his 1993 planning by assuming that the exchange rate would be $1.50 = £1.00 throughout the year to 1993. If anything, he felt the £ was more likely to rise against the $, rather than to fall further, though either was quite possible. Mr Rolls had been feeling for some months that American interest rates might fall soon, which he expected would weaken the dollar.

The question was: what dollar selling price to charge in 1993? At much less than $200 per unit, the trolley would seem underpriced compared with its US rivals. On the other hand, it might be hard to increase sales volume if the price remained at $200. There was also a danger, if sales volume expanded too far, of reaching the domestic UK production limit of about 9000 units per year.

The latest sales forecast for the home market was for sales of 5000 units at £100 each in 1993. HOT had less confidence in the American sales forecasts. The company's best guess was that export sales volume in 1993 at various prices would be as follows:

| | |
|---|---|
| $120 | 8000 units |
| $150 | 6000 units |
| $180 | 4000 units |
| $200 | 3000 units |
| $225 | 2000 units. |

*Question*
What $ price per unit do you think HOT should charge for the American export market in 1993, assuming the following foreign exchange rates:

(a) £1 = $1.50
(b) £1 = $1.80
(c) £1 = $2.00?

7  Kaiser Kopters Limited is wholly owned by Kaiser Luft GmbH, a German producer of civilian helicopters. As from January 1993, Kaiser Kopters will be selling the new KL Hans-Off automatic pilot model. The transfer price to the UK company has been set at DM 118 000, and the net selling price in the United Kingdom will be £55 000. Budgeted sales for 1993 are 1000 KL helicopters.

Kaiser Kopters expect to incur fixed costs of £7.8 million in 1993, in addition to variable selling costs of £2000 per helicopter. The average exchange rate for 1993 is forecast at £1 = DM 2.95. No forward currency deals are to be arranged.

*Question*
For 1993, calculate the following:

(a) the breakeven level of sales;
(b) the budgeted amount of profit;
(c) the budgeted amount of profit that would result if the exchange rate were: (i) £1 = DM 3.25; and (ii) £1 = DM 2.65.

8  Presto Sums Limited was formed to produce electronic calculators. Sales were estimated at 5000 units per quarter, at an average price of £30 per unit; so production was set at this level. Stocks were planned to build up at the start, since the first quarter's sales were not expected to exceed 3500 units. By the end of the first quarter, it seemed that even that sales estimate had been too optimistic, and production for the second quarter was accordingly cut back to 2000 units.

Direct costs of production (all variable) averaged £20 per unit, and fixed production overheads amounted to £20 000 per quarter. The company sold 2000 units in the first quarter and 4000 units (at a price reduced by 5%) in the second quarter. When the managing director saw the company's profit and loss accounts (set out below in summarized form) for the first two quarters, he was astonished.

| | 1st quarter £'000s | 2nd quarter £'000s |
|---|---|---|
| Sales revenue | 60 | 114 |
| Opening stocks | — | 72 |
| Cost of production | 120 | 60 |
| Available | 120 | 132 |
| Less: Closing stocks | (72) | (30) |
| Cost of goods sold | 48 | 102 |
| Gross profit | 12 | 12 |

*Questions*

(a) Write a brief but clear memo to the managing director explaining why profits were the same in each quarter despite sales volume having doubled in the second quarter.
(b) How could a different accounting treatment of stocks produce different results?

(c) Compare the half-year's results under the two methods, and explain the difference.

(d) Which of the two accounting methods do you think does a better job of giving a 'true and fair view'? Why?

(e) Comment on the business performance of Presto Sums in its first six months.

(The solutions to Problems 3–8 will be provided in the *Instructors' Manual*.)

# CHAPTER 5 *Decentralized management*

## 5.1 Divisions of companies

Legal responsibility for ultimate management of a company's affairs rests with its board of directors. This often consists of a mix of executive and non-executive directors (the chairman may be either). As business organizations have grown larger and more international, the main board of directors has tended to manage a group's portfolio of businesses. Lower levels of management then manage the separate businesses themselves, usually delineated either on a geographical or on a product basis.

Even in such groups, certain functions (for example, legal and finance) are likely to remain under the direct control of top management. A key aspect of decentralization is for self-contained business units to operate as separate divisions of a company or group. A division will often have its own board of directors, perhaps with one or more main board directors as members. A division may legally comprise a limited company which is a subsidiary (usually wholly owned) of the parent (or holding company).

### 5.1.1 Divisions contrasted with parent companies

A division differs from its parent company in several respects: independence, finance and attitude to risk.

1 *Independence* No division is entirely independent. A group's top management is always likely to have some say in the following aspects:
   (a) appointing senior divisional managers;
   (b) agreeing long-term objectives and overall strategy;
   (c) approving annual budgets;
   (d) arranging necessary finance; and
   (e) approving major capital spending.
   There may also be common corporate policies for personnel, accounting, etc.
2 *Finance* A parent company has three main sources of long-term capital: retained profits, issuing more equity shares and long-term borrowing. But a division usually has only one: an allocation of funds

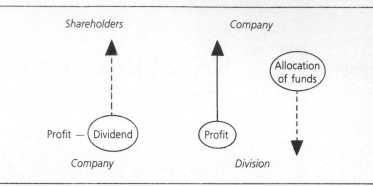

Figure 5.1 *Decisions about cash*

from the corporate pool. In this sense, *all* a division's funds are external to it. Division managers will probably deal far more with marketing, operations and personnel management than with long-term financial policy.

There is no legal requirement to maintain a division's capital, even in money terms. It is therefore possible to shrink a division's business fairly rapidly simply by not reinvesting in it. Any group which lets each division automatically retain and reinvest its internally generated cash is abdicating one of its most powerful strategic tools. Figure 5.1 compares the relationship of the parent company with its shareholders and that of the company with its divisions. In each case, it is the company's main board of directors that makes the essential decisions about cash: how much to pay out in dividends to shareholders, and how much to reinvest in each of its divisions.

3 *Attitude to risk*   A division manager may not view risk in the same way as a corporate manager. The latter will assess not only an activity's specific risk, but also its (portfolio) effect on the rest of the group's business. The division manager may be reluctant to risk a major failure for the division, even though it might not cripple the whole group. In contrast, the corporate manager may be willing to accept such risks if he sees a high enough chance of large returns. Thus, a division manager may be more averse to high-risk projects than a corporate manager. A similar difference in attitude may apply between a company's shareholders and its top management, and for the same reason (see Figure 5.2).

**5.1.2 Responsibility centres**

In order to let managers control units which are not too big, many large companies are split into a number of smaller units. There are two different main types of decentralization:

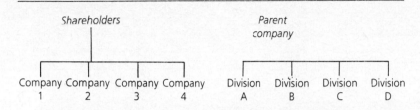

Figure 5.2 *Portfolios held by shareholders and by a parent company*

1 Functions, such as production, engineering, sales, research.
2 Divisions, such as product groups or geographical locations.

The economics of an industry may dictate a functional form of business, where only top management can decide some important trade-offs. Managers may be highly specialized, but perhaps in danger of not seeing the wood for the trees. In functional units it may be easy to measure inputs but not outputs (or vice versa).

Divisions can allow even fairly junior managers to aim for profits, subject to constraints such as market share and research spending.

There are four major types of responsibility centre: cost centres, revenue centres, profit centres and investment centres; though not all units will neatly match one of the four. Choosing the most suitable kind of centre is important in achieving effective financial control.

Three possible ways of viewing the objectives of responsibility centres are as follows:

1 Maximize outputs for a given amount of inputs.
2 Minimize inputs for a given amount of outputs.
3 Maximize the excess of outputs over inputs, for a given amount of investment.

**Cost centres** are appropriate for operations serving only customers within the group. For instance, a motor vehicle engine production plant would normally be a cost centre because it supplies the group's assembly plants. Financial performance is judged against standard costs (or, if available, the market value of equivalent products).

**Revenue centres** are suitable for sales operations which depend on supplies from within the group. This is especially true where selling costs are low and/or selling prices are set elsewhere in the group (since both affect profit). The branches of national supermarkets, with central purchasing and national pricing, fit into this category.

When a business unit's customers and suppliers are both (to a large extent) external to the whole group, the manager may be able to influence profit significantly. For this reason, diversified conglomerates, for

Table 5.1 *Financial responsibilities of centre managers*

| Type of centre | Manager responsible for | | | |
| --- | --- | --- | --- | --- |
| | Costs | Revenues | Profit or loss | Investment |
| Cost centre | Yes | No | No | No |
| Revenue centre | No | Yes | No | No |
| Profit centre | Yes | Yes | Yes | No |
| Investment centre | Yes | Yes | Yes | Yes |

example, normally treat each of their separate businesses as **profit centres** (section 5.2 discusses profit centres in more detail).

**Investment centres**, like profit centres, deal mainly with external suppliers and customers; but they also have a large degree of control over investment decisions. In practice, no profit centres or investment centres are likely to be entirely independent; and the difference between them is not always very clear.

Table 5.1 summarizes the financial responsibilities of managers in each of the four types of centre.

## 5.2 Profit centres

### 5.2.1 Advantages

Profit centres may be suitable in managing a business in the following circumstances:

1 Where divisions have direct access to markets both for suppliers and for customers.
2 Where division managers possess a fair amount of independence.
3 Where business between divisions is not too important.

Table 5.2 lists some possible advantages of treating divisions of a company 'as if' they were (largely) independent of top management control.

### 5.2.2 Disadvantages

Where any of the three conditions noted in 5.2.1 above is lacking, profit centres may do more harm than good. In particular, profit centres may

Table 5.2 *Possible advantages of treating divisions as profit centres*

- Uses division managers' specialized market knowledge
- Makes local managers responsible for making trade-offs
- Encourages initiatives
- Motivates managers to perform well in areas they control
- Spotlights poor performance by emphasis on 'bottom line'
- Permits management by exception
- Helps train future top managers
- Frees top management time and energy for other tasks

Table 5.3 *Possible disadvantages of treating divisions as profit centres*

- Duplicates staff activities
- Underuses corporate competence
- Risks mistakes by division managers which top managers might avoid
- Overemphasises short-term results
- Confuses division's results with managers' performance
- Difficult to identify suitable profit centres
- Hard to arrange for goal congruence
- Complicated by transfer price problems

be inappropriate where a division manager has only limited freedom in the following areas:

1 What goods or services to provide.
2 Who to sell to.
3 What prices to charge.
4 Who to buy from.

Consider an extreme case where Division S produces only for Division C, and central management decides the transfer price. If Division S may not sell to any other customers, but is required to make only to Division C's orders, and cannot amend the price, then it has little influence over profits. The main task is controlling costs, while achieving acceptable quality. It would probably be better to regard Division S as a cost centre; and to judge performance by comparing actual cost with (flexible) budget, as well as checking the various aspects of quality.

Table 5.3 shows some possible disadvantages of treating divisions as profit centres.

## 5.3 **Measuring divisional performance**

Four specific problems arise when measuring divisional profit or return.

### 5.3.1 **Measuring return**

**1. Depreciation**

Depreciation represents the charging of a fixed asset's net cost (i.e. original cost less ultimate proceeds) over its useful life. As Figure 5.3 illustrates, there is a need to estimate the magnitudes of three amounts, and to choose the method of depreciation.

(a) *Determining cost* may be simple for fixed assets purchased from external suppliers, including legal costs and installation charges. When companies manufacture fixed assets internally, however, they may omit overhead costs.
(b) *Estimating ultimate proceeds* is often ignored in practice. This can result

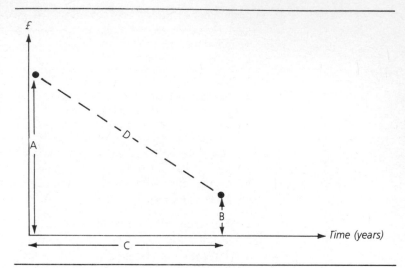

Figure 5.3 *The four estimates used in depreciation*

in charging too much depreciation during the asset's life, and being left with a profit on disposal at the end.

(c) *Estimating the useful life* of a fixed asset usually depends on economic (market) factors rather than on technical or legal ones. In practice, many companies group fixed assets together and assume all assets in the same class have similar lives.

(d) *Choosing a method*. The main methods are:
   (i) Straight-line: charging an equal amount each year, i.e. a constant percentage of original cost. This is the simplest method, and the most common in the United Kingdom.
   (ii) Declining balance: charging each year a constant percentage of the declining net book value. This is the approach normally taken for tax purposes (i.e. for tax deductible capital allowances).
   (iii) Usage (or machine-hour): relating the asset's life not to time, but to usage or output. The effect of this method is to make depreciation a variable expense.

### 2. Interest payable

Any external long-term borrowing will usually relate to the parent company and not to separate divisions. So most divisions will not pay any external interest. Where a division has its own bank overdraft, short-term interest will be payable. Unless the division manager has authority to determine the size of his division's bank overdraft (which would be unusual), it is probably best to relate profit before interest to total capital employed, including bank overdraft. (A possible alternative would be to relate profit after interest to equity capital only.)

### 3. Tax

Some groups do not allocate the total corporate tax charge between divisions, but judge divisions' performance on a before-tax basis. This is for a number of reasons.

(a) Tax charges of all the divisions may not add up to the company's total tax charge. Some taxable corporate income or expenses may not be split between divisions; or divisions may not use deferred tax accounting.

(b) A division manager may not entirely control his division's tax charge, since tax rules may vary (over time, according to location, capital intensiveness, etc.).

(c) Even if profits in one division can legally be set off against losses in another, it is doubtful whether one division's performance should be affected by other divisions' tax position.

### 4. Inflation adjustments

Allowing for the effects of inflation will help avoid misleading comparisons between divisions with fixed assets of varying lives. It will also improve the usefulness of trends over time within a division. Current cost accounting may be more appropriate in divisional accounting than in external financial reporting. (But there is still a need for constant purchasing power accounting to make **residual income** comparisons over time — see section 5.3.3.)

5.3.2 **Measuring investment**

Six aspects of investment require brief comment.

### 1. Opening, average or closing investment

In calculating **return on investment** measures from external published accounts, it is easiest to use end-of-period investment as the denominator. Internally, however, the choice seems to be between beginning-of-period and average investment. There will normally be little difference; but the longer the period concerned, and the bigger the change within the period, the more reason there is to prefer an average figure.

### 2. Valuation of assets

Revaluing some fixed assets upwards increases investment, and may also affect depreciation (and thus reduce return). Without explicit inflation adjustments, regular revaluations of fixed assets may be desirable, say every five years, at least for land and buildings.

Methods of stock valuation can significantly affect short-term profits. Divisions in completely different kinds of business may want to use different methods of stock valuation, but will need to apply them consistently over time.

### 3. Accumulated depreciation on fixed assets

Unless there are regular replacements of fixed assets, using net book value of fixed assets may mean a division's capital employed seems to shrink as fixed assets grow older. One way to solve this (largely academic) problem is for budgets to allow for the apparent ROI or residual income increase over time, and the probably sharp fall when major new capital investment occurs.

### 4. Cash and debtors

Using actual figures for both cash and debtors is simplest; but the critical question is whether a division really controls either amount. Groups which centralize cash management (as is common) should allocate divisions some reasonable amount — perhaps a fixed percentage of sales. Similarly with debtors; but where a division controls collection, then it should use actual trade debtors owing.

### 5. Current liabilities

In computing investment, there is a strong argument for deducting current liabilities from total assets. Unless trade creditors are paid centrally, using actual liabilities is best even though this might encourage divisions to delay payment unduly, with possible loss of goodwill to the whole company. Bank overdrafts should be deducted if, but only if, they are both (i) really short-term, and (ii) negotiated separately by each division.

If profit before tax is the measure of divisional performance, it is probably best *not* to deduct the current tax liability in measuring a division's capital employed. (Otherwise, the higher the actual tax payable, the higher the before-tax ROI!)

### 6. Long-term liabilities

Many divisions have no long-term liabilities. Even if they have, a company's top management nearly always decides long-term financial policy. This suggests including any long-term liabilities as part of long-term capital employed. Divisions should also include any deferred tax liabilities as part of capital employed.

**5.3.3 Calculating return on investment and residual income**

Table 5.4 shows a hypothetical summarized profit and loss account and balance sheet for Paradise Division.

Table 5.4 *Paradise Division's 1991 accounts*

| Profit and loss account Year 1991 | (£'000) | Balance sheet at 31 December 1991 | (£'000) |
|---|---|---|---|
| Sales revenue | 1 500 | Fixed assets, net | 400 |
| Cost of goods sold | 850 | Current assets | 1 300 |
| Gross profit | 650 | Current liabilities | (500) |
| Admin. expenses | 350 | Net assets | 1 200 |
| PBIT | 300 | Equity | 900 |
| Interest payable | 50 | Long-term debt | 300 |
| Profit before tax | 250 | Capital employed | 1 200 |
| Tax | 100 | | |
| Profit after tax | 150 | | |

Return on investment (ROI) is calculated as: profit before interest and tax (PBIT) divided by net assets (= capital employed), that is:

$$ ROI = \frac{PBIT}{\text{net assets}} = \frac{300}{1200} = 25\% $$

Residual income (RI), a less familiar measure, is calculated as: profit, less interest on capital employed, that is:

| | (£'000s) |
|---|---|
| PBIT | 300 |
| Less: capital charge[1] | 240 |
| = residual income | 60 |

[1] @ 20% (say) on net assets (£1200k).

In effect, residual income reduces accounting profit by charging a notional interest expense on equity capital, as well as on other long-term capital. Residual income (like ROI) can be calculated either before-tax (as above) or after-tax.

5.3.4 **Comparing return on investment and residual income**

ROI and RI are alike in the following respects:

• Both rely upon adequate accounting measurement of profit and of capital employed.
• Both can be used to plan, control and evaluate divisions' performance.
• Both can use budget figures as a standard against which to compare actual results.
• Both can be used as the basis for profit-sharing.

Table 5.5 *Differences between ROI and RI*

|  | Return on investment | Residual income |
|---|---|---|
| 1. Form of measurement | Percentage ratio | Money amount |
| 2. Involves same rate of return for all assets? | Yes | Not necessarily |
| 3. Profit (or loss) | Relates to capital | Is residual |

On the other hand, Table 5.5 summarizes three key differences between ROI and RI.

Using residual income, a division will want to go on expanding as long as it can find investment projects which promise a return higher than the required rate of return (see Chapter 7). This makes economic sense, as the aim is to maximize residual income. Using ROI, however, a division might not want to accept such projects if they only promise to return less than the present rate of ROI.

### Example 5.1

Division A of a company has been earning a 30% ROI, Division B 8%, and the company as a whole 17%. Each division is considering two new capital investment projects of similar risk, returning 10% and 20% respectively.

Using the return-on-investment approach, the company as a whole might want both divisions to reject the first project and accept the second. But Division A might want to reject both projects (since they would both be expected to reduce the division's ROI); whereas Division B might want to accept both.

With the residual income approach, however, using an interest rate of 17% should induce each division to reject the 10% project and accept the 20% project — thus achieving goal congruence between each division and the company as a whole.

Now consider Case study 5.1.

### Case study 5.1

*Problem*
Chesterfield Division's summarized profit and loss account and balance sheet for 1991 are shown below. The capital charge for residual income is to be 20%.

*Question*
Calculate the division's ROI and RI for 1991.

| 1991 Profit and Loss Account | | Balance Sheet at 31 December 1991 | |
|---|---|---|---|
| | (£'000s) | | (£'000s) |
| Sales revenue | 2400 | Fixed assets (net) | 783 |
| Cost of goods sold | 1723 | Current assets | 1220 |
| Gross profit | 677 | Current liabilities | (453) |
| Other expenses | 491 | | |
| PBIT | 186 | Net assets | 1550 |
| Interest payable | 83 | Equity | 730 |
| Profit before tax | 103 | Long-term debt | 820 |
| Tax | 32 | | |
| Profit after tax | 71 | Capital employed | 1550 |

### Solution

$$\text{ROI} = \frac{\text{PBIT}}{\text{net assets}} = \frac{186}{1550} = 12\%$$

$$\begin{aligned}
\text{RI} &= \text{PBIT} - (20\% \times £1550\text{k}) \\
&= £186\ 000 \quad £310\ 000 \\
&= -£124\ 000
\end{aligned}$$

**5.3.5 Other performance indicators**

Whether a company uses return on investment or residual income in looking at the performance of divisions, the question arises: is it an adequate criterion? Should a single one-year financial measure of profit provide the sole basis for judging business unit performance or managers' performance? It may seem convenient to use a single measure, but there are dangers — two in particular being 'short-termism' and lack of balance.

A single measure may overemphasize short-term financial performance at the expense of longer-term profits. For instance, there may be pressure to cut back on discretionary costs (see section 2.2.4) such as advertising, training, and research and development.

Critics sometimes accuse the City of 'short-termism', though in theory stock market prices reflect the discounted present value of future cash flows for *ever*! If investors were really over-discounting the longer-term future, presumably they perceive more uncertainty than their critics think exists; but it is hard to prove who is right. Such complaints come strangely from politicians — whose own preoccupation with election dates in the near future is notorious!

There may be important factors which a single performance measure for the current year cannot easily include. To overcome this danger, the

General Electric Corporation (US) many years ago identified eight key result areas: profitability; market position; productivity; product leadership; personnel development; employee attitudes; public responsibility; and the balance between short-term and long-term goals. There were measurement problems with several of these items (which General Electric seemed to handle rather well). But the essential purpose was to emphasize the need for a *balanced* view of performance.

A number of UK public sector businesses now publish performance indicators in their annual reports. Examples are British Rail reporting what proportion of passenger trains arrive late, the Post Office reporting what proportion of first-class letters fail to arrive the next day, and the National Health Service reporting on average waiting times. This seems to be a useful way of directing attention to trends over time in quality of output. It can, however, take considerable effort to develop suitable indicators of performance (as universities are now beginning to discover).

Hopwood looked at different US approaches to financial performance evaluation. He contrasted a 'budget-constrained' style, focusing on short-term performance, with a 'profit-conscious' style, concerned with achieving long-term goals. He found the profit-conscious style produced less job-related tension, much less accounting manipulation, and better relations with both superiors and colleagues (Hopwood, 1974).

## 5.4 **Before and after**

There may be important differences, as Table 5.6 shows, between methods used for capital investment project evaluation in advance, and those used for divisional performance appraisal after the event. Some writers have suggested that instead of using accounting profits or losses as the basis for the latter, using cash flows could avoid many of the differences. The asterisks against each item in Table 5.6 show which way cash-flow accounting would probably tend. Items 1a and 4 would remain difficult points to overcome. After the event, it may often be very hard to identify incremental amounts resulting from projects which the on-going business has thoroughly absorbed. (This is a major difficulty in attempting post-project audits.) Nor will it be possible to make useful guesses after the event about the actual degree of risk involved. (This, of course, is not easy *before* the event either!)

Figure 5.4 illustrates point 1 in Table 5.6, the contrast between looking at incremental amounts relating to discrete projects over a project's whole life and looking at overall totals relating to the whole business unit for a single period. Modern thinking has tended to downgrade techniques which strongly emphasize discrete projects, and to reinstate older approaches which try to consider the impact of particular decisions on the business as a whole.

Table 5.6 *Investment evaluation in advance compared with performance appraisal after the event*

| In advance<br>Main methods: NPV, IRR | After the event<br>Main methods: RI, ROI |
|---|---|
| 1a. Incremental amounts | 1a. Overall totals |
| 1b. Relating to discrete 'projects' | *1b. Relating to whole business unit |
| 1c. Over all (or most) of project's life | *1c. For a single period (often one year) |
| *2a. Cash flows | 2a. Profits (or losses) |
| *2b. Ignoring depreciation | 2b. After charging depreciation |
| *2c. After tax | 2c. Often before tax |
| 3a. May be constant purchasing power units (= Year 0 money) | *3a. Usually monetary units (distorted by inflation) |
| 3b. Often discounted | *3b. Not discounted |
| 3c. Implicit reinvestment assumption | *3c. No reinvestment assumption |
| 4. Uncertainty clearly relevant | 4. Uncertainty often ignored |

*Note:* * indicates which way cash-flow accounting would probably tend.

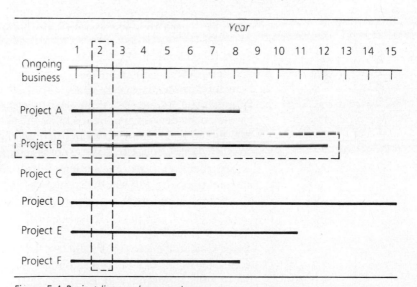

Figure 5.4 *Project lives and accounting years*

## 5.5 Transfer pricing

Corporate management will usually make ultimate decisions about sourcing (or at least establish rules to enable divisions to decide), and lay down rules for negotiating transfer prices between divisions. Any system for setting transfer prices should be fairly simple; and division managers need to accept it as fair since it will affect their division's reported performance. Some arbitration system may be required to settle disputes; but top management will rarely want to interfere in setting a price for a specific transfer of goods or services between divisions.

## 5.5.1 Sourcing

There may be sound business reasons for transferring goods between two divisions, rather than letting one division buy from outside. Control of supply may be important, there may be commercial secrets involved, or the outside supplier may be seeking to expand his business at the company's expense. An inside division which can match outside firms in price (and, of course, in quality) will normally be entitled to the business if it wants it. But even in such a case, a purchasing division might still prefer to buy outside, either to maintain more than a single source of supply, or to ensure that outside suppliers continue to quote realistic prices.

## 5.5.2 Pricing

Assuming there is no overriding economic reason for two divisions to deal with each other, a common rule is to transfer goods and services between divisions at long-run market price, with either buying or selling division free to choose whether or not to deal with another division. This requires divisions to have access to outside markets, and to be free to negotiate with each other. For example, ICI's 1990 Annual Report (p. 38) says: 'The Group's policy is to transfer products internally at external market prices.'

In some cases, there may be no outside market (e.g. for specialized intermediate products); or the market price may be difficult to discover; or the goods dealt in may not be quite the same. Sometimes it may be possible to reach a suitable proxy for a market price (e.g. by allowing for known differences in quality). But where no equivalent market price exists, there are three main options: use 'cost plus mark-up' as the transfer price; use different transfer prices for buyer and seller; or change the profit centre set-up.

### 1. Cost plus mark-up

Some kind of standard cost should be used, since using actual cost would enable the selling division to pass on the cost of production inefficiencies. To provide an incentive to reduce costs, the selling division might be allowed to go on charging the former price for a limited period.

If transfer prices are based on full costs, the selling division's fixed costs will seem to the buying division to be variable costs. From the corporate viewpoint, this might induce wrong decisions. Where volume is small, this may not matter; but in principle it may be better to use marginal costs. Where volume is substantial, there may be a case for a two-part transfer price, consisting of the following:

(a) an explicit share of the selling division's fixed costs; plus
(b) a variable cost per unit.

Whichever cost figure is used, some mark-up needs to be added in order to determine the transfer price. Otherwise, a profit centre will nearly always prefer to sell outside, at a profit, rather than inside, at cost. The simplest method is to use a normal profit margin on sales or a normal rate of return on the assets employed.

### Example 5.2

Roberts Computers comprises several manufacturing and several assembly divisions. The Carlton division has allocated 40% of its production capacity to meet the Warner division's chip requirements for next year. Calculate the transfer price per unit for the six million MPX chips which Carlton is to supply to Warner next year, given:

(i) transfer prices are based on a 'two-part' cost, plus 5%;
(ii) Carlton's budgeted fixed costs are £4 million a year;
(iii) the variable cost of MPX chips to Carlton is 40p each.

To calculate the total transfer price we determine the share of Carlton's fixed costs that Warner is to bear; add the total variable cost for the output required, and then add 5% to the total cost.

Thus, total transfer price:

$$= [(40\% \times £4m) + (6m \times £0.4)] \times 1.05$$
$$= [£1.6m + £2.4m] \times 1.05$$
$$= £4.2 \text{ million}$$

The transfer price per unit = £4.2m ÷ 6m units = 70p each. Note that in a two-part transfer pricing system the transfer price per unit depends on the volume of parts being transferred.

### 2. Different transfer prices for buyer and seller

One way to avoid the buying division viewing the seller's fixed overheads as variable is to credit the seller with standard full costs and charge the buyer only standard marginal costs. That should avoid distorting buyer–division decisions away from corporate interests. But the total of all the divisions' reported profits would exceed the total company profit: the difference would become a corporate overhead. One problem with this method is that neither the buyer nor the seller would feel responsible for controlling the seller's fixed overheads.

### 3. Change the profit centre set-up

If there is no suitable market price, and neither 1. nor 2. above seems right, the profit centre set-up itself may be unsuitable. If the volume of internal business is large, two divisions may be so closely linked that it makes little sense to treat them both as independent profit centres. It might be better to combine them into a single profit centre, perhaps with the supplying division being only a cost centre.

Vancil's (1979) study found that the transfer pricing policies of 239 companies were based on the following methods:

|  | (%) |
| --- | --- |
| Variable cost | 5 |
| Full cost | 25 |
| Cost plus | 17 |
| Negotiation | 22 |
| Market price | 31 |
|  | 100 |

### 5.5.3 Capacity and competition

When the supplying division is at or near full capacity, then the transfer price ought at least to cover the full cost of production. The supplying division would presumably not want to use its limited capacity for intra-group sales at lower prices than it could get by selling outside.

But in conditions of industry over-capacity, many suppliers might resort to 'distress pricing' at marginal cost plus a small mark-up. Assuming the supplying division, too, is operating well below capacity, it should be prepared to transfer goods or services itself at only a little above marginal cost. This should induce the buying division to buy internally, rather than from external suppliers. If the supplying division were to insist on maintaining a full-cost pricing policy in such conditions, it might rapidly lose most of its customers, internal as well as external, if demand is price-sensitive.

### 5.5.4 International transactions

Transfers inside a single country are internal to the group, and outside parties have no say in transfer pricing decisions. But transfers across national boundaries also concern the national tax authorities, because suitably adjusted transfer prices could transfer profits from high-tax countries to low-tax countries, thereby reducing the group's overall tax bill. (Likewise, transfer prices could affect the amount of import tariffs.)

Artificial attempts to reduce tax liabilities could well upset a country's tax officials, if they discover it; and might result in some form of penalty. Indeed, many tax authorities possess the power to modify transfer prices in computing tariffs or taxes on profits — though a genuine arms-length market price should pass muster.

International groups have to worry about possible currency fluctuations; they may also seek to use transfer prices to evade restrictions on remitting dividends, where these still exist. (Financing overseas subsidiaries by means of loans rather than equity is another way to achieve the same end.) Setting international transfer prices, therefore, requires a delicate balance between satisfying shareholders and governments, and in assessing longer-term as well as short-term impact.

## 5.6 Measuring managerial performance

### 5.6.1 Control

The basis of controlling a division's performance is usually the budget, which should be agreed as a result of informed discussion. No single measure can encompass all aspects of performance (see section 5.3.5); and accounting problems can distort any financial measurement (such as ROI or RI). The 'single criterion' fallacy can tempt division managers to concentrate on manipulating numbers; but it is one of top management's tasks to establish a sensible and realistic budget climate. For instance, there may be good reasons for failing to achieve an agreed budget.

The need to balance short-term and long-term aspects requires subjective judgement. The emphasis in the financial literature has changed from 'maximizing profits' to 'maximizing shareholders' wealth'; but the latter requires the use of an interest rate to discount expected future cash flows back to their present-day value (see section 7.3). Choosing a suitable interest rate is itself subjective and difficult, and liable to a large margin of error.

Some expenses may not be fully controllable by a division manager, especially in the short term (for example, depreciation and rent). Leaving them out may give a misleading picture of a business unit's financial performance, but including them may make it hard to hold the division manager fully responsible for results. 'Controllability' should not be regarded as an 'all or nothing' criterion. Many profit centre managers try to 'muddle through' by using their network of acquaintances, whom they do not in any sense control. Hence, the practical importance of doing favours, trading gossip, and so on.

Including apportioned expenses *informs* division managers about expenses which contributions from the divisions must cover, and may also *induce* them to query seemingly high corporate overheads. On the other hand, it can cause pointless argument about the basis of apportionment.

Even where one can distinguish between controllable and non-controllable expenses, the resulting report form may be in danger of being too complicated (see Table 5.7).

### 5.6.2 Motivation

One of the major benefits of decentralized management is the chance it offers to develop managers for more senior positions. Giving division managers responsibility and authority can lead them to behave in a much more entrepreneurial way, almost as if they were running their own firm.

Table 5.7 *Divisional profit statement*

| | (£'000) | (£'000) |
|---|---:|---:|
| Sales to outside customers | 9 848 | |
| Transfers to other divisions at market value | 512 | 10 360 |
| Less: Variable cost of goods sold and transferred | 5 578 | |
| Variable divisional expenses | 815 | 6 393 |
| *Contribution to fixed costs and profit* | | 3 967 |
| Less: Controllable divisional overhead | 1 201 | |
| Depreciation on controllable fixed assets | 1 015 | 2 216 |
| *Controllable operating profit* | | 1 751 |
| Less: Interest on controllable investment | | 210 |
| *Controllable profit before tax* | | 1 541 |
| Less: Non-controllable divisional overhead | 300 | |
| Central expenses chargeable to division | 250 | |
| Interest on non-controllable investment | 191 | 741 |
| *Net profit before tax* | | 800 |
| Less: Corporation tax | | 264 |
| Net profit after tax | | 536 |

However, top management cannot abdicate completely, since they must answer to shareholders for earning adequate profits.

When a company comprises divisions which neither compete nor trade with each other, a high degree of divisional authority is often healthy. However, if divisions are competing with each other, or if there is much trading between them, then allowing managers to do what is best for their divisions might harm the best interests of the group as a whole.

The aim is goal congruence, which means inducing division managers to improve their own divisions' results, while acting in the best interests of the group. This requires an effective system of performance appraisal, and suitable transfer pricing rules. It also means that division managers need to *know* what corporate objectives are. Where there are problems, head office may need to arbitrate; but if this happens too often, it can undermine divisional management's autonomy, and thus impair motivation.

The balance is often difficult between the following objectives:

1 Developing top-level managers.
2 Giving division managers a high degree of autonomy.
3 Achieving goal congruence between divisional and group objectives.

Getting the balance more or less right will go a long way towards enabling managers to demonstrate superior performance. There is a difference between measuring a business unit's results and measuring its manager's performance. Unless top management understands this, a good manager may be unwilling to accept responsibility for a bad division (which may urgently need his services).

5.6.3 **Agency theory**

Agency theory deals with the relationship between agent and principal: how to give the agent incentives to achieve the principal's goals, and how to monitor his actions. Agent and principal may respectively be top management and shareholders; or divisional management and top management. Measuring an agent's effort directly is extremely difficult, at reasonable cost, but it is possible to assess effort indirectly by measuring profit or return on capital employed.

From a practical viewpoint, one wonders whether company shareholders ought to become more involved in their role as principal. Otherwise, company directors end up being both principal and agent, and setting their own contracts. Recent attention to increases in some directors' pay illustrates the point. In the current debate about 'corporate governance', one suggestion worth pursuing is the proposal to change company law so that shareholders could increase the level of dividends proposed by the directors.

5.7 **Chapter summary**

Most large companies have a number of more or less independent divisions, whose separate performance they can measure. Divisions may match one of four types of responsibility centre: cost centre, revenue centre, profit centre, or investment centre.

Treating divisions as profit centres may have benefits in using local knowledge and encouraging initiatives. But profit centres may not be suitable where top management limits the freedom of divisions with respect to suppliers or customers or selling prices.

The basis of measurement for profit centres (or investment centres) may be either return on investment (ROI) or residual income (RI). In measuring such divisions' performance, there must be agreement about what constitutes 'return' and what constitutes 'investment'. Other performance indicators may also be useful.

Transfer pricing policy affects the prices that supplying divisions charge to other divisions in the group. This might be as low as marginal cost, or as high as market price, or full cost plus mark-up. Transfer pricing policy should aim to maximize long-run group profits; it needs to consider use of capacity, competition and management motivation. For international transactions it must also allow for tax and currency aspects.

It may be misleading to relate a division's performance directly to that of its management. Managers can be responsible only for those aspects which they control (or at least significantly influence).

## 5.8 **Review questions**

1 Name three respects in which a division differs from its parent company.
2 What are the four major types of responsibility centre?
3 List four possible advantages of profit centres.
4 List four possible disadvantages of profit centres.
5 What problems arise when measuring a division's 'return'?
6 What issues have to be decided to determine the amount of a division's 'investment'?
7 What are the two main ways of measuring divisional performance?
8 What is the formula for return on investment?
9 How is residual income measured?
10 How might residual income be superior to return on investment in enhancing goal congruence?
11 What does 'goal congruence' mean?
12 Identify five differences between methods used for (ex ante) capital investment project evaluation and those used for (ex post) divisional performance appraisal.
13 What options are available when setting a transfer price between two (profit-centre) divisions, if there is no market price available?
14 What are the advantages of a 'two-part tariff' basis for transfer pricing?
15 What problems does agency theory deal with?

To maximize learning, please *write out* your answers on a separate sheet of paper. *Then* check with the answers in Appendix C, pp. 237–8.

## 5.9 **Problems**

1 Using the abbreviated ICI profit and loss account and balance sheet for 1990 set out below, calculate ICI's ROI. What is the resultant RI obtained, using a capital charge of 18%?

Profit and loss account for 1990

| | £m |
|---|---|
| Turnover | 12 906 |
| Net operating costs | 11 877 |
| Trading profit | 1 029 |
| Net income from Assoc. Cos | 154 |
| Net short-term interest | (51) |
| Profit before loan interest | 1 132 |
| Loan interest | 155 |
| Profit before taxation[1] | 977 |
| Taxation | 338 |
| Profit after taxation[1] | 639 |

[1]on ordinary activities

Balance sheet as at 31.12.1990

| | £m |
|---|---|
| Fixed assets (net) | 5 430 |
| Current assets | 5 369 |
| Current liabilities | (3 406) |
| Net assets | 7 393 |
| Equity | 4 671 |
| Loans | 1 670 |
| Other long-term liabilities | 1 052 |
| | 7 393 |

(See solution in Appendix C, p. 238.)

**2** Edinburgh Leisure plc has two major business segments, brewing and entertainments. The Edinburgh breweries division supplies the Holiday entertainments division with all its lager beer requirements, reserving 20% of its production capacity for this purpose. Holiday entertainments division plans to use 45 000 ten-gallon barrels of lager for 1993. The transfer price has to be agreed based upon a 'two-part' cost plus 6%. The Edinburgh breweries division has a variable cost per ten-gallon barrel of £36 and their 1993 fixed costs are budgeted at £2.15m.

(a) Calculate the total transfer price for Holiday entertainments division's 1993 requirements.
(b) How much is this per barrel?
(c) If demand was actually 10% more than planned and these additional requirements were provided at variable costs plus 6%, what would the new average transfer price per barrel be?

(See solution in Appendix C, p. 238.)

**3** General Manufacturing Ltd supply parts for the automobile and domestic appliance industries. The company comprises two divisions, Foundry Division and Machine Division. Both divisions are treated as profit centres and are allowed to buy and sell as they think fit, although a significant amount of inter-divisional trading takes place.

Foundry Division have recently given the following unit cost quote to Machine Division, regarding an automotive component, for which a total of 20 000 units is required:

| | Unit cost (£) |
|---|---|
| Material cost | 9.75 |
| Direct labour cost | 2.65 |
| Depreciation[1] | 3.10 |
| Other fixed overheads (excluding depreciation) | 1.80 |
| Variable overheads | 1.35 |
| Admin. costs (divisional and head office) | 2.20 |
| Mark-up | 2.10 |
| Quoted price | 22.95 |

[1]excluding tooling which is to be supplied by the customer.

The general manager of Machine Division has tried unsuccessfully to negotiate a lower price. He knows that Foundry Division has considerable spare capacity (even on one-shift working). Also, the material cost of £9.75 is quoted at cost, even though material prices have since dropped by 20%. He has therefore asked the managing director to intervene and 'instruct' Foundry Division to supply at £12.95 per unit.

Machine Division have been quoted a price of £19.95 per unit by an external supplier.

The general manager of Foundry Division has responded by saying that his division cannot afford to sell at a loss. Also, this contract would prevent him from disposing of machinery which originally cost £450 000 and has a net book value of £45 000. It is expected to fetch about £80 000 net of removal costs.

*Questions*

(a) Is it more advantageous to the company for Foundry Division to make the component for Machine Division than for them to buy from the external supplier? (Support your answer with financial data.)
(b) What 'instructions' should the managing director give?

Identify any assumptions you make.

**4** Peach Printers recently launched a new printer which was assembled in its Singapore plant and shipped to its Malaysian distributors in Kuala Lumpur. Duty of $350 per unit is paid on shipments.

Variable cost of production in Singapore is as follows:

|  | Per unit $ |
| --- | --- |
| Labour | 420 |
| Materials | 520 |
| Variable overheads | 460 |
|  | 1400 |

Peach Malaysia, a subsidiary of Peach Printers, sells (only) this printer in Malaysia for R 13 000. It pays its distributors a commission of 3% of the selling price of the printers. Variable selling overheads (excluding commission) are R 600 per unit and fixed costs amount to R 300 000 per month. The purchase price of printers from Singapore (including freight and duty) is R 5900 per unit.

The budget level of sales is 60 units per month. If the sales price is reduced to R 11 800, volume is expected to increase by 20%.

The current exchange rate is R 1 (Malaysian Ringgit) = $0.65 (Singapore).

*Questions*

(a) Calculate Peach Malaysia's breakeven point using the existing selling price and volume.
(b) Calculate Peach Malaysia's expected annual profit: (i) with the existing price and volume; and (ii) with the reduced price and increased volume.
(c) Calculate the marginal profit the Singapore company makes on the sale of

1 extra printer to Malaysia (in Singapore dollars).
(d) What would you advise the managing director of Peach Malaysia to do?

**5** Versatile Vehicles Limited makes specialized vehicles, and each manufacturing division operates as a separate profit centre. Division A normally purchases its engine requirements (5000 a year) from Division E at a unit price of £175; but Division E has recently informed Division A that, as from next month, the unit price will increase to £200.

Division A has ascertained that it can still purchase an equivalent engine for £175 from another (external) supplier, and has decided to do so. Division E has appealed to the group chairman to reverse the decision. E's variable costs are £140 per engine; and E's fixed costs are £40 per engine.

*Questions*
Determine whether Division A should be allowed to purchase externally in each of the following cases (give reasons):

(a) Assuming that there are no other uses for E's internal facilities.
(b) Assuming that there are no other uses for E's internal facilities *and* that the unit price from external suppliers drops a further £40.
(c) Assuming that by not producing 5000 engines for A, E could use its internal facilities for other products which would produce an annual contribution of £170 000.

(The solutions to Problems 3–5 will be provided in the *Instructors' Manual*.)

| CHAPTER **6** | *Making decisions* |

## 6.1 **What is relevant?**

This chapter mainly deals with business decisions for which one can assess the financial results fairly closely. Sections 6.2, 6.3 and Chapter 7 deal with three types of major business issue for which relevant cost and revenue data can help make better decisions: make-or-buy; use-of-capacity; and capital investment. Some cost and revenue data may be irrelevant or even misleading. Table 6.1 summarizes four basic features that determine which costs and revenues are likely to be relevant.

We now discuss each of these features in turn, in order to understand the distinction between the relevant and the irrelevant. In practice, however, the four relevant features listed in Table 6.1 are interrelated and overlapping rather than being discrete.

### 6.1.1 **Future**

Only future costs and revenues are relevant not past ones.

**Example 6.1**
An investor paid £6 a share for 1000 shares in ABC plc. Later he needed the money; but since the shares had fallen to £4.50 he preferred not to sell, reasoning that, if he did, he would make a loss of £1500 (= £1.50 per share).

The fallacy is that he has already made the loss, whether he sells now or not. The market value of the shares is £4500; and what he paid for them originally is not relevant. It is a **sunk cost**. His choice is between £4500 cash (what he could sell the shares for in the immediate future) and continuing to hold the shares.

### 6.1.2 **Incremental**

Only incremental (extra or lesser) costs and revenues are relevant, not those costs and revenues which remain unchanged. (Incremental costs are also referred to as differential or avoidable costs.)

**Example 6.2**
Two years ago, KPC Limited acquired for £100 000 a specialized machine with an estimated useful life of five years. A major customer has just told KPC that it will not be needing the products made on the machine beyond the next three months. The machine makes no other products nor does it have any other use in

Table 6.1 *Features of relevant and irrelevant costs and revenues*

| Relevant | Irrelevant |
| --- | --- |
| Future | Past (sunk costs) |
| Incremental | Unchanged |
| Cash flows | Accounting profits |
| | Depreciation charges |
| | Accounting book values |
| Whole enterprise | Costs or revenues moved between departments |

Table 6.2 *Alternative expenditures and savings*

| Alternative | Further expenditure | Savings or receipts | Net savings/receipts |
| --- | --- | --- | --- |
| (i) | Nil | None, unless the machine can be used at some future date | Nil |
| (ii) | Nil | £2 000 | £2 000 |
| (iii) | £400 | £5 000 | £4 600 |
| (iv) | £20 000 | £45 000 | £25 000 |

its present state. A production engineer suggests four alternatives for the machine:

(i) keep it in store in case it might be useful in future;
(ii) sell it for scrap for £2000;
(iii) cannibalize it (i.e. remove useful parts) at a cost of £400, thereby avoiding the need to spend £5000 in future to overhaul other machines;
(iv) spend £20 000 to modify the machine in order to avoid buying another (different) machine for £45 000.

Three maintenance men work in the machine shop (at a total cost of £54 000 per year). There will be no change in their number or salary whichever alternative is chosen.

Table 6.2 shows the resultant expenditures and savings. In each case, we ignore the past costs (sunk costs) of £100 000 and the unchanging maintenance costs of £54 000. Only the incremental (avoidable) further expenditure and the future savings or receipts matter in the decision now. Alternative (iv) appears to be the best, giving a net saving of £25 000 (£45 000 savings − £20 000 further expenditure).

However, to help in making better future decisions, some lessons might be learned from past ones. For example, is it wise to invest in specialized equipment to satisfy the orders of one customer, without an adequate long-term sales contract?

6.1.3 **Cash flows**

Decision makers need to use future incremental cash flows rather than accounting profits, book depreciation charges or accounting book values. This allows for the timing of cash flows before reaching a final decision, if necessary by discounting them (see Chapter 7).

**Example 6.3**

The Four Ps Advertising Agency acquired a ten-year lease on offices in London four years ago, for a cost of £500 000. The accounting net book value of the lease now stands at £300 000. The Agency is considering moving to Milton Keynes which would allow operating savings (excluding lease costs) of £35 000 per year. The move itself would cost £10 000. Suitable leasehold premises are available at £240 000 for an initial period of six years. The Agency could sub-let the leasehold premises in London for the remaining six years for £180 000. Does it make financial sense to move? Table 6.3 summarizes the cash flows involved.

A £70 000 net cash outflow now could bring cash inflows (operating cost savings) of £35 000 per year for the next six years. Ignoring timing, this gives a total net cash benefit of £140 000. So, unless there are significant adverse factors (e.g. loss of customers, staffing problems, tax considerations, etc.), moving to Milton Keynes appears the better (financial) alternative.

The decision to move to Milton Keynes will result in a first year accounting book loss of £120 000 (£300 000 net book value − £180 000 realizable value) on the sale of the London lease. But this is irrelevant. It has already occurred.

Table 6.4 shows how the move to Milton Keynes would affect reported profits for the next six years. Over the six-year period the effect on profits is as follows:

(£85 000) + £225 000 (= 5 years × £45 000) = +£140 000

The six years' net profit result is the same as for the cash flow approach. The difference between accounting profits/losses and cash flows boils down to timing differences. This is always true, providing that at the end of the period under

Table 6.3 *Cash flows resulting from moving to Milton Keynes*

| Timing | Event | Cash flow (£'000) | |
|---|---|---|---|
| Now | Sale of London lease | +£180 | |
| Now | Cost of Milton Keynes lease | −£240 | |
| Now | Cost of moving to Milton Keynes | −£ 10 | |
| Now | | −£ 70 | = −£ 70 |
| Years 1 to 6 | Operating cost savings per year | +£ 35 | = +£210 total |
| | | | = +£140 |

Table 6.4 *Effect on profits from moving to Milton Keynes*

|  | Year 1 (£'000) | Years 2–6 (£'000) |
|---|---|---|
| Book loss on sale of London lease | (£120) | — |
| Cost of moving to Milton Keynes | (£10) | — |
| Savings in London lease depreciation £300 000/6 | £50 | £50 |
| Cost of Milton Keynes lease depreciation £240 000/6 | (£40) | (£40) |
| Savings in operating costs | £35 | £35 |
|  | (£85) | £45  per year |

review there is no difference between the alternatives in the assets held by the business. (In our example, both leases expire in six years' time and are therefore directly comparable.)

### 6.1.4 Whole enterprise

The whole enterprise should be considered, not just the department making the decision.

**Example 6.4**
Static Products Ltd are thinking of dropping one of their product lines. This will release 2000 square feet of floor space in the factory for which they have recently signed a ten-year lease agreement. Sales volume of the remaining four product lines, which currently use 8000 square feet of floor space, are not expected to increase; nor are there plans for any new products in the future. If floor space costs £20 per square foot per year, what incremental saving in floor space costs will dropping the product line produce?

The answer is none. Lease costs for the business will not fall. Unless Static Products can find other use for the floor space there is no saving. The floor space costs 'saved' by dropping one product line are merely shared among the remaining four product lines.

If the company had (wrongly) included the floor space cost in making the decision, they might well have dropped the product line instead of retaining it (at least for the time being). With this line of (incorrect) reasoning, other product lines may then follow as the total floor space costs have to be shared among fewer product lines. The full costing approach might thus lead to closing the whole plant when in fact keeping going (for the time being) would be financially better.

### 6.2 Make-or-buy decisions

Businesses must often decide whether to make a product themselves or to buy it from another firm. If there is confidence that suppliers and in-house sources can equally well provide:

- the required technical competence;
- the desired level of quality;
- prompt and reliable delivery; and
- the necessary support services,

then the financial aspects may be decisive.

### Example 6.5

Simon Goode, the purchasing officer of Dynamic Products Ltd, recently discovered that it cost £65.00 each to manufacture TRM units internally. He invited two outside suppliers to tender for the part and received quotes of £45.80 and £47.00 per unit. Apparently, Dynamic Products could save money by buying the TRM unit rather than making it.

Before proposing this to the Make/Buy Committee, Mr Goode took another look at the detailed cost sheet, shown in Table 6.5.

Table 6.5 *TRM unit cost sheet*

|  | *(£)* |
|---|---|
| Labour cost (1 hour at £8.00 per hour) | 8.00 |
| Material cost | 9.00 |
| Manufacturing overhead (at 600% of labour cost) | 48.00 |
| Total standard manufacturing cost per unit | 65.00 |

Given that manufacturing overhead is 80% fixed and 20% variable, what should Simon Goode recommend? We need to identify the relevant costs for this decision. How much will Dynamic Products actually save if the TRM unit is bought from an outside supplier?

Only 20% of the overheads are variable, which amounts to £9.60 per unit (£48.00 × 20%). So the incremental savings from outsourcing would amount to £26.60 per unit (£8.00 labour, £9.00 material and £9.60 overhead). Since the cheapest outside quote is £45.80, Dynamic Products should continue to make the TRM unit in-house. Had the cost advantage from continuing to make the TRM unit been relatively small, we would then need to look at other differential costs — such as interest on the cost of holding inventories needed for internal manufacture.

Alternatively, if the overhead had been 20% fixed and 80% variable, then the total savings would have been £8.00 + £9.00 + £38.40 = £55.40. It would then be cheaper to buy outside for £45.80 (or even at £47.00).

Before reaching a final decision, the Make/Buy Committee need to consider other relevant issues (such as quality, delivery, reliability, potential price increases). Financial information is important, but often so are other (non-financial) factors.

Clearly, using 'full costs' may lead to poor decisions. Since many firms maintain standard (full) cost information, there is a constant danger of misusing it. The damage done may be worse than that resulting from less sophisticated approaches (e.g. 'gut feel').

Now consider Case study 6.1.

## Case study 6.1

### Problem

Shrival Engineering have suffered from falling demand in recent years and now have significant spare capacity in their foundry and machining operations. Two years ago they decided to buy, rather than produce in-house, a cast and machined iron component. The following current data indicates that the purchase price is still cheaper than the in-house manufacturing cost:

|  | In-house cost per unit (£) | Purchase price per unit (£) |
|---|---|---|
| Material | 6.90 | |
| Mfg labour | 6.00 | N/A |
| Mfg overhead | 15.00 | |
| Total | 27.90 | 25.90 |

Manufacturing overhead is calculated at 250% of manufacturing labour cost. The various overheads are split between fixed and variable costs as shown below:

|  |  |  | Fixed | Variable |
|---|---|---|---|---|
| Depreciation charges | 90% | = | 90% | — |
| Supervision | 8% | = | 6% | 2% |
| Indirect labour | 80% | = | 40% | 40% |
| Utilities | 40% | = | 8% | 32% |
| Rates | 12% | = | 12% | — |
| Other | 20% | = | 18% | 2% |
| Manufacturing overhead rate | 250% | = | 174% | 76% |

### Question

Should Shrival Engineering continue to buy the component (cast and machined) from their outside supplier?

### Solution

The decision should be based on the additional costs of producing the component in-house. Because of Shrival's spare capacity, the only additional costs per unit involved appear to be the variable costs.

|  | (£) |
|---|---|
| Material | 6.90 |
| Manufacturing labour | 6.00 |
| Manufacturing overhead (76% × £6.00) | 4.56 |
| Total incremental manufacturing cost | 17.46 |

Purchase price from outside is £25.90 per unit; therefore, the company should manufacture in-house at an incremental cost of only £17.46 per unit.

Note that if Shrival continues to make use of its spare capacity, the company will eventually reach the point where it will incur additional fixed costs. Shrival would need to take these incremental costs into account in make-or-buy decisions.

Alternatively, if the outside supplier has spare capacity, it is quite possible that he will offer to supply at a lower price still. Thus, it might be more advantageous for the outside supplier to continue to supply, but at a much lower price. In times of excess industry capacity, buyers are in a very strong bargaining position.

## 6.3 Use-of-capacity decisions

In the short term, a business often cannot much alter its operating capacity, so management has to decide how to use the available facilities to best advantage.

### Example 6.6

Maggie Stewart, the owner of Flair Hair, a ladies hairdressing salon, is considering opening the shop for extra hours and offering a half-price 'hair-do' for lady pensioners, using semi-skilled hairdressers undergoing training at the local college. The 28 additional opening hours will be 6.00–10.00 p.m. Monday through Friday, and 9.00 a.m.–1.00 p.m. and 2.00–6.00 p.m. on Sunday. Three semi-skilled students will each be paid £5 per hour. It is reckoned that they will handle about two customers per hour each, with an average customer price of £10.00 each. Additional electricity and consumable costs are estimated at £9.00 per additional hour of opening.

Assuming that there is no transfer of existing customers to the pensioner business, calculate the expected financial impact of this decision, as follows:

Incremental revenue:

= £10.00 each × 2 per hour × 3 staff × 28 hours per week
= £1680 per week

Incremental costs:

= (£5.00 per hour × 3 staff × 28 hours per week)
+ (£9.00 per hour × 28 hours per week)

= £420 + £252 per week

= £672 per week

Surplus of incremental revenue over incremental costs:

= £1680 − £672 per week

= £1008 per week

The financial information suggests that this is a good idea. Before making a final decision, Maggie should consider what other incremental costs might be incurred (e.g. advertising, supervision (possibly herself), more wear and tear on facilities and equipment). She might also consider the impact of possible changes to her proposed prices.

Now consider Case study 6.2.

---

## Case study 6.2

### Problem

Integrated Systems Ltd makes electronic control systems. The production manager has recently suggested discontinuing the dual reflex actuator (DRA) unit, which is sold separately, due to its low and declining demand levels and because it sells at a price below its full standard cost of £510 per unit. The current sales volume is 200 units per month and, while very little adverse customer reaction is likely, the sales director points out that it still makes a contribution to profit of £5000 a month, as follows:

|  |  | (per unit) |
|---|---|---|
| Sales price |  | £400 |
| Manufacturing cost: |  |  |
| Labour | £75.00 |  |
| Material | £187.50 |  |
| Mfg overhead — variable | £112.50 | £375 |
| Contribution |  | £25 |

(× 200 = £5000 per month)

The plant facilities manager reckons that discontinuing the DRA unit would allow him to dispose of the machinery (which has a nil book value) for little more than scrap value (about £5000). The costs of dismantling and disposal would be about

£1000. Integrated Systems could use the vacated space (some 10 000 square feet) for spare parts currently stored in a nearby warehouse which the company rents for £3000 per month. The cost of moving the spare parts storage to the main site would be about £4000. Floor space on the main site is costed at £12 per square foot per year.

*Question*
What action would you recommend?

### Solution
Relevant information for ceasing manufacture of the DRA unit is as follows:

|  |  |  |
|---|---|---|
| (i) | Loss of contribution | £5000 per month |
| (ii) | Disposal value of machinery | £5000 |
| (iii) | Dismantling machinery and disposal costs of machinery | £1000 |
| (iv) | Saving on warehouse cost | £3000 per month |
| (v) | Moving costs | £4000 |

|  | Positive effects | Adverse effects |
|---|---|---|
| Once-off | (ii) £5000 | (iii) £1000 |
|  |  | (v) £4000 |
| Monthly | (iv) £3000 per month | (i) £5000 per month. |

The result is a net cash flow of £2000 per month. On the figures, Integrated Systems Ltd should continue producing the DRA unit for the time being. Note that the incremental saving on floor space is £3000 per month (warehouse rent) and not £10 000 per month (main site). The opportunity cost of releasing space in the main site building is (apparently) only £3000 per month — the savings from avoiding renting the warehouse. Had we (incorrectly) used the main site floor space cost of £10 000 per month, we would have made the opposite (i.e. wrong) decision.

In bad times, the problem is what to do with surplus capacity. In good times, firms may have to deal with excess demand. In the longer term, possible solutions might include increasing capacity to supply (see Chapter 7) or increasing selling prices to reduce demand.

In the short term, the **limiting factor** of supply may be materials, skilled labour, equipment or space. Maximizing profit then means maximizing the contribution per unit of the limiting factor.

**Example 6.7**

Eye-D TV Products make high-definition television sets in three models (ITV, JTV, KTV) using the same production equipment for each. Details are as follows:

|                            | ITV | JTV | KTV |
| -------------------------- | --- | --- | --- |
| Sales price (£ per unit)   | 450 | 550 | 625 |
| Contribution (£ per unit)  | 225 | 297 | 310 |
| Units per hour             | 10  | 7   | 6   |

Which model will result in most contribution (and therefore profit), given that Eye-D can sell (at existing prices) whatever they make?

KTV has the highest contribution per unit, JTV the highest contribution margin to sales (54%). But with equipment capacity limiting output, ITV gives the largest contribution per hour at £2250 (£225 × 10). This is more than either JTV (£297 × 7 = £2079 per hour) or KTV (£310 × 6 = £1860 per hour).

Non-profit seeking organizations would aim to maximize net benefit from the limited resource. For a NHS hospital this might be surgeons, hospital beds, operating theatres, etc. Where there is more than one limiting factor (e.g. eventually sales volume too), in theory linear programming techniques may help reach the optimum solution.

## 6.4 Cost–benefit analysis

It may be difficult to measure the costs or (more likely) the benefits of certain business activities, such as: research, training, donations to charity, or providing an after-sales service or a low-price staff canteen or free sports facilities for employees. **Cost–benefit** analysis involves trying to quantify in money terms all the costs and benefits relating to a decision.

In deciding about such things in our personal lives, pure gut feel can be important. For example, Adam Smith pointed out that in taking a job, as well as the pay one may want to consider other pros and cons. These may include the agreeableness of the job, the difficulty of learning it, security of tenure, the level of responsibility, and the chance of success. Presumably, many people decide to get married on other than purely financial criteria.

Private commercial calculations of profit or loss, based on costs and benefits arising to the enterprise, may be misleading in seeking to assess net welfare gains for the whole community. For example, a project which pollutes the environment may seem profitable to the enterprise if there is no way to 'charge' it for the pollution. Or another project, such as lighting a passageway, may not seem worth doing if it is impossible to assess how many and how much people benefit from it. Part of the problem stems from the difficulty of developing adequate rules governing property rights.

Hence, the cost—benefit approach is of special interest in the public sector where market prices may often not apply. Cost—benefit analysis tries to value all relevant non-market costs and benefits (as well as using ordinary market prices where available) in order to determine whether on balance a particular project is worthwhile or not. Examples include the location of another London airport, or requiring car passengers to wear seat-belts. Clearly, it is not easy to value the noise from an airport, people's travelling time, or the lives supposedly saved by wearing seat-belts.

Public sector cost—benefit analysis often uses 'shadow pricing' — what receivers of external benefits would be willing to pay for them, or what those who bear external costs would accept as fair compensation. Clearly, such shadow prices are hypothetical!

## 6.5 **Risk and uncertainty**

Business managers usually have to plan, control and make decisions on the basis of **uncertain** estimates, even though they may know some figures for sure, such as some suppliers' prices for the next few months.

Where adverse events could seriously damage their business, managers need to understand the range and likelihood of possible outcomes. Two ways to cope with uncertainty are: **sensitivity analysis**; and subjective probabilities and **expected values**.

### 6.5.1 **Sensitivity analysis**

In decision making, the first step is usually to make a single best estimate (best = most likely) for each variable. One might then also make optimistic and pessimistic estimates for each. The spreads may not be symmetrical: for instance, capacity constraints may prevent a firm exceeding budgeted sales volume by much, whereas there could be a sharp decline in a recession.

Another approach is to vary the most likely estimate for each item (of cost, volume or revenue) in turn, to see how much it affects the overall results. Some items will not matter much even if they change by a large percentage. So one needs to identify the critical items where even a fairly small percentage change could make quite a large difference to the overall result.

It is not much use to try changing each item by a fixed percentage, say 10%; for some items could vary by much more, while others may be unlikely to change by nearly as much as 10%. A better method is to define an optimistic estimate of income as one which there would be only (say) a 1 in 10 chance of exceeding. (There would be only a 1 in 10 chance of falling short of the pessimistic estimate of income.)

It is not easy to allow for interdependence among variables. But merely to combine the pessimistic estimates of the most sensitive items would be far too gloomy. If 'pessimistic' means a 1 in 10 chance of a worst outcome, for example, with four completely independent variables there would be only a 1 in 10 000 chance of such a combined outcome! Sensitivity analysis may answer the question 'what if?'; but it does not say how likely 'if' is.

## 6.5.2 Subjective probabilities and expected values

Some authors distinguish between risk and uncertainty. They use the term 'risk' where the chance of each possible outcome occurring is known (as in roulette or with dice). Uncertainty exists when, as is usual in business, one can only estimate the odds subjectively (i.e. guess).

Suppose that, for a new product, a firm reckons that sales of 600, 400, 300 or 100 units are possible, with the chances of each outcome (in order) being 0.1, 0.3, 0.4 and 0.2. By weighting the possible outcomes by their estimated chances of happening, we can calculate an expected value of sales volume of 320 units (see Table 6.6). We can do the same for the estimated profit at each possible level of sales, to arrive at an expected profit of £42.

Attaching subjective probabilities to uncertain future events allows arithmetical manipulation of the numbers. It may even mislead people into pretending that their decision making is scientific. But what confidence can we have in guesses about the chances of various outcomes? Can we even be sure we have considered every possible event? (Events which in advance were thought to be impossible quite often seem afterwards to have been inevitable.)

What does it really mean to apply subjective estimates of probabilities to one-off events (which are not going to recur)? In deciding whether or not to become a professional footballer, for example, does it make sense for someone to say: 'I guess the odds against my becoming a top-class football star are 200 to 1; against my becoming a run-of-the-mill third division player, 5 to 1; etc.'; to multiply the estimated after-tax rewards in each case by the estimated chance of it happening; and then to decide by choosing the alternative with the highest expected value?

Table 6.6 *Subjective probabilities and expected values*

| Sales volume | Profit (loss) | Probability of happening | 'Expected' sales | 'Expected' profit |
|---|---|---|---|---|
| 600 | £210 | 0.1 | 60 | £21 |
| 400 | £90 | 0.3 | 120 | £27 |
| 300 | £30 | 0.4 | 120 | £12 |
| 100 | (£90) | 0.2 | 20 | (£18) |
| | | 1.0 | 320 | £42 |

Not many people would really have much confidence in such a procedure for important decisions.

If we know the true odds, there is no uncertainty, only risk. But we are not safe in extrapolating frequencies for future events from statistics of past occurrences in similar cases. For we are then merely *assuming* that the past will repeat itself. ('Trends go on until they stop.') And what about unprecedented events? What are the odds against the Ukraine joining the European Community not later than December 2004?

When dealing with unique events, we can never know if our estimate of the odds was correct — even after the event. Some approaches may help us to think about a problem, by breaking it up into a number of simpler sub-problems.

### 6.5.3 Managing risk and uncertainty

Business risk refers to how a business invests its resources, financial risk to how it finances them. Financial risk relates to borrowing to finance net assets. This is risky because the business must make regular interest payments and must repay the amount borrowed on the due date. For any fluctuation in profits before interest, such financial gearing increases the volatility of the profits for equity shareholders. In contrast, equity capital is less risky for the business, since it implies no legal commitments in terms of dividends or capital repayments.

A firm can reduce business risk in a number of ways. Table 6.7, which is certainly not comprehensive, lists three kinds of business actions: contractual, flexible and uncertainty-reducing. Some actions may either reduce risk or increase it, depending on the circumstances (e.g. diversifying into different (less well-understood) businesses; or building spare capacity).

Table 6.7 *Ways of reducing uncertainty*

| | Contractual | Flexible | Uncertainty-reducing |
|---|---|---|---|
| Sales | Produce goods only against firm orders, not for stock | Avoid over-dependence on a few customers or products | Extensive market research before launching new products |
| Purchases | Arrange long-term supply contracts | Arrange more than one source of supply | Stockpile raw materials |
| Assets | Insure as much as possible | Use general-purpose rather than highly specialized equipment | Retain high liquid resources |
| Employees | Contracts of service usually not enforced against employees by UK courts | Pay partly by commission or bonus rather than flat rate | Promote from within rather than hire from outside |

A general approach to reducing uncertainty may be to spend time, as well as money, in trying to gain more information. This, too, may be risky! It is hard to avoid the conclusion that, in a sense, nearly all human action which commits resources in one way rather than another is speculative.

| 6.6 **Chapter summary** | People making business decisions must forecast the relevant costs and revenues, that is, the incremental future cash flows for the whole enterprise. Three important decision areas where this applies are: make-or-buy; use-of-capacity; and capital investment (Chapter 7). |
|---|---|
| | Make-or-buy decisions should consider not only the financial results, but also other important aspects such as suppliers' technical competence, quality, delivery and support services. |
| | Firms with spare capacity may often make decisions using variable cost as the opportunity cost. At full capacity the choice is what to make, or whether to increase selling prices or to expand. |
| | In the public sector, there is often no market to put a money value on benefits (and perhaps costs). Cost–benefit analysis, which uses a more subjective approach to decision making in such cases, can also apply to some business decisions. |
| | Most business decisions involve some risk or uncertainty. Sensitivity analysis measures how changes to variables might affect the financial outcome, while subjective probabilities can be used to estimate expected values. Business risk refers to the way a firm invests resources, financial risk measures the extent to which it borrows funds. |

## 6.7 **Review questions**

1 Identify three business decisions that require relevant cost information.

2 What are the four basic principles that identify which costs and revenues are relevant?

3 How should on-going costs and revenues be dealt with in financial decision making?

4 Division A of a company is considering dropping one of its product lines. If Central Office overheads are apportioned to divisions on the basis of divisional revenue, how should Division A include savings of Central Office overheads in their decision analysis?

5 What sort of non-financial matters should a company consider before deciding to buy a component part from outside suppliers instead of making it internally?

6 Since many businesses aim to make a profit, surely depreciation and profit implications are relevant in decision making! Do you agree?

7 What does cost–benefit analysis involve?

8 What is the difference between risk and uncertainty?

9 Name two ways of dealing with uncertainty.

10 What is sensitivity analysis?

11 Why is it unsatisfactory to always adjust 'more likely' figures by 10% when analysing sensitivities?

12 In what circumstances may 'subjective probabilities' be useful?

13 What are the drawbacks to using 'subjective probabilities'?

14 How are 'expected values' calculated?

15 Identify two ways of reducing risk by:
   (a) contractual arrangements;
   (b) flexible operating;
   (c) uncertainty-reducing.

To maximize learning, please *write out* your answers on a separate sheet of paper. *Then* check with the answers in Appendix C, pp. 238–9.

## 6.8 Problems

1 Nippey's Garage sells new and used cars and provides after-sales service. Business activity has grown rapidly in recent years. The servicing, repair and MOT test facilities, and the five garage staff, are fully utilized from 8.00 a.m. to 6.00 p.m. Monday to Friday, and from 8.00 a.m. to 1.00 p.m. on Saturdays (50 working hours). In fact, some potential customers are going elsewhere rather than wait two weeks or more for an appointment.

Nippey's general manager is considering recruiting five garage service and repair staff to work from 6.00 p.m. to midnight on Monday to Friday (30 working hours). He believes this shift would rapidly become fully utilized.

Existing financial information for the servicing and repair activities reveals the following:

|  | £ per hour |
|---|---|
| Charge-out rate to customer | 15.00 |
| Labour costs (including NHI, pensions, etc.) | 7.50 |
| Equipment depreciation | 2.00 |
| Floor-space costs (including rates) | 2.50 |
| Other overheads | 1.50 |
| Total costs | 13.50 |
| Profit margin | 1.50 |
|  | 15.00 |

Higher labour rates of £9.50 would be incurred for the new late shift. With the additional proposed use of existing equipment, its estimated life is only two-thirds of its current estimated life. About one-third of the 'other overheads' are variable.

*Questions*

(a) Determine which is the better alternative:
   (i) commence a late-shift operation; or
   (ii) continue to limit customers due to capacity restrictions.
(b) What other alternatives would you consider before making a final recommendation?

2 Waterton Football Club was considering introducing an away-supporters' ban, thus limiting attendance to home-club supporters only. Attendance at matches would be adversely affected by the absence of away supporters, but it was reckoned that this would be partly offset by attracting more home supporters. For the first season as a whole, the following estimates were made:

|  | Away-supporters' ban | |
|---|---|---|
|  | With £m | Without £m |
| Gate receipts | 2.4 | 2.5 |
| Programme sales | 0.1 | 0.15 |
| Policing costs | 0.06 | 0.2 |

Cost of new system:

| | | |
|---|---|---|
| equipment[1] | 0.2 | — |
| running costs | 0.1 | — |
| Staffing costs on | | |
| match days | 0.04 | 0.1 |
| Players' costs | 1.8 | 1.8 |
| Other running costs | 0.5 | 0.5 |

[1]the equipment was expected to last at least three years.

*Questions*

(a) What is the financial effect on the football club?
(b) Are there any other factors that need to be considered?

**3** Roy Essex was considering utilizing six currently unused robots for a cost-savings project. The robots had been replaced by more modern equipment after only two years of use and were now stored in a nearby warehouse. The robots cost a total of £2.4 million and were being depreciated on a straight-line basis over ten years. With eight years to go, the net book value stood at £1.92 million. Roy gathered from the equipment supplier that the second-hand value for the six robots was about £0.8 million.

Generally, when equipment was transferred within the company it was transferred at its net book value. Roy knew his project could not afford the net-book-value cost, but he felt it was a shame that the robots should remain unutilized.

*Questions*

(a) What costs are relevant?
(b) How should the company deal with this situation?

**4** Wilfred Dudley Ltd had nearly completed a specialized piece of capital equipment when its customer went bankrupt. After searches, two other possible customers (Elton Ltd and Protheroe Ltd) for the equipment were found who might be interested subject to certain modifications being carried out.

Elton wanted the equipment to be completed to its original specification and then certain extra features to be added. Protheroe wanted the equipment in its present condition but without its control mechanism and with certain modifications. The costs of these additions and modifications were as follows:

| | Elton | Protheroe |
|---|---|---|
| Direct materials | | |
| (at cost) | £1400 | £350 |
| Direct wages | | |
| Dept A | 1 man for 3 weeks | — |
| Dept B | 2 men for 5 weeks | 1 man for 3 weeks |
| Dept C | 2 men for 8 weeks | 1 man for 5 weeks |
| Variable overhead | 15% of direct wages | 15% of direct wages |
| Special delivery charge | £1700 | £450 |

Fixed production overhead is absorbed as follows:

| | | |
|---|---|---|
| Dept A | 120% of direct wages | (£140 per man per week) |
| Dept B | 80% of direct wages | (£120 per man per week) |
| Dept C | 40% of direct wages | (£100 per man per week) |

The costs of the equipment as originally estimated and incurred so far were as follows:

| | Original quotation | Work done so far | Work yet to be done |
|---|---|---|---|
| | £ | £ | £ |
| Direct materials | 26 150 | 21 490 | 4 685 |
| Direct wages | 15 000 | 13 400 | 2 100 |

| Overhead: | | | |
|---|---|---|---|
| variable | 2 250 | 2 010 | 315 |
| fixed | | | |
| production | 12 500 | 10 500 | 2 400 |
| fixed selling | | | |
| and | | | |
| administration | 2 500 | 2 100 | 400 |
| | 58 400 | 49 500 | 9 900 |

The price to the original customer allowed for a profit margin of 20% on selling price. An advance payment of 15% of the price had been received when the order had been confirmed.

The following additional information is related to the possible conversions:

- Direct materials for the additions for Elton Ltd would need to be bought from suppliers, but those for modifications for Protheroe Ltd are in stock and, if not used for Protheroe Ltd, would be used on another contract in place of materials that would now cost £750.
- Dept A is slack at present, but to ensure the availability of skilled personnel it must keep three men on its payroll even though the current and projected load for the next few months is only 50% of capacity.
- Dept B is working normally.
- Dept C is extremely busy: it is currently yielding a contribution to overhead and profit of £3.20 per £1 of direct labour.
- If the work for either Elton or Protheroe is undertaken, supervising overtime of £500 and £350 respectively would be incurred. Such costs are normally charged to fixed production overhead.
- The cost of the control mechanism that Protheroe does not require was £4500. If taken out (at a cost of 1 man-week's work in Dept B), it could be used on another contract in place of a different mechanism which could be bought for £3500.

If neither of the conversions is carried out, some of the materials in the original equipment would be used on another contract in place of materials that would have cost £4000, but would need 2 man-weeks of work in Dept B to make them suitable. The remaining materials would realize £3800 as scrap. The drawings for the equipment, which would normally be included in the selling price, could be sold for £500.

*Questions*

(a) Calculate the minimum price that the company should accept from Protheroe for the converted machine.
(b) Calculate the minimum price at which it would be more advantageous to sell to Elton if the company received an offer from Protheroe of £18 000 for the converted machine.

Explain clearly how you reach your recommended figures in both cases.

5 Tarpit Machines Ltd made complex industrial machinery that involved assembling thousands of parts, ranging from small nuts to large castings. In the past, the company had tended to buy most such parts from outside suppliers, rather than making them in-house. A new managing director was reviewing many of the company's practices, and had asked Bill Short, the company's chief accountant, to recommend a policy on 'make-or-buy' decisions for component parts.

Labour rates did not vary much, so Tarpit charged direct labour costs (and variable overheads) to products at a uniform average rate per hour. To avoid unit costs varying widely, the company also charged fixed overheads at a uniform rate per direct labour hour. (Otherwise, low production volume would produce unduly high fixed overhead costs per unit; and vice versa.)

Twice a year, Tarpit totalled direct labour, variable overhead and fixed overhead costs;

and divided each by total direct labour hours for the past six months. Present practice was to use this figure (together with material costs) to estimate the cost of making parts for the next six months, assuming that Tarpit would make a one-year supply in a single production run. Latest unit cost figures were as follows:

| | |
|---|---|
| Direct labour | £4.50 |
| Variable overhead | £5.25 |
| Fixed overhead | £4.00 |
| Basic cost of manufacturing | £13.75 |

Bill Short wondered which costs Tarpit should properly use in make-or-buy decisions. He believed that in the short run nearly all costs (apart from materials) were fixed, but that in the long run one could regard all costs as variable. In his view, the two key factors were fixed overheads and the level of plant activity. In looking at making a part instead of buying from outside suppliers, he thought Tarpit should omit fixed overheads from its cost estimates when the plant was working under capacity.

Relations with suppliers might suffer if Tarpit made parts itself when the plant was below capacity, but tried to buy them outside when the plant was full. Suppliers would seek other customers, and Tarpit might not be sure to get delivery when it wanted. Moreover, suppliers' prices included marketing and financial costs, as well as profit. Should Tarpit's estimates of the cost of making parts therefore include a fair share of marketing, financial and other expenses?

To help the purchasing department make specific make-or-buy decisions on parts, Bill Short suggested two different cost figures. One included all costs. The other, excluding fixed overheads, he called 'marginal manufacturing cost'. He believed it should serve as a valuable guide when the plant was below capacity.

*Questions*

(a) Annual requirements for a solid steel stud are 25 000 units. Total materials cost will be £1600, and direct labour hours will total 280. Determine: (i) what cost estimates would Tarpit make; (ii) what would Tarpit decide if the outside purchase price is £0.18 per unit; and (iii) would the decision be correct?

(b) The case suggests excluding fixed overheads from the cost estimates when the plant is under capacity. Do you believe, as this implies, that Tarpit should *include* fixed overheads when the plant is working at capacity?

(c) How should Tarpit decide 'make-or-buy' questions? What factors might lead either to understating or to overstating the apparent cost of making in-house?

**6** The showroom manager of Posh Car Dealers Ltd was considering ways to improve financial performance. Posh Cars sold new expensive cars to wealthy individuals and companies. Although they did take some cars in part exchange, they found a buyer for the second-hand car before finalizing the new car sale. New cars were therefore effectively sold for cash.

During the last month, 9 cars were sold at List Price (average £28 000) less 10% discount. Posh Car Dealers bought the cars at List Price less 25% discount.

A statement of the latest month's financial performance for the Posh Car showroom showed the following:

| | £ |
|---|---|
| Sales | 226 800 |
| Cost of sales | 189 000 |
| Gross profit | 37 800 |
| Expenses: | |
| salaries, etc. | 14 500 |
| rent and rates | 4 650 |

| heating and lighting | 800 |
|---|---|
| telephone | 370 |
| miscellaneous | 280 |
| Profit before interest and tax | 17 200 |

Two proposals were being considered as possible ways of improving financial performance:

- Sell cars at List Price less 15% instead of List Price less 10%. It was thought that this would increase sales from an average of 9 cars per month to 13 cars per month. Expenses would be unchanged.
- Increase the hours of business from 50 hours per week to 68 hours per week by staying open later in the evening and opening on Saturday and Sunday afternoons. This was thought likely to increase sales from an average of 9 cars per month to 11 cars per month. Total salaries would increase by £4800. The remaining variable expenses would increase in proportion to the increased opening hours of business The fixed monthly expenses are:

| Rent and rates | £4650 |
|---|---|
| Heating and lighting | £50 |
| Telephone | £20 |
| Miscellaneous | £130 |

*Questions*

(a) Evaluate the two proposals. Which of the two (if either) would you recommend?
(b) If the (separate, but related) Posh Car Dealers Ltd service and repair garage operation which has variable costs of 60% of its sales revenue was able to increase its sales revenue by: (i) £12 000 in the next year for proposal 1, or (ii) £6000 in the next year for proposal 2, how (if at all) does this affect the proposals? No change in fixed costs is expected.

7 Antonio was reviewing his strategy for his small bakery business. Demand had improved over the last few years and he was now working at about 90% of full capacity. Although it was easily possible to increase production staff hours further, the production bottleneck would be the baking oven.

The profit and loss account for the last 12 months analysed by product line was as follows:

| | Bread | Pastry | Cakes | Total |
|---|---|---|---|---|
| | | (£'000s) | | |
| Production costs: | | | | |
| Ingredients | 28 | 20 | 10 | 58 |
| Labour | 10 | 9 | 18 | 37 |
| Depreciation | 5 | 8 | 1 | 14 |
| Repairs and maintenance | 2 | 3 | — | 5 |
| Rent and insurance | 4 | 4 | 4 | 12 |
| Power, light and heat | 1 | 1 | 1 | 3 |
| Total production costs | 50 | 45 | 34 | 129 |
| Admin. and sales costs | 16 | 13 | 12 | 41 |
| Total costs | 66 | 58 | 46 | 170 |
| Sales | 84 | 69 | 62 | 215 |
| Profit | 18 | 11 | 16 | 45 |

The allocation of labour and ingredients costs was reckoned to be fairly accurate. Depreciation and repairs and maintenance was apportioned according to estimated equipment usage. The remaining production costs being relatively small, amounts were divided equally between the three product lines. Admin. and sales costs were apportioned in proportion to sales revenue.

Antonio regarded his costs to be fixed with the exception of production labour and ingredients costs which he believed to be 100% variable.

*Questions*

(a) Which of his product lines should Antonio prefer to increase sales revenue on, assuming the output and sales could be increased further but still within capacity constraints? Explain your answer.

(b) If one of Antonio's production workers is off sick and he is therefore unable to meet the day's production schedule, which of the product lines would you recommend reducing output on? Explain why.

(c) There is sufficient production capacity to increase production output by: (i) 10% on bread; (ii) 6% on pastry; (iii) 20% on cakes. Rank the product lines in the order that enables Antonio to improve profitability most.

**8** The Beck Company manufactures sheet metal that can either be sold as basic sheet metal for £200 per ton or processed further and sold as alloyed sheet metal for £330 per ton. Beck have about 1% of the basic sheet metal market and about 2% of the alloyed sheet metal market (for which the market price was, until recently, £360 per ton).

The sales manager has suggested that Beck discontinues making alloyed sheet metal and uses its entire production capacity for basic sheet metal production and sales. (The production equipment can be used for either basic or alloyed sheet metal.) The production equipment is currently working at full capacity, half on basic sheet steel and the other half on alloyed sheet steel, producing thirty tons of basic sheet steel and thirty tons of alloyed sheet steel per day.

The existing cost structure of both basic sheet metal and alloyed sheet metal is as follows:

| | Cost per ton (£) | |
|---|---|---|
| | Basic sheet metal | Alloyed sheet metal |
| Variable costs: | | |
| Materials | 100 | 40 |
| Direct labour | 20 | 20 |
| Variable overhead | 20 | 20 |
| Fixed costs: | | |
| Fixed overhead | 40 | 40 |
| Total cost | 180 | 180 + 120 = 300 |
| Operating profit | 20 | 30 |
| Price | 200 | 330 |

*Questions*

(a) Should the Beck Company stop producing alloyed sheet steel and devote the entire production facilities to producing basic sheet steel? Justify your conclusion with appropriate figures.

(b) What is the lowest price at which the Beck Company should continue with alloyed sheet steel production?

(c) What additional factors need to be considered?

(The solutions to Problems 3–8 will be provided in the *Instructors' Manual*.)

# CHAPTER 7 *Capital investment decisions*

## 7.1 **Capital projects**

### 7.1.1 **What is investment?**

The key distinction between the previous chapter and this one is that of *time*. Chapter 6 focused on relatively short-term decisions; but the benefits from capital investments typically accrue over many years.

Capital investment means spending money now in the hope of getting sufficient returns later. Investment as such is not good: companies invest money in order to make a profit.

Three main kinds of capital investment are: replacing equipment, to reduce costs or improve quality; expanding productive capacity, to meet growing demand; or providing new facilities, to make new products.

### 7.1.2 **Key steps in the process**

There are several key steps in the capital investment process (see Table 7.1). Probably the most important is the first — generating worthwhile ideas for capital investments. These ideas may result from identifying business opportunities or from responding to recognized problems. Only a small proportion are likely to emanate from accountants. Most will come from sales, marketing, production, engineering, R&D, and other functional personnel. Good ideas from these people are vital to the success of most businesses.

Reaching a sensible answer may depend on asking the right questions. For example, for a capital investment the choices may be:

1 Whether or not to buy machine H;
2 whether to buy machine H or machine J;
3 whether to buy machine H now or later.

After looking at possible alternatives to each project, detailed engineering estimates, market forecasts, and so on, will be needed. Capital investment projects may often cover the whole range of business: production, marketing, organization, strategy. Hence, large projects involve groups of people from many parts of a business, and often cover quite long periods of time.

If there are many alternatives to consider (step 3), it may prove

Table 7.1 *Key steps in the capital investment process*

1.  Generate ideas — opportunities and solutions to problem.
2.  Acquire relevant information.
3.  Consider possible alternatives to achieving aim.
4.  Establish specific project details, costs *and benefits*.
5.  Evaluate financial and non-financial consequences and make a decision.

If to proceed:
6.  Implement and control project.
7.  Monitor results and (selectively) post audit.

worthwhile to screen out any clearly unsatisfactory ones before spending too much time on them.

It can be hard to estimate a project's future net benefits. What consumers will want in a few years' time, what competitors will be up to, how production methods may change — all are uncertain. Yet they may affect the project's life, sales volume, selling prices, costs. An expansion or new-product project may promise to increase sales revenue by more than operating costs. A cost reduction project, in contrast, may not affect sales revenue at all: reduced future operating costs are the net benefits of the project (compared to what would happen without it).

In trying to tell how much net improvement will result from a project, the forecast of sales revenue is often critical. For example, publishers may be able to calculate production costs quite closely, with a fixed selling price, but sales volume may be very uncertain; or petrol companies may be fairly sure how much petrol they will sell, but not what the selling prices will be. On the other hand, shipbuilding on a fixed-price contract would provide certain sales revenue, but uncertain costs and timing.

In most organizations, what goes on informally is at least as important as the formal system. The internal politics of capital budgeting is often crucial. In any case, the financial estimates may not be the most critical aspects of capital investment projects.

Even after the final decision to invest, there remains the vital process of implementing the decision. This process cannot simply be taken for granted: it may take many months (or even years); and mistakes here can be very costly.

Finally, after the event some companies have a system of post-project audit. This may involve checking the amount and timing of the capital investment outlay. Or it may involve a full-scale reappraisal to check on the accuracy of the original estimates of operating cash flows as well as capital spending. One of the main aspects to review is the basis of the original assumptions about the economic climate, market size, market share, cost of supplies, etc. The purpose is not so much to apportion blame if things have gone wrong, as to learn how to do better in future.

### 7.1.3 Organization for capital budgeting

In addition to a method of looking at each capital project's expected profit, companies must have a system of capital budgeting. This involves planning the total amount of capital spending over the next year or two, and breaking it down into a monthly or quarterly spend which will form part of the cash-flow budget. This is needed in order to arrange suitable financing. Such plans are often updated quarterly, since both the amounts and the timing of payments for capital projects can change quickly. The phasing may change if business conditions make it desirable to slow down or speed up capital spending. In extreme cases, even approved projects may have to be cancelled.

Capital investments may be for very large sums of money. Once implemented, they are often not reversible since, for much specialized plant and equipment, there may be no second-hand market. And, even if there were a potential buyer, it may only be possible to sell at a reduced price. Moreover, large investments may have important strategic implications. So businesses tend to be wary about capital spending. They look carefully before they leap, and have thorough procedures for proposals to pass through before approval. The larger the amount of money involved, the higher up the organization the capital project must go for approval. If such approval sometimes seems to be merely 'rubber-stamping', the reason is probably that extensive informal discussions have already taken place before the formal submission of the project.

## 7.2 Simple appraisal methods

Profitability is often expressed as an annual rate of return on investment.

### 7.2.1 Average accounting rate of return on investment

**Example 7.1**

Table 7.2 illustrates two rival proposals for capital investment, each lasting for three years. Project A requires an initial investment of £6000, Project B of

Table 7.2 *Project A versus Project B*

|  |  | Project A (£'000) | | Project B (£'000) | |
|---|---|---|---|---|---|
| Investment outflow | Year 0 |  | −6 |  | −12 |
| Cash inflows | Year 1<br>Year 2<br>Year 3 | +3<br>+4<br>+8 | +15 | +7<br>+8<br>+9 | +24 |
| Net profit (3 years) |  |  | +9 |  | +12 |
| Average annual profit |  |  | +3 |  | +4 |
| $\dfrac{\text{Average annual profit}}{\text{Initial investment}}$ |  | $\dfrac{3}{6}$ = 50% | | $\dfrac{4}{12}$ = 33% | |

£12 000. Project A will produce cash inflows of £3000 in Year 1, £4000 in Year 2, and £8000 in Year 3; while Project B will produce cash inflows of £7000 in Year 1, £8000 in Year 2, and £9000 in Year 3. Deducting the initial investment for each project from its total cash receipts gives the total net profit.

If we deduct the initial investment from total cash inflows, in effect charging 'depreciation', Project B produces a higher total net profit (12 versus 9). The projects have the same life (three years), so Project B also produces a higher average annual profit (return) than Project A (4 versus 3).

But if we divide the average annual profit by the initial amount invested, Project A produces a higher rate of return on investment than Project B (50% versus 33%).

The average rate of return on investment (expressed as an annual percentage) does tell us something about a capital project's profitability. But the averaging process eliminates relevant information about the timing of the returns.

### Example 7.2

Suppose we now compare Project A (as before) with Project C. Project A's profits (NB: not its cash inflows) are £1000, £2000 and £6000 in Years 1, 2 and 3 respectively; while Project C's, let us suppose, are £6000, £2000 and £1000. The order is reversed.

The average rate of return on investment is the same for both projects: 50% a year (£3000/£6000). The only difference is that Project C gives a return £5000 higher than Project A in Year 1, but £5000 lower in Year 3. In total, this difference averages out; but the extra £5000 received in Year 1 under Project C can, of course, be invested for two years, to yield a positive return. Thus, taking this opportunity cost into account, Project C is better than Project A.

But the average rate of return calculation does not reveal this conclusion, since it ignores the timing of the returns.

### 7.2.2 Payback

Probably even more widely used than 'rate of return on investment' is the **payback** method. This shows how many years it will take before a capital project pays back the original amount invested (i.e. before the cumulative cash returns exceed the initial investment). The shorter the payback period, the better.

For the payback period, it is usual to look at cash receipts from a project rather than accounting profits. Thus, in calculating a project's net cash inflows, only cash expenses should be deducted from sales revenues, not depreciation.

### Example 7.3

Let us now use again the figures for Project A and Project C, each costing £6000, assuming that cash is received evenly throughout the year (see Table 7.3).

Table 7.3 *Cash flows for Project A and Project C*

|  |  | Project A (£'000) | Project C (£'000) |
|---|---|---|---|
| Investment | Year 0 | −6 | −6 |
|  | Year 1 | +3 | +8 |
| Cash inflows | Year 2 | +4 | +4 |
|  | Year 3 | +8 | +3 |

The payback period for Project A can easily be calculated. £3000 is repaid in Year 1, and £4000 in Year 2. Thus, Project A's payback period is one-and-three-quarter years. (One year at £3000 plus three-quarters of a year at £4000 equals the initial investment of £6000.) Similarly, we can calculate Project C's payback period as nine months. Only three-quarters of the £8000 cash inflow in Year 1 is needed to recover the initial investment of £6000.

The payback method of project appraisal does have one clear advantage over the average rate of return on investment method: it takes timing into account. It is also simple to calculate and easy to understand. But the payback method ignores cash receipts *after* payback. This is vital: there can be no profit unless we get back more than the original investment.

**Example 7.4**
Suppose that in Year 4, Project A produced a cash inflow of £20 000, while Project C produced only £1000. According to the payback method, that would not change the relative attractiveness of the two projects: Project C would still look better than Project A. This clearly does not make business sense!

Thus, while it may be a useful measure of risk (the sooner the payback, the less the risk), the payback method does not measure profit.

In practice, payback is often used as a rough 'screening' device. But there are better ways to estimate the profitability of capital projects.

## 7.3 Measuring profit over time

### 7.3.1 The time value of money

Capital investment involves spending money now in the expectation of getting larger returns later. To tell whether the returns are large enough, we need a way to compare returns in the future with investment now; to compare money amounts over time.

A given amount of money now is worth more than the same amount of money in future. Why? Because it can be invested today to yield a return in the meantime.

Table 7.4 *Future values of '£1 000 now', at 20% a year*

|  | End of Year 0 (now) (£) | End of Year 1 (£) | End of Year 2 (£) | End of Year 3 (£) |
|---|---|---|---|---|
| Future values | 1 000 ⟶ | 1 200 ⟶ | 1 440 ⟶ | 1 728 |
| Present values | ⎧ 1 000 ⟵ | 1 200 | | |
| | ⎨ 1 000 ⟵ | | 1 440 | |
| | ⎩ 1 000 ⟵ | | | 1 728 |

Interest rates do not merely represent inflation: they also allow for time preference and risk. Some types of investment (e.g. in the stock market) are more risky than others (e.g. bank deposits) and are therefore expected to command a higher return.

Let us suppose that we can invest money today to yield 20% a year, so that £1000 invested today will accumulate (compounding annually) to the amounts shown as follows:

In 1 year's time, to £1000 × 1.20 = £1000 × 1.200 = £1200
In 2 years' time, to £1000 × $(1.20)^2$ = £1000 × 1.440 = £1440
In 3 years' time, to £1000 × $(1.20)^3$ = £1000 × 1.728 = £1728

Thus, using an interest rate of 20% a year, the future value of '£1000 now' is £1728 at the end of three years. Or, looking at it the other way round: the present value of '£1728 to be received at the end of 3 years' is £1000 now (see Table 7.4).

What, then, is the present value of '£1000 to be received at the end of three years'? Clearly, it must be £579, as follows:

$$\frac{£1000}{(1.20)^3} = \frac{£1000}{1.728} = £579$$

We can prove this by showing what would happen if we invested £579 at 20% a year. Each year the effect of compound interest is to add 20% of the start-of-year cumulative amount invested, as follows:

After 1 year the amount becomes: £579 + £116 = £695
After 2 years the amount becomes: £695 + £139 = £834
After 3 years the amount becomes: £834 + £166 = £1000

Thus, we can show the present value of £1000 to be received at any future date (see Table 7.5).

Assuming an interest rate of 20% a year, the present value of any amount (call it 'a') to be received at the end of three years is 0.579a. Thus, 0.579 is the **discount factor** for three years at 20% a year. It is equivalent

Table 7.5 *Present values of '£1 000 in future', at 20% a year*

|  | End of Year 0 (now) (£) | End of Year 1 (£) | End of Year 2 (£) | End of Year 3 (£) |
|---|---|---|---|---|
| Future values | 579 ⟶ | 695 ⟶ | 834 ⟶ | 1 000 |
| Present values | ⎧ 834 ◀─────── 1 000 | | | |
|  | ⎨ 695 ◀─────────────── 1 000 | | | |
|  | ⎩ 579 ◀───────────────────────── 1 000 | | | |

to $1/(1.20)^3$. (We shall use discount factors correct to three decimal places. This is quite accurate enough for most purposes.)

In effect, this gives us an exchange rate over time. Just as compound factors tell us the future values of present-day money amounts, so discount factors tell us the present value of future money amounts. (See Appendix B for table of discount factors.)

### 7.3.2 **Net terminal value**

We have been assuming that we can always invest any sum of money now to yield an annual return of 20%. In practice, it is not always easy to estimate accurately this rate of interest (the opportunity cost of capital).

If the relevant opportunity cost is 20% a year, then that is the required rate of return on a capital investment project (sometimes called the **hurdle rate**). If money costs 20% a year, why invest in a capital project expected to yield less than 20% a year? We need to get a higher return from capital projects for the investment to be worthwhile. (At this stage we ignore possible differences in riskiness.)

Using an annual interest rate enables us to compare money amounts receivable, or payable, at different points in time.

### Example 7.5

Rapid Transport Company Limited is considering expanding its fleet of vehicles by one 20-ton truck costing £24 000. It would operate for four years and then be scrapped, so the straight line depreciation charge will be £6000 per year. The company expects net cash flows from the extra business to be £6000, £7000, £9000 and £11 000 in years 1–4. Should Rapid Transport acquire the truck?

We have enough information to compare the two alternative courses of action, as follows:

(i) Invest £24 000 in buying the truck, and receive the cash inflows listed.
(ii) Do not buy the truck — in which case the company will merely earn the going interest rate of 20% a year on the £24 000.

The financial consequences are set out in Table 7.6. Since we are looking at a project with a 4-year economic life, we need to allow for the re-investment of

Table 7.6 *Net terminal value for new truck proposal*

| End of year | Cash flow (£) | | | Compound factor | | Amount at end of year 4 (£) |
|---|---|---|---|---|---|---|
| 0 (now) | − 24 000 | × | $(1.2)^4$ | [2.074] | — | − 49 766 |
| 1 | + 6 000 | × | $(1.2)^3$ | [1.728] | + 10 368 ⎫ | |
| 2 | + 7 000 | × | $(1.2)^2$ | [1.440] | + 10 080 ⎬ | + 42 248 |
| 3 | + 9 000 | × | $(1.2)$ | [1.200] | + 10 800 ⎪ | |
| 4 | + 11 000 | × | 1.0 | [1.000] | + 11 000 ⎭ | |
| Net terminal value | | | | | | − 7 518 |

cash inflows received before the end of year 4. Then we can compare the two alternatives as at the end of year 4. We assume cash received during the life of the project can be invested to earn the going interest rate of 20% a year. Thus, for instance, the £9000 cash received at the end of year 3 can be invested to earn 20% interest in year 4, accumulating to a total of £10 800 by the end of year 4. Similarly for other cash receipts at various times.

Clearly, the investment in the truck is not worthwhile. Its **net terminal value (NTV)** is negative (− £7518). This means that Rapid Transport would be better off choosing alternative (ii) and earning 20% a year on the £24 000 for 4 years (to accumulate to £49 766 by the end of year 4), rather than choosing alternative (i) and buying the truck — which provides only £42 248 by the end of year 4.

## 7.4 Discounted cash flow methods

The **net present value (NPV)** method of investment appraisal (like the net terminal value method we saw in 7.3.2) calculates a project's profit by comparing cash payments and cash receipts at the *same* point in time. Rather than looking at the end of a project's life, however, it looks at the start. It does so by discounting expected future cash flows back to the present (i.e. back to the end of year 0), and then comparing the total present value of the future cash receipts with the initial capital investment in the project.

### 7.4.1 Net present value

The NPV method multiplies future cash flows by a suitable discounting factor (this is equivalent to dividing by the appropriate compounding factor). The discounting factor depends on two things: the discount rate being used, and the number of years in future that the cash flow arises.

**Example 7.6**
Looking again at the Rapid Transport project, we see that its net present value is negative. Hence the project is not financially worthwhile. The cost of investing in the project is £24 000 now, while the present value of the cash receipts in future

Table 7.7 *Net present value for new truck proposal*

| End of year | (1)<br>Cash flow<br>(£) | (2)<br>Discount factor<br>(at 20% per year) | (1) × (2)<br>Present value<br>(£) | (£) |
|---|---|---|---|---|
| 0 (now) | − 24 000 | 1.000 | — | 24 000 |
| 1 | + 6 000 | 0.833 | +4 998 ⎫ | |
| 2 | + 7 000 | 0.694 | +4 858 ⎪ | |
| 3 | + 9 000 | 0.579 | +5 211 ⎬ | + 20 369 |
| 4 | + 11 000 | 0.482 | +5 302 ⎭ | |
| Net present value | | | | − 3 631 |

is £20 369. Thus the project amounts to a proposal to pay out £24 000 now in order to acquire the rights to future cash flows which have a (present) value of £20 369. That is hardly smart business: it represents a loss (in present value terms) of £3631 (see Table 7.7).

Note that we round off all amounts to the nearest pound. There is no advantage in seeking more accuracy. Our figures for cash flows are usually no more than estimates; and the discount rate used is nearly always only a rough approximation.

In determining the net present value and net terminal value, we have assumed that cash flows arise only at year ends. In practice, they may occur evenly throughout the year, but our assumption is usually more convenient and is unlikely to change our decision. Remember that nearly all the numbers we use are only estimates.

The principles used to calculate net present value are exactly the same as those used for net terminal value. Hence, both methods always give the same signal about whether or not a project is worthwhile. The only difference is that NPV compares amounts at the start of the project, NTV at the end.

The numbers from the Rapid Transport project show that NPV is roughly equivalent to NTV:

NPV (EOY 0) − £3631 × 2.074 = NTV (EOY 4) − £7531

or

NTV (EOY 4) − £7518 × 0.482 = NPV (EOY 0) − £3624

(If it were not for rounding errors, the numbers would be precisely equivalent.)

In practice, firms use the net present value method rather than the net terminal value method. Managers prefer to think in terms of present values, rather than in terms of future values. Also, NPV enables us to compare different projects as at the same point in time (EOY 0); whereas, if different projects have different lives, they would have different terminal dates (which would make it hard to compare NTVs directly).

The great advantage of the net terminal value method, at least in a textbook, is to clarify the precise meaning of the interest rate used in discounted cash flow methods. The compounding approach of the NTV method makes the opportunity cost nature of the interest rate quite explicit.

**Discounted cash flow (DCF)** methods involve forecasting both the amount and the timing of **incremental cash flows** which are expected to result if a particular project is undertaken, but not otherwise. Note that DCF methods deal with cash flows and *not* with accounting profits, income and expenses. Hence, non-cash expenses such as depreciation should be ignored in estimating future cash flows. To tell whether a project is expected to be profitable, we simply see whether or not the present value of the project's discounted cash inflows exceeds (the present value of) the cash investment involved.

In other words, we first value the project, and then compare that amount with the project's cost. This may simply be the initial amount of the cash investment, though sometimes projects consist of several cash payments spread out over time, which themselves need to be discounted back to present value terms. If the project's value is more than its cost (i.e. if it has positive net present value), then it is worth undertaking on financial grounds; it will increase the owner's wealth. Table 7.8 shows a way of picturing this valuation process.

The net present value method, in theory, will always give the correct answer — if one assumes the following:

1 The amounts and timing of the cash flows are correctly forecast.
2 The opportunity cost of capital is correctly estimated.
3 There are no non-financial aspects to a capital project.

Table 7.8 *Valuing a capital asset*

| | Present | | Future |
|---|---|---|---|
| Physical reality | Capital asset | ⟶ | Flow of services |
| | v. | | ↓ |
| Money values | Present value | ⟵ | Net cash inflows |

The sweeping and unrealistic nature of these necessary qualifications makes it clear that, in practice, no method of analysis can be guaranteed to give a precisely 'correct' answer.

Now consider Case study 7.1.

---

### Case study 7.1

*Problem*

Saturn Software, a small but growing software company, is considering installing a hot-drinks machine to provide free hot drinks for staff during the working day. Management felt that if free, high-quality hot drinks were immediately available, then time spent by individuals brewing tea and coffee (using their own equipment) could be significantly reduced. This saving would result in less overtime being worked and postpone the need to recruit additional staff.

The hot-drinks machine would cost £3000 to buy and would incur further costs for provisioning and maintenance (by the machine manufacturer) of £4000 per year. Savings resulting from more efficient use of staff are estimated to be about £5200 per year over the five years estimated life of the drinks machine.

*Questions*

What is the present value of the proposed Saturn Software investment in the hot-drinks machine if a 20% discount rate is applicable? What decision should be made? (Ignore corporation tax and inflation.)

*Solution*

| End of year | Net cash flow (£) | Discount factor (at 20%) | Present value (£) |
|---|---|---|---|
| 0 (now) | −3000 | 1.000 | −3000 |
| 1 | +1200 | 0.833 | +1000 |
| 2 | +1200 | 0.694 | +833 |
| 3 | +1200 | 0.579 | +695 |
| 4 | +1200 | 0.482 | +578 |
| 5 | +1200 | 0.402 | +482 |
| Net present value | | | +588 |

Because the net cash flows are the same for years 1 to 5 (annuities), we could alternatively use the cumulative discount tables from Appendix B, Table B.2. These give a cumulative discount factor of 2.991 for 5 years @ 20% (which, multiplied by £1200 gives £3589).

Decision: install hot-drinks machine.

**7.4.2 Internal rate of return**

Another method of discounting cash flows is often used instead of the net present value method. This is the **internal rate of return (IRR)** method (also called the DCF yield method).

The net present value method lists the amount and timing of all the expected future cash flows from a project; the internal rate of return method does the same. The NPV method then applies a pre-selected (criterion) discount rate, to see whether the net total of all the discounted cash flows is positive or negative. If the NPV is positive, then the project is worthwhile (from a financial point of view); if the NPV is negative, then it is not.

In contrast, the internal rate of return method determines, by trial and error, what is the (initially unknown) **discount rate** that when applied to the same cash flows will produce a net present value of exactly zero. That discount rate is the project's internal rate of return. It must then be compared with the **criterion rate**, to see whether or not the project is worthwhile.

**Example 7.7**

In Table 7.7 we found an NPV of −£3631 for Rapid Transport's new truck proposal. The IRR of this proposal is therefore less than 20% because the NPV at a 20% discount rate is negative. So, let us recalculate the NPV using (i) a 15% discount rate and (ii) a 10% discount rate (see Table 7.9).

From Table 7.9 we can see that the project's IRR lies between 10% and 15%, a little closer to 15%. We can estimate the IRR by interpolation, as follows:

$$IRR = 15\% - 5\% \left[ \frac{(1274)}{1274 + 1508} \right] = 12.7\%$$

Table 7.9 *Calculating IRR by trial and error*

| End of year | Cash flow (£) | Discount factor (at 15%) | (at 10%) | Present value (at 15%) (£) | (at 10%) |
|---|---|---|---|---|---|
| 0 (now) | − 24 000 | 1.000 | 1.000 | − 24 000 | − 24 000 |
| 1 | + 6 000 | 0.870 | 0.909 | + 5 220 | + 5 454 |
| 2 | + 7 000 | 0.756 | 0.826 | + 5 292 | + 5 782 |
| 3 | + 9 000 | 0.658 | 0.751 | + 5 922 | + 6 759 |
| 4 | +11 000 | 0.572 | 0.683 | + 6 292 | + 7 513 |
| Net present value | | | | − 1 274 | + 1 508 |

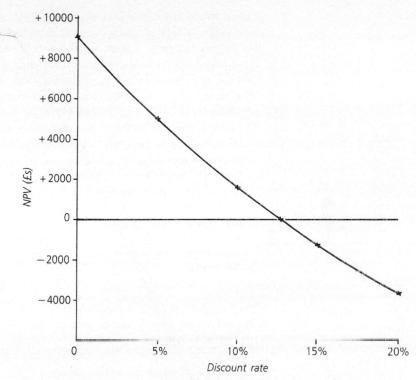

Figure 7.1 *Net present value of Rapid Transport project at various discount rates*

This IRR of 12.7% would need to be compared with the company's required minimum hurdle rate in order to conclude whether 12.7% is an acceptable return. It is possible to draw a picture showing what the net present value amounts to for a whole range of discount rates (see Figure 7.1).

Three values in particular are worth noting:

**1** Using a 0% discount rate, the NPV is +£9000.
**2** The net present value is zero at a discount rate of 12.7%. This is the internal rate of return.
**3** Using a 20% discount rate (the criterion rate), the NPV is −£3631.

A project with a higher internal rate of return may not always be better than a project with a lower IRR, for two main reasons. First, the amount invested may be different. Is a 50% IRR better than 25%? Perhaps not, if the 50% is earned on an investment of £100, while the 25% is earned on an investment of £10 000.

The second reason is that IRR, in effect, assumes **reinvestment** at the project's own (internal) rate of return. But this may not be the actual opportunity cost of capital; which makes it hard to compare two different projects, especially if they have different lives.

Even where one of the DCF methods (NPV or IRR) appears to show that a project will be profitable, it is still important for managers to identify the general economic reasons for the project. In other words, *why* can a particular project make a profit? If no specific reason can be identified, then the apparent result of the financial evaluation must be doubtful. All experienced managers know how easy it is to include very optimistic assumptions to make a project look good!

In addition to the DCF calculations, other factors such as strategic considerations and competitors' actions may need to be considered. The final decision for marginal capital investment proposals often depends on the ability of proposers to sell their idea. A good track record from previous capital investments will also carry weight at the final decision stage.

Now consider Case study 7.2.

---

### Case study 7.2

*Problem*
You are now invited to calculate the IRR for Saturn Software's hot-drinks machine proposal (see section 7.4.1). We found that with a 20% discount factor the NPV was £588. The IRR must therefore be above 20%. Try 25% and 30%; and use the cumulative discount factors from Table B.2 of Appendix B.

*Solution*
At 25% discount rate NPV = (£1200 × 2.689) − £3000 = +£227
At 30% discount rate NPV = (£1200 × 2.436) − £3000 = −£77

$$\text{By interpolation IRR} = 30\% - 5\% \left[ \frac{77}{77 + 227} \right] = 28.7\%$$

For the IRR to be determined, the NPV must = 0
And for NPV = 0 the cumulative discount factor must equal:

$$\frac{\text{the initial investment}}{\text{the annual cash flow}} = \frac{£3000}{£1200} = 2.5$$

By inspecting along the 5-year row in Table B.2 in Appendix B the cumulative discount factor reaches 2.5 somewhere between 28% and 30% discount rate. If we interpolate between 28% and 30% we would get a cumulative discount factor of 2.5 at a discount rate as follows:

$$28\% + 2\% \left[ \frac{(32)}{32 + 64} \right] = 28.7\%, \text{ as before.}$$

## 7.4.3 **Discount rate premium for risk**

When computing a project's NPV we have to select a discount rate in advance. This normally reflects (i) the company's cost of capital; (ii) the extent of essential projects which give no financial return; and (iii) the riskiness of the project concerned.

The long-term sources of finance are equity (retained profits or new issues of shares) and debt (borrowing). A company's **weighted average cost of capital (WACC)** depends on the mix and after-tax cost of equity and debt. For example, if the proportion of equity to debt is 70/30, and the cost of equity is 18% and the cost of debt 7%, then the weighted average cost of capital is as follows:

$$(0.7 \times 18\%) + (0.3 \times 7\%) = 14.7\%$$

Most companies invest in some necessary projects giving no direct financial return (e.g. for safety or to protect the environment). Projects which do yield financial returns will need to make up for those that do not. Thus, in the example above, the discount rate may need to be somewhat higher than the weighted average cost of capital — perhaps 16.0% instead of 14.7%.

Some companies use different discount rates for different types of project, to allow for differences in risk. For example, cost saving projects may bear a lower discount rate than new product projects. (Conversely, one large company uses a lower discount rate for certain high-risk technical projects, as a safeguard against being left behind in the technology race.) How much to increase (or reduce) the average discount rate to allow for high (or low) risk projects is hard to judge.

No method of estimating the cost of equity capital is precisely accurate. Over the years, the stock market has yielded average returns on equities of about 7% a year more than on risk-free securities (gilts). Hence, we may regard 7% as the required risk premium to apply to capital investment in the average project.

Table 7.10 summarizes the results of a 1986 survey of 100 large UK firms (Pike *et al.*, 1988). It shows that by no means all companies use

Table 7.10 *Popular capital investment appraisal methods*

| | Total | | Frequency of use in 1986 in 100 large UK firms | | | |
| --- | --- | --- | --- | --- | --- | --- |
| | | | Always | Mostly | Often | Rarely |
| Payback | 92 | = | 47 | 24 | 16 | 5 |
| Internal rate of return | 75 | = | 42 | 13 | 11 | 9 |
| Net present value | 68 | = | 23 | 14 | 15 | 16 |
| Average accounting rate of return | 56 | = | 18 | 10 | 15 | 13 |

discounted cash flow methods at all; and those that do may also use one or both of the simple methods (see section 7.2).

Section 6.5 mentioned other ways to deal with risk. Another survey of 146 large UK companies found that about 40% often or very often used sensitivity analysis, 39% a subjective/intuitive assessment of risk, and 17% probability analysis. Methods of adjusting for risk (by the 133 companies that did so) most frequently included raising the required rate of return (42%), shortening the payback period (34%), and adjusting estimated cash flows subjectively/intuitively (63%) (Ho *et al.*, 1991).

## 7.5 Taxation

### 7.5.1 Writing-down allowances

Corporation tax is levied on **taxable profit** rather than on the profit reported in the accounts. In computing taxable profit, depreciation of fixed assets charged in arriving at accounting profit is disallowed. Instead, tax **writing-down allowances** are available for certain kinds of capital spending. On plant and equipment, for example, the allowance is 25% of cost in the year of purchase and 25% of the reducing balance in each subsequent year (see Table 7.11).

The writing-down allowance is not a cash flow but a tax-deductible **expense**. It reduces taxable profit, and hence results in lower subsequent corporation tax payments. Table 7.11 shows that the writing-down allowance (wda) falls as the years go by. For practical purposes, we can often ignore the corporation tax effects of the later project years.

Table 7.11 *Writing-down allowance for plant and machinery*

|  |  | *(£'000)* |
|---|---|---|
| Cost of equipment |  | £250.0 |
| Year 1[1] writing-down allowance | (25% of 250) | 62.5 |
| Tax written-down value | Year end 1 | 187.5 |
| Year 2 writing-down allowance | (25% of 187.5) | 46.9 |
| Tax written-down value | Year end 2 | 140.6 |
| Year 3 writing-down allowance | (25% of 140.6) | 35.1 |
| Tax written-down value | Year end 3 | 105.5 |
| Year 4 writing-down allowance | (etc.) | 26.4 |
| Tax written-down value | Year end 4 | 79.1 |
| Year 5 writing-down allowance |  | 19.8 |
| Tax written-down value | Year end 5 | 59.3 |
| Year 6 writing-down allowance |  | 14.8 |
| Tax written-down value | Year end 6 | 44.5 |

*Note:* [1]Year 1 is the accounting year in which the equipment was purchased.

There are special provisions for short-lived assets, such as computer hardware. If such assets are disposed of within five years, any surplus (deficit) of the proceeds compared with the tax written-down value will be subject to a balancing charge (allowance). After five years, the asset's tax written-down value is transferred into the main pool of plant and equipment for subsequent wdas. For industrial buildings, there is a wda of 4% per year of the cost of the new building (for 25 years). Offices, shops and wholesale warehouses do not qualify for any tax allowances (except in enterprise zones).

## 7.5.2 **Corporation tax**

The rate of corporation tax is 33% for taxable profits above £1.25 million. On taxable profits up to £250 000 the tax rate is 25%. (Between £250 000 and £1.25 million the marginal tax rate is 35%.)

We need to estimate a capital project's tax effect on the whole company. Table 7.12 shows a company's extra tax payments resulting from a project requiring £250 000 investment in plant and equipment, with extra revenue of £220 000 per year and allowable expenses of £120 000 per year (excluding book depreciation).

We assume the investment in plant and equipment occurs in the year before any incremental revenue arises. Where a project reduces taxable profits (as in year 0 in Table 7.11), the company's overall tax bill will fall. This results in a positive incremental tax cash flow (in year 1), assuming that the rest of the company has taxable profits against which to offset the loss arising from the project. Companies not currently paying tax can carry forward losses or writing-down allowances for future use.

The tax payments lag by a year. UK corporation tax is normally payable nine months after the accounting year end (or fifteen months after the average point of earning taxable profits); but as a rule we discount only at whole year intervals. Because corporation tax is paid in arrears, the profit in year 5 gives rise to a tax payment in year 6 (see Table 7.12).

Table 7.12 *Incremental corporation tax payments*

| | 0 | 1 | 2 | 3 (£'000) | 4 | 5 | 6 |
|---|---|---|---|---|---|---|---|
| | | | | *End of year* | | | |
| Sales revenue | — | +220.0 | +220.0 | +220.0 | +220.0 | +220.0 | — |
| Expenses (excl. depn.) | — | −120.0 | −120.0 | −120.0 | −120.0 | −120.0 | — |
| Writing-down allowance[1] | −62.5 | −46.9 | 35.1 | 26.4 | −19.8 | −14.8 | — |
| Taxable income | −62.5 | +53.1 | +64.9 | +73.6 | +80.2 | +85.2 | — |
| Corporation tax payable @ 33% | — | +20.6 | −17.5 | −21.4 | −24.3 | −26.5 | −28.1 |

*Note:* [1]wda ignored after year 5.

## 7.6 Capital disinvestment

Capital disinvestment means reducing the assets a business holds.

Possible limits to a project's economic life may stem from the following factors:

### 7.6.1 Why projects end

1 Physical exhaustion of equipment.
2 Technical obsolescence of equipment or process.
3 Market factors, such as changing consumer tastes.

Amounts recoverable at the end of a project's economic life may represent the following items:

1 Value of land or buildings.
2 Scrap or second-hand value of equipment.
3 Working capital, such as stocks and debtors.

These items will appear as positive cash flows at the end of a project, together with any tax-related cash flows.

Even where a firm expects to recover part (or all) of its investment at the end of a project, the time value of money is still relevant. Capital has an opportunity cost as long as it is invested in a project; so a firm must discount back to present value any amounts it expects to recover at the end of a project.

A project's life may change after it has started. Sometimes a firm may need to abandon a project early, if conditions or estimates have changed — perhaps even before it comes on stream. One can decide when to stop a project by comparing the remaining NPV of the (continuing) project, with the NPV of stopping the project and selling the assets. Another option for self-contained projects might be to sell them as a going concern to another company.

In appraising long projects, it is normal to use an arbitrary **horizon** period of 10, or perhaps 15, years. Firms do not consider cash flows beyond the horizon even if they expect the project to last longer. With a fairly high discount rate this makes little difference. (For example, with a 20% a year discount rate, extending the horizon from 15 to 30 years for a project with equal annual cash inflows would increase the total present value of all the cash inflows only by about 6½%! The discount factor would increase from 4.675 to 4.979.)

### 7.6.2 Working capital and its recovery

In addition to investment in fixed capital assets, many projects also involve investment in working capital, that is, in stocks and debtors. This is likely to be true of projects involving expansion or new products, but less likely for cost reduction projects.

Stocks in the form of raw materials, purchased parts, work-in-progress and finished goods need to be built up before any goods can be sold. (Purchases on credit terms may partly offset their cash flow impact.)

Table 7.13 *Project incremental cash flows*

|  | End of year | | | | | | |
|---|---|---|---|---|---|---|---|
|  | 0 | 1 | 2 | 3 (£'000) | 4 | 5 | 6 |
| *Capital* | | | | | | | |
| Capital expenditure | − 250.0 | | | | | −[1] | |
| Corporation tax | | + 20.6 | + 15.5 | + 11.6 | + 8.7 | + 6.5 | + 4.9 |
| Stocks | − 40.0 | | | | | + 40.0 | |
| Debtors | − 56.0 | | | | | + 56.0 | |
| Creditors | + 30.0 | | | | | − 30.0 | |
|  | − 316.0 | + 20.6 | + 15.5 | + 11.6 | + 8.7 | + 72.5 | + 4.9 |
| *Revenue* | | | | | | | |
| Sales revenue | | + 220.0 | + 220.0 | + 220.0 | + 220.0 | + 220.0 | |
| Expenses | | − 120.0 | − 120.0 | − 120.0 | − 120.0 | − 120.0 | |
| Corporation tax | | | − 33.0 | − 33.0 | − 33.0 | − 33.0 | − 33.0 |
|  | | + 100.0 | + 67.0 | + 67.0 | + 67.0 | + 67.0 | − 33.0 |
| Net cash flow | − 316.0 | + 120.6 | + 82.5 | + 78.6 | + 75.7 | + 139.5 | − 28.1 |

*Note:* [1]assuming no recovery of fixed capital at end.

Credit sales, of course, also imply an investment in debtors (accounts receivable). At the end of a project's life, stocks, debtors and creditors will fall to zero.

Table 7.13 shows the main types of incremental cash flows arising from a project involving an increase in sales revenue. The working capital part is inside the box. The table separates capital and **revenue** items, and splits the net tax cash flows between them. Note that the working capital items have no tax effects.

Check that you can see where the year 3 tax receipts of £11.6k and payments of £33.0k have come from. (Of course, this is equivalent to the net payment of £21.4k in Table 7.12.)

## 7.7 Inflation

### 7.7.1 What inflation means

So far we have ignored the effects of **inflation** on the cash flows of capital investment projects. But in many countries inflation is too high to overlook. In the United Kingdom, it averaged nearly 10% a year between 1970 and 1990; and the rate in 1990 was about 9%. Given that many projects last for ten years or more, such a rate of inflation implies that by the end of a project prices may be at least twice as high as at the start. For a twenty-year project started in 1970, the UK multiple would actually have been nearly *seven times*!

We need to distinguish between general inflation (an increase in the general average level of prices, as measured by the Retail Prices Index) and specific price changes of particular goods and services. For instance, in the mid-1980s house prices were rising at a much faster rate than the general rate of inflation; but, around 1990, they were static or falling slightly in money terms, and thus actually fell quite sharply in **real terms**.

The prices of different goods and services may well change at different rates, rather than all reflecting precisely the general rate of inflation. So one may often need to forecast specific price changes for component items in a capital project. Selling prices, material costs, wages — such prices may be critical for a project's success or failure. Only in very simple cases will it be good enough to assume that inflation will affect all items in the same way over a period of years.

Inflation is not just a technical detail affecting the numbers: it can have a profound impact on business projects. For example, if the United Kingdom has faster inflation than other countries for several years, then sooner or later the pound may have to devalue against other currencies. That can have significant effects on many projects (e.g. on export prices, cost of imported materials, etc.). Or high domestic inflation may lead in future, as it has in the not-so-distant past, to some form of price control. This, too, can have devastating effects on business profits, since it often amounts to compelling businesses to cut their prices in real terms.

### 7.7.2 **Tax**

Writing-down allowances (depreciation for tax purposes) are based on original cost: they are not adjusted for inflation. But of course, if sales revenue or expenses increase as a result of inflation, that will affect the amount of corporation tax payable.

Now examine Case study 7.3.

---

### Case study 7.3

*Problem*
To understand the effect of inflation on a project's net cash flows, look again at Table 7.12 (on page 137). Assume the cash flows for sales revenues and expenses need to be adjusted to allow for expected inflation of 10% a year (from year 0).

*Question*

Recalculate the amount of corporation tax cash flows, using the format shown in Table 7.12.

**Solution**

| | End of year | | | | | | |
|---|---|---|---|---|---|---|---|
| | 0 | 1 | 2 | 3 | 4 | 5 | 6 |
| | | | | (£'000s) | | | |
| Sales revenue | — | +242.0 | +266.2 | +292.8 | +322.1 | +354.3 | — |
| Expenses | — | −132.0 | −145.2 | −159.7 | −175.7 | −193.3 | — |
| Writing-down allowance | −62.5 | −46.9 | −35.1 | −26.4 | −19.8 | −14.8 | — |
| *Taxable income* | −62.5 | +63.1 | +85.9 | +106.7 | +126.6 | +146.2 | — |
| Corporation tax @ 33% | | +20.6 | −20.8 | −28.3 | −35.2 | −41.8 | −48.2 |

Notice again the one-year time-lag between the taxable income and the related tax payment. You may like to verify that after the first tax cash flow, a receipt of £20.6k in year 1, the other corporation tax amounts are higher than the earlier amounts shown in Table 7.12. The increases reflect 33% of the increases in the amounts of taxable income year by year, that is 33% of, respectively: £10.0k; £21.0k; £33.1k; £46.4k; and £61.0k. Thus, the amounts of tax have increased by: £3.3k; £6.9k; £10.9k; £15.3k; and £20.1k.

Because the writing-down allowances have not changed as a result of the 10% a year inflation — being based on original money cost — the amount of taxable income has not simply increased by 10% a year. The effect of inflation on taxable income is not so simple.

7.7.3 **Working capital**

Working capital investment is also subject to inflation. Stock levels which stay constant in physical terms will require an increasing level of financial investment. Likewise, if debtor days remain constant, the money investment in debtors will increase as selling prices increase. (Similarly, creditors will grow as supplier prices increase.) The incremental working capital cash flow will be the increase (or decrease) in working capital compared to the previous year.

**Example 7.8**

If a five-year project involves a £66 000 investment in working capital at the end of year 0, show the amount of investment in working capital, and the resulting incremental cash flow year by year, assuming an inflation rate of 10% a year.

|  | End of year | | | | | |
|---|---|---|---|---|---|---|
|  | 0 | 1 | 2 | 3 | 4 | 5 |
|  | | | (£'000s) | | | |
| Total working capital | 66.0 | 72.6 | 79.9 | 87.8 | 96.6 | 0[1] |
| Incremental cash flow | −66.0 | −6.6 | −7.3 | −7.9 | −8.8 | +96.6 |

[1] assumed all working capital recovered at the end of year 5.

The sum of all the incremental cash flows is 0, because we assume that we recover all the investment in working capital in full at the end of year 5. The essential point is that working capital held constant in real terms still involves incremental money cash flows each year. We must allow for these even if we set out the cash flows in real terms, not in money terms (see section 7.7.4).

## 7.7.4 How to cope with inflation

In principle, there are two ways to cope with inflation in discounted cash flow appraisal of capital investment projects. Perhaps the easiest to understand is to forecast all cash flows in money terms, allowing for specific price changes, and then to discount these future money amounts at a nominal (or money) discount rate (opportunity cost of capital) which includes an allowance for general inflation.

If the rate of inflation is expected to vary, it may become rather messy using a different discount rate for the net present value method from year to year over the life of the project; and, in fact, few companies seem to do so. (It is, of course, not feasible to vary the discount rate using the internal rate of return method.)

An alternative approach is to forecast specific money cash flows as above; then to discount twice — once to allow for the expected general inflation rate, and once using a real discount rate, to allow for the real opportunity cost of capital. The starting point for estimating such a real discount rate may be the yield on index-linked gilt-edged securities, which may be taken to represent the real risk-free rate of return. (Any item whose money price is expected to rise, but less fast than general inflation, will then (correctly) appear to have its price falling in real terms.)

The real discount rate should be lower than the money discount rate by the rate of inflation. For example, if the money discount rate is 18%, but 7% inflation is expected (which the 18% presumably includes), then the real discount rate to use would be only 11%. (Strictly speaking, it should be 1.18 − 1.07 = 1.1028 (i.e. 10.28%), not 1.18 − 1.07 = 1.11 (i.e. 11%); but it would be spurious accuracy to insist on this!)

In some ways, it may seem less trouble to forecast cash flows in real terms (in effect, in terms of 'year 0 pounds' throughout), and then just discount by the same real discount rate each year. But such an approach has three snags, as follows:

1 Only in the simplest cases is it adequate to assume that inflation is going to affect all items to the same extent.
2 The tax authorities base writing-down allowances on original money

Table 7.14 *Table 7.13 adjusted for 10% a year inflation*

| | 0 | 1 | 2 | End of year 3 (£'000) | 4 | 5 | 6 |
|---|---|---|---|---|---|---|---|
| *Capital* | | | | | | | |
| Capital expenditure | − 250.0 | | | | | | |
| Corporation tax | | + 20.6 | + 15.5 | + 11.6 | + 8.7 | + 6.5 | + 4.9 |
| Working capital | − 66.0 | − 6.6 | − 7.3 | − 7.9 | − 8.8 | + 96.6 | |
| | − 316.0 | + 14.0 | + 8.2 | + 3.7 | − 0.1 | + 103.1 | + 4.9 |
| *Revenue* | | | | | | | |
| Sales revenue | | + 242.0 | + 266.2 | + 292.8 | + 322.1 | + 354.3 | |
| Expenses | | − 132.0 | − 145.2 | − 159.7 | − 175.7 | − 193.3 | |
| Corporation tax | | | − 36.3 | − 39.9 | − 43.9 | − 48.3 | − 53.1 |
| | | + 110.0 | + 84.7 | + 93.2 | + 102.5 | + 112.7 | − 53.1 |
| Net cash flow | − 316.0 | + 124.0 | + 92.9 | + 96.9 | + 102.4 | + 215.8 | − 48.2 |
| Discount factor (10%) | 1.000 | 0.909 | 0.826 | 0.751 | 0.683 | 0.621 | 0.564 |
| Net cash flow in year 0 (£s) | − 316.0 | + 112.7 | + 76.8 | + 72.7 | + 69.9 | + 134.0 | − 27.2 |
| Original cash flows per Table 7.13 | 316.0 | + 120.6 | + 82.5 | + 78.6 | + 75.7 | + 139.5 | − 28.1 |
| *Difference* | — | − 7.9 | − 5.7 | − 5.9 | − 5.8 | − 5.5 | + 0.9 |
| consisting of: | | | | | | | |
| 1. Working capital | | − 6.0 | − 6.0 | − 6.0 | − 6.0 | − 6.0 | |
| 2. Writing-down allowances | | − 1.9 | − 2.7 | − 2.9 | − 2.8 | − 2.5 | − 2.1 |
| 3. Tax on profits | | | + 3.0 | + 3.0 | + 3.0 | + 3.0 | + 3.0 |

cost. So, in times of inflation, they will be falling in real terms; and real cash flows must reflect that fact (which seems to be easy to overlook — see section 7.7.2).

3 The cash-flow impact of inflation on working capital is rather complicated. In particular, even if working capital seems to be constant in real terms (e.g. number of days' stock, number of days' debtors), there will still be a need for some incremental cash-flow investment in money terms. This is not equivalent to a zero investment in real terms (see section 7.7.3)!

The last two of the above points are illustrated in Table 7.14, which repeats the items in Table 7.13, but assuming 10% a year inflation. There are three reasons why the numbers in Table 7.14, when discounted back into real terms, are not identical with the original numbers in Table 7.13, as follows:

1 The increase in working capital amounts (in year 0 £s) to £6.0k a year from years 1 to 5. This, of course, is a real increase.

2 The writing-down allowances gradually lose value in real terms, being based on original money cost. The higher the inflation rate, the larger the real loss.

3 Tax on profits, being lagged by one year, is reduced in real terms by £3.0k a year from years 2 to 6.

## 7.8 Life-cycle costing

Often we can identify an asset's **cost** as either its purchase price or the cost of making it. But many long-life assets will have much larger total costs over their whole life, including running costs and maintenance. Managers should base investment decisions on estimates of the amount and timing of all an asset's costs over its whole life, as well as technical performance and user satisfaction. This approach is known as **life-cycle costing** (or **terotechnology**, from the Greek *tereo*, to take care of).

Life-cycle costing may be especially useful in organizations which:

- operate in capital intensive industries;
- are thinking of buying or developing expensive new technology;
- have substantial replacement programmes; or
- are sensitive to down-time disruption.

The life cycle of a physical asset may comprise a number of stages: specify, design, manufacture/build, install and commission, operate, maintain/overhaul, close down/decommission, and dispose. All these stages need to be considered before the initial commitment to invest.

For example, in assessing huge projects such as nuclear power stations, it is not enough to consider only construction costs, or even construction costs plus running costs. For that would be to ignore the massive costs of decommissioning nuclear power stations and making them safe. Nuclear Electric provided over £10 000 million for just such items in its 1991 balance sheet! Going for the option which was apparently cheapest in the short term could work out very costly indeed in the long run.

### Example 7.9

Mayflower Hospital is about to replace its old boiler equipment, either by a coal-fired system or by an oil-fired system. Finance costs 15% a year, and other estimated costs are as follows:

|  | Coal (£'000) | Oil (£'000) |
|---|---|---|
| Initial cost of boiler | 70 | 100 |
| Annual operating costs | 60 pa | 45 pa |

If the hospital expected the new boiler system to last at least fifteen years, which system should be chosen?

On the basis of initial cost only, the hospital would choose coal. But coal's lifetime costs are much higher than oil's, as we can see when we include the discounted annual operating costs of each system:

|                                    | Coal (£'000) | Oil (£'000) |
|------------------------------------|-------------|-------------|
| Initial cost of boiler             | 70          | 100         |
| Annual operating costs[1]          | 351         | 263         |
| Total life-cycle costs             | 421         | 363         |

[1] = annual costs × 5.847 — see Appendix B

On this basis, oil is clearly much cheaper than coal. Unless there are other overriding considerations favouring coal, oil should be chosen.

If the decision seemed closer, it might be useful to try sensitivity analysis. How much would fuel costs need to change to alter the decision? What difference would it make if the life were much shorter (or much longer) than fifteen years? What if the discount rate were significantly different from 15% a year?

## 7.9 Chapter summary

Capital investment means spending money now to obtain larger, but uncertain, future benefits. Two main kinds of capital project are: replacing equipment, to reduce costs or improve quality; and increasing productive capacity, to expand output or to provide new products.

Accounting rate of return is the average annual profit expected, as a percentage of the amount invested; which ignores the timing of returns. Payback measures the time before a project's cash receipts equal the initial investment; but it fails to measure profit. Firms still often use these simple methods in conjunction with DCF approaches.

To compare money amounts over time, we use an interest rate which combines: pure time-preference, an inflation premium, and a risk premium. This represents the opportunity cost of capital: what else the money could earn if not invested in the project.

Net present value (NPV) results from applying a pre-selected discount rate to expected future cash flows; a positive NPV signals that a project is worthwhile. The internal rate of return (IRR) is that discount rate which produces a NPV of zero. A company's weighted average cost of capital (adjusted for risk) can help determine a suitable hurdle rate for capital projects.

To assess after-tax cash flows, one must allow for writing-down allowances (tax depreciation), and the time-lag in tax payments.

Capital projects may come to an end due to physical exhaustion, technical obsolescence, or market factors. Amounts may then be recovered in respect of: land or buildings, second-hand or scrap value of equipment, and working capital. Companies often use a horizon period of 10 years in appraising projects.

Not all goods will increase in price at the same rate as the Retail Prices Index (general inflation). So one must usually forecast specific price changes for sales, purchases, wages, etc. Money forecasts need to be discounted at an inflation-inclusive discount rate, real cash flows at a real (inflation-exclusive) discount rate. Two tricky items are: tax writing-down allowances, which are based by law on historical costs; and working capital, which may require extra real investment even when real sales volume remains constant.

Life-cycle costing (terotechnology) aims to minimize the present value cost of long-life investments. It is especially relevant where ongoing project costs are large compared with the initial purchase cost.

## 7.10 Review questions

1 What is (probably) the most important step in the capital investment process?
2 What is the purpose of post auditing projects?
3 How is the payback period of a project calculated?
4 What important factor does payback ignore?
5 What is the formula for calculating the average accounting rate of return?
6 In what respect is the average accounting rate of return method deficient?
7 Explain the term 'present value'.
8 What is net present value?
9 Distinguish between a discount rate and a discount factor.
10 Explain the term 'internal rate of return'.
11 What is a writing-down allowance?
12 What is meant by 'weighted average cost of capital'?
13 What type of discount rate should be used for discounting cash flows when:
    (a) inflation has been *excluded* in the forecast future cash flows;
    (b) inflation has been *included* in the forecast future cash flows.
14 What ways are there of allowing for uncertainty in project evaluation?
15 What is sensitivity analysis?

To maximize learning, please *write out* your answers on a separate sheet of paper. *Then* check with the answers in Appendix C, pp. 241–2.

## 7.11 Problems

1 A new toll road is expected to produce net cash receipts of £300m a year when it is completed. Assume that the road will be operational for 25 years. The road will take five years to complete; and the cash outflows are expected to be: £800m at the end of year 0, and £500m a year for years 1 to 5.

*Question*
What is the project's IRR?

2 Chiltern Council was reviewing two alternative schemes for the building and running of a new library. The choice was between a low-cost conventional building and a hi-tech building. Features of the latter included: optimum orientation of the building; less glazing; north-facing rooflight; photo-sensitive override controls for the lighting system; sealed environment — no opening windows; double glazing; cavity wall insulation.

Estimates of the building costs and running costs (in terms of present-day prices) for the estimated 50-year life are as follows:

| | Conventional (£'000s) | Hi-tech (£'000s) |
|---|---|---|
| Design, construction and installation | 1400 | 1600 |
| Annual running costs: | | |
| labour | 26 | 26 |
| energy | 10 | 5 |
| materials | 1 | 1 |
| depreciation | 28 | 32 |
| Maintenance costs: | | |
| labour | 16 | 12 |
| materials | 7 | 5 |
| Demolition and disposal costs | 10 | 10 |

*Question*

Calculate the present value cost of each scheme, using a 4% real discount rate. Which scheme is cheaper over the 50-year life?

**3** H. Stephenson Limited is considering an investment project which will require the investment of £500 000 in new fixed assets and £120 000 in additional stocks. The annual sales revenue from the project is forecast to be £800 000, and the annual running costs £600 000 (including depreciation of £100 000). The project's life is expected to be five years.

(a) Show the cash flows year by year.
(b) Show the profit forecast year by year.
(c) Should the project be accepted if the firm's minimum required IRR is 20%?

(Ignore inflation and taxation.)

**4** The cash flows for two projects are as follows:

| End of year | 0 | 1 | 2 | 3 | 4 |
|---|---|---|---|---|---|
| H cash flows (£'000s) | −1000 | +500 | +400 | +350 | +300 |
| J cash flows (£'000s) | −1000 | +400 | +400 | +400 | +400 |

*Questions*

(a) Which of these two projects has the higher net present value at a discounting rate of 15% a year? By how much?
(b) What is the payback period of each project?
(c) Graph the net present value of project J at discount rates of 12%, 18%, 24% and 30%. Estimate the IRR from the chart.

(Ignore inflation and taxation.)

**5** Project T requires an initial investment of £200 000 (which is non-returnable) and is expected to produce cash inflows of £70 000 a year for five years.

*Question*

Is it worth investing in the project if the opportunity cost of capital is 15% a year?

(Ignore inflation and taxation.)

**6** Project XL requires a cash investment of £360 000 in a new machine that is to be completely depreciated in equal instalments over its expected four-year life. The project's accounting profits are expected to amount to £40 000 a year in years 1 and 2, and to £70 000 a year in years 3 and 4.

*Questions*

(a) What is the average accounting rate of return?
(b) Draw up a schedule of the amount and timings of cash flows for Project XL.
(c) What is the payback period?
(d) If the discount rate is 20% a year, what is the net present value?
(e) What is Project XL's IRR?

(Ignore inflation and taxation.)

**7** Project Y is expected to produce accounting profits of £240 000 a year over its eight-year life. The initial investment in fixed capital equipment is £1 200 000, and the firm uses straight-line depreciation.

*Questions*

(a) What is the average accounting rate of return?
(b) Draw up a schedule showing the amount and timing of Project Y's cash flows.
(c) What is the payback period?
(d) Graph Project Y's net present value, using discount rates from 0 to 30% inclusive, at 10% intervals.
(e) From the graph, what is Project Y's IRR?
(f) Check your estimated IRR by calculation from the tables.

(Ignore inflation and taxation.)

**8** Globe Gears Limited is about to choose between three projects. Project A is for the purchase of a new machine; Project B is for a promotional campaign to boost sales; and Project C is for the rationalization of part of the production department. The cost and expected returns for each project are as follows:

| End of year | Project A (£) | Project B (£) | Project C (£) |
|---|---|---|---|
| Initial outlay: | | | |
| 0 | 100 000 | 100 000 | 100 000 |
| Cash inflows: | | | |
| 1 | 10 000 | 40 000 | 30 000 |
| 2 | 20 000 | 30 000 | 30 000 |
| 3 | 30 000 | 30 000 | 30 000 |
| 4 | 30 000 | 20 000 | 30 000 |
| 5 | 30 000 | – | 20 000 |
| 6 | 34 000 | – | 10 000 |
| Total: | 154 000 | 120 000 | 150 000 |

*Questions*

(a) Calculate for each project: (i) average accounting rate of return; (ii) payback period; and (iii) IRR.

(b) State, with reasons, the project you would rank as of greatest value to the firm on purely financial grounds.
(c) What other factors might you consider before making a final choice?

(Ignore inflation and taxation.)

**9** New Supa-calc requires investment in a factory of £2.0 million, in equipment of £1.5 million, and in working capital of £1.0 million. Assume that all cash outflows occur at the same time; and that, after eight years, working capital will be recovered in full, the equipment will be sold for £200 000, and the factory will then have a value of £500 000.

*Question*

What is the net present value of the capital investment cash flows, assuming a discount rate of 20%?

(Ignore inflation and taxation.)

**10** Sales volume of new Supa-calc is expected to be 100 000 units in year 1, 250 000 units in year 2, and 500 000 units a year for each of the next six years. The selling price per unit will be £6.00 for years 1 to 4 and £5.00 for years 5 to 8. Variable costs are expected to be: (i) production costs of £2.40 per unit in years 1 and 2, and £2.00 per unit in years 3 to 8; and (ii) selling costs equal to 5% of sales revenue, with advertising costs of £100 000 in year 1, £60 000 in year 2 and £40 000 per year thereafter.

*Questions*

(a) Set out a schedule of the amount and timing of the operating cash flows, assuming all receipts and payments are for cash (not on credit), and that all cash flows take place at the end of the year to which they relate.
(b) What is the net present value of the cash

flows, assuming a discount rate of 20% a year?

**11** Grampian Limited has just developed a new product, the bastick, and must now decide whether or not to produce and sell it. Development required three man-years of work by employees in the research department; on average, these employees earned £35 000 a year. Various special materials and components cost £500 000.

Manufacture of basticks would mean purchasing a special machine costing £3 500 000. Its residual value at the end of eight years would be £300 000 (at today's prices). The bastick's selling price would be £82 per unit, which would increase in line with inflation. Expected sales at that price are 50 000 units a year for eight years.

Production of the bastick would require: materials costing £26 per unit; 15 labour hours per unit at a wage rate of £2 per hour; and variable overhead costs would increase by £16 per unit. All these costs would increase in line with general inflation. Production of the bastick should not increase Grampian's total fixed costs (other than depreciation); but allocated fixed overheads will be £10 per unit.

Assume that sales and production costs occur on the last day of each year. Ignore taxation and calculate in real terms. Assume that for this kind of project, 6% a year is a suitable real discount rate.

*Questions*

(a) Should Grampian produce and sell basticks?
(b) Calculate the minimum annual sales volume at which making basticks would be just worthwhile, assuming that all the other original estimates hold good.
(c) Explain in general terms what sort of adjustments you would make were you

to take inflation into account. If the figures which did include inflation differed from the calculations in real terms, which would guide you? Why?

**12** The management of Hart and Young Limited (HAY) are thinking of investing £3.0m in new equipment in order to make and sell a new product. The investment would qualify for 25% tax writing-down allowances.

The new product would also use existing equipment with a net book value of £950 000. If HAY do *not* introduce the new product, they will sell this equipment for £800 000. Its tax written-down value is nil. At the end of the project, the acquired equipment will realize about £150 000. The existing equipment used on the project would then fetch about £10 000. Its net book value by then would be nil.

HAY expects sales revenue for the new product to be as follows:

| | |
|---|---|
| 1993 | £2.0m |
| 1994 | £2.6m |
| 1995 | £2.8m |
| 1996 | £3.0m |
| 1997 | £3.3m |
| 1998–2002 | £3.5m per year |

Variable expenses are expected to be about 40% of sales revenue.

The project would result in extra fixed costs of £500 000 per year (including £100 000 depreciation). In addition, the £1.5m already spent on product research will have to be recovered. A proportion of head office costs (i.e. 10% of £3.0m = £300 000 per year) will also be charged against the project, even though total head office costs should not change if the project goes ahead.

HAY currently have a working capital to sales ratio of 20%; the new product will require similar working capital levels.

The rate of corporation tax is 33%; but, because of accumulated losses and the level of capital investment over the next ten years, HAY is unlikely to pay mainstream corporation tax for the foreseeable future.

If the project goes ahead, HAY intends to raise £1.0m on a long-term basis at an interest rate of about 15% a year. The company requires a minimum internal rate of return of 20% a year.

*Question*
Calculate the project's net present value, and recommend whether or not the project should go ahead.

**13** The management of Cavana Limited are thinking about a proposal to make and sell a new product by installing in existing premises new plant costing £100 000. The space has no other obvious use in the foreseeable future. Being in a special development area, Cavana expects to receive a tax-free cash grant of 22% of the new plant's cost about one year after the investment.

A 25% writing-down allowance applies to the cost of new plant for tax purposes. (Ignore writing-down allowances after the fifth operating year.) The company pays corporation tax on profits (at a current rate of 33%) about one year after its accounting year end, and expects to be paying tax for the foreseeable future.

The initial investment in working capital comprises £80 000 of stocks and £40 000 debtors. As a result of this proposal, creditors will increase by about £30 000. Investments in working capital do not attract tax allowances.

The project will last for about five years, after which time the plant will be worth about £10 000 (at today's prices) and Cavana will recover the working capital investment in full.

Cavana expects sales revenue of £200 000 for each of the next five years and operating

costs (including £20 000 per year depreciation) of £170 000 per year. However, inflation will affect sales prices (but not volumes) and out-of-pocket costs. The annual rate of inflation is expected to be about 8%; it will also affect working capital requirements and the plant's resale value.

*Question*
Should Cavana accept the proposal, if the company requires a minimum after-tax nominal rate of return of 20% a year:

(a) Ignoring inflation?
(b) Taking inflation into account?

Identify any significant assumptions you make.

**14** Ancastle Ltd, a small food company, is considering whether to introduce a new beverage called GULP. For appraisal purposes, the life of the GULP project is to be taken as 10 years (though the company hopes it will, if introduced, last much longer).

Ancastle is subject to corporation tax at 25% on profits, and requires 20% a year after tax as the minimum acceptable rate of return on new product proposals.

All the figures set out below relate to the GULP project. They represent the best estimates that Ancastle's managers can make; but obviously they are all subject to a margin of error.

Fixed capital assets:

|  | Buildings (£'000s) | Plant and equipment (£'000s) |
|---|---|---|
| Cost (all payable at start) | 800 | 1200 |
| Residual value | 480 | 120 |
| Book depreciation on cost (straight line) | 2½% | 10% |
| Tax capital allowances | 4% on cost | 25% on WDV[1] |

[1]Written-down value (= declining balance).

Operating cash flows:

Sales revenue (£'000s): Year 1 — 600; Year 2 1200; Year 3 — 2000; Year 4 (and later years) — 3000.

Cost of goods sold (including book depreciation): 60% of sales revenue. In addition, special promotion expenses of £200 000 a year for years 1 to 5, and £100 000 a year thereafter.

Working capital:

20% of sales revenue (assumed payable at the end of the year to which it relates). All recoverable at the end of the project.

*Questions*

(a) Prepare a statement showing the amount and timing of the cash flows expected to result from the GULP project.

(b) Calculate the net present value of the GULP project, and recommend whether the company should go ahead with it.

(The solutions to Problems 3–14 will be provided in the *Instructors' Manual*.)

CHAPTER **8**  *Budgets*

8.1 **Budgetary control**

**Budgets** are business plans expressed in money and covering a period of time, agreed in advance for all or part of a firm. Many firms prepare budgets for balance sheet items (e.g. fixed assets, debtors, stocks), as well as for profit and loss account items (e.g. sales, expenses). Budgets are not neutral forecasts of future events: managers accept a personal commitment to help make them happen. Nor are they merely ideal targets: budgets must be capable of achievement.

The following sections discuss how budgets:

- set objectives;
- co-ordinate activities;
- motivate managers;
- transmit information;
- assess performance;
- help effective action.

8.1.1 **Achieving objectives through budgets**

An organization's aims (as discussed in Chapter 1) will influence top management's approach to budgets. The various parts of a business will express objectives in terms of sales revenue, profits, and so on.

Many budget techniques are also useful in organizations which may not be aiming for profit (e.g. schools, churches, armed services, etc.). Entities which do not sell goods or services on the market may choose to budget their output in physical rather than money terms, looking at both quantity and quality. (Physical quantities as well as money may also be useful in budgeting inputs.)

Judging a business's performance entirely on the basis of current profits is unwise, since many decisions have longer-term effects. For example, a manager might improve current profits by spending less on research; but it could be disastrous in the long run. Using more than one yardstick to measure business success is more sensible than judging managers or business units by any single accounting number, however cleverly devised. In practice, managers are normally judged on their track record over a period of years.

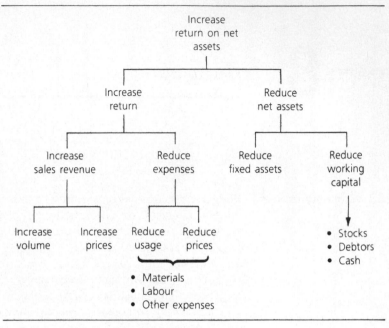

Figure 8.1 *Financial split of operating objectives*

Perhaps the single most important financial measure of operating performance is return on net assets. To summarize what a financial budget covers, Figure 8.1 sets out the main headings that a business must consider when trying to improve its performance. It is important for top managers to keep their long-term objectives in mind. Otherwise they may persist with certain short-term goals — originally chosen as steps on the way towards the ultimate objectives — even after conditions have changed.

8.1.2 **The budget cycle**

Developing the master budget involves the following steps:

1 State basic assumptions and company objectives.
2 Forecast general economic and industry conditions.
3 Develop detailed sales budgets, suitably split (e.g. between areas, market sectors, products, customers, etc.).
4 Prepare production budgets, including materials, labour and overheads, analysed between different products, locations, etc.
5 Prepare budgets for administration and other expenses.
6 Prepare capital spending budgets.
7 Prepare cash budgets.
8 Combine all the above into the master budget: the overall budgets for

profit and loss account, balance sheet and cash flow (receipts and payments).

Many companies require all subordinate units to adopt certain central assumptions for a budget period, such as the rate of population growth, the rate of general inflation, and so on. It is a matter of judgement which assumptions to make centrally and use throughout a firm, and which to leave to each department to make for itself.

Most businesses prepare budgets annually, but normally split the one-year budget into much shorter periods, such as months or 4-week periods. Many activities do not occur evenly throughout the year, so a monthly budget amount need not be exactly one-twelfth of the equivalent item in the annual budget.

For some businesses, the annual budget represents only the first year of a longer planning period. The one-year budget will often contain more refinement of detail than three-year or five-year plans. And managers may feel a stronger commitment to the one year budget.

It is also possible to prepare **rolling budgets**, which add a month or quarter at the end while dropping off the month or quarter just finished. This means that detailed budgets always stretch twelve months into the future; whereas with 'fixed' annual budgets there can come a time when they cover only a month or two ahead. The question is whether the benefit from rolling budgets outweighs the extra costs of preparing them.

## 8.2 **The budget process**

### 8.2.1 **Construction of budgets**

The starting point for a business budget is usually to estimate the achievable sales revenue for the period. Salesmen can try to assess the quantity and type of products or services which both existing and new customers are likely to purchase. The marketing department may make a separate estimate of sales, based on general industry conditions. After discussion, an agreed sales budget will detail quantities, types of products, prices, and perhaps customers. The annual budget is normally divided into monthly budgets, often not equal in size. If the business is seasonal or is changing rapidly, setting realistic monthly budgets will need great care.

Once a budget for sales volume has been set, it is then possible to establish a budget for production. People, materials and equipment need to be provided in the right amounts and types, and at the right times, to deliver the level of output required to achieve the sales.

Figure 8.2 outlines the early stages in building up a budget for a manufacturing company. Establishing the sales revenue budget first lets other business functions budget to achieve that sales volume. Functions such as R & D, training and advertising would require separate budgets.

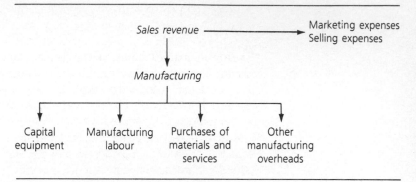

Figure 8.2 *Construction of a manufacturing organization budget*

Any other objectives (e.g. changing levels of stocks held, new sources of finance, etc.) can also be allowed for.

The resulting budgets for the profit and loss account and balance sheet constitute the first draft of the master budget, the overall plan which the company as a whole will work towards achieving.

8.2.2 **Co-ordination**

Budgets help co-ordinate business operations: for example, between production and sales, by revealing end-of-period stocks in budgeted balance sheets. They also force managers to plan ahead, and may often reveal needs for action which might otherwise have been overlooked, at least for some time (e.g. storage requirements, financing needs, etc.). Since lead times can often be extensive, firms should plan far enough ahead to give adequate warning of such needs in good time.

The budget procedure nearly always contains elements of feedback; and if the original budgets reveal problems in specific areas, that may trigger suitable changes. It may also be possible to adjust the timing of certain events to avoid bunching, especially in relation to **critical resources**, which may be money, manpower, raw materials or physical facilities.

Capital budgets should fit in with operating budgets. Thus, if managers justify capital investment on the basis of the operating savings it will produce, then subsequent budgets should include such savings.

The first draft of a master budget often fails to satisfy everyone. There may be doubts about achieving sales or production levels, or the budgeted level of profit may not satisfy top management. Some of the budgeting process may need repeating, possibly more than once, in order to achieve a master budget that all parties can accept. Given the likelihood of feedback, it is essential to leave enough time for the process of agreeing the budget.

### 8.2.3 **Motivating managers**

Most students work with more purpose if they know they are going to be tested. Likewise, business managers tend to work more effectively if they know that their performance (and that of their business unit) is to be compared with an agreed budget. Managers may feel more personal commitment where they have themselves helped to prepare the budget. (Their detailed knowledge may anyway make that a good idea.)

At the two extremes, budgets could be dictated from above (top-down), or simply emerge from below (bottom-up). In practice, different levels of management often agree budgets by a process of negotiation. The final budget will often lie between what top management would really like, and what junior managers reckon is feasible. (But ambitious junior managers might sometimes even budget for better results than top management demands. In the same way, students can be more severe than teachers when marking themselves.)

Ultimately, however, it is for top managers to judge whether a proposed budget represents adequate performance. A budget that is either too easy or too hard to achieve will usually provide less effective motivation than a budget which is difficult but achievable. A more satisfactory outcome is likely where there exists a high degree of trust between different levels of management; and experience in both setting and achieving budgets.

Top management may expect junior managers not quite to achieve their (stretching) budget **targets**. Hence, it may not be wise to plan on the basis that budgets will be achieved. Optimum performance may occur when managers agree budgets at a level somewhat above the most likely outcome. This implies that unfavourable variances may often occur — and that (in moderation) they may not be a 'bad thing'.

### 8.2.4 **Zero-base budgeting**

In many firms, preparing next year's budget is a routine task to be done without disrupting normal business. As a result, it is easy to overlook gradual changes taking place which may affect the cost structure or other basic aspects of the business. In contrast, **zero-base budgets** challenge the amounts — indeed, the very existence — of *all* items. For each activity, the business needs to identify the following:

1 Its purpose.
2 The expected outcome for different levels of expenditure.
3 Possible alternative courses of action.

Table 8.1 summarizes the main differences between normal and zero-base budgeting.

Because zero-base budgeting absorbs so much time and effort, few organizations would have enough managers to be able to review the entire business each year. (Nor would the benefits be likely to justify

Table 8.1 *'Normal' budgeting versus zero-base budgeting*

|  | Normal budgeting | Zero-base budgeting |
| --- | --- | --- |
| Frequency | Annual | Every 3–5 years |
| Time and effort | Often significant | Very substantial |
| Starting point | Last year's budget/actual | Zero |
| Basis for budget | Last year +/−% | Separate decision packages |
| Amount | Single sum | Range of cost/benefit options |
| Involves | Manager and boss | Cross-functional team |
| Needs awareness of | Function | Whole business |
| Priorities | Not stated | Ranks 'musts' and 'wants' |
| Alternatives | Only implicit | Explicit review |

it.) A three- to five-year cycle is probably more suitable, perhaps on a rolling basis, reviewing only part of the enterprise each year.

Ordinary budgeting probably often starts with last year's actual, and then adjusts a bit at the margin. Zero-base budgeting is much more radical: it questions the cost/benefit rationale for *everything*. This process requires a team which knows about the enterprise as a whole; though where necessary it may be possible to delegate some of the work to people with a better detailed knowledge of particular areas.

Managers rank activities in order of importance: 'musts' first, then mere 'wants'. This makes it easier to decide whether to approve a particular programme, and how much to spend on it. The process also involves looking at other ways to achieve the same end result, as well as weighing up the cost/benefit implications of different quality levels.

Zero-base budgeting is most effective for discretionary expense centres. It is less likely to be worthwhile in businesses where legal and operational constraints control costs — though in any case it may be extremely healthy to challenge assumptions from time to time. Members of the team — whose job is to make recommendations, not decisions — should not accept too easily everything they are told. Resource-users are often quite skilled at defending their empires.

Many local authorities are now looking closely at their options, on a zero-base approach. As a result, some have decided to subcontract certain services (such as refuse collection) to outside firms. This would have been unheard of not many years ago. It illustrates the zero-base approach — that there are no 'sacred cows'.

For example, Leslie Chapman, a regional director in the Ministry of Works, analysed savings achieved (amounting to about one-third of the total budget) as follows: '15 per cent by cutting out work altogether, and 85 per cent ... by economies whose results were still acceptable to those directly affected ... sub-divided in four ways. 15 per cent was saved

Table 8.2 *Decision packages for a business school*

---

*Long courses*
1.  Full-time MBA
2.  Full-time PhD
3.  Part-time MBA
4.  Part-time PhD

*Short courses*
5.  General management
6.  Subject-specific
7.  Company-specific

*Research activities*
8.  Contract research
9.  Faculty research
10.  Student research

*Administrative activities*
11.  General administration
12.  Computer facilities and services
13.  Library facilities and services
14.  Building maintenance
15.  Equipment provision and maintenance
16.  Marketing and public relations

---

by using different methods; and 15 per cent by using different standards; 10 per cent was saved by accepting a different speed of response and service; and 60 per cent was saved by a different use of Directly Employed Labour' (Chapman, 1979). His very impressive book gives many examples of improvement, based essentially on the zero-base budget approach.

The essence of zero-base budgeting is dividing a business into specific decision packages (activities) that together comprise the whole enterprise. The intention is not necessarily to reduce costs, but to look at value for money from each programme. Sometimes it may pay to increase expenditures.

Table 8.2 shows a possible split of programmes for a postgraduate business school. One of the obvious problems is that it is difficult in practice to separate parts of the activity — for example, the library facilities are related to research.

## 8.3 Preparing budgets

To illustrate how a business can develop its annual budget, let us consider Green's Garden Sheds Ltd, whose accounting year runs from 1 October to 30 September.

### 8.3.1 Sales

The company makes three types of garden shed: Goliath, General and Gnome. Based on previous sales volumes and prices, the sales manager reckons that sales for the year ending 30 September 1993 will be as follows:

| Shed type | Sales volume (units) | Price (£/unit) | Sales revenue (£) |
|---|---|---|---|
| Goliath | 190 | 480 | 91 200 |
| General | 320 | 300 | 96 000 |
| Gnome | 600 | 190 | 114 000 |
| | | | 301 200 |

### 8.3.2 Manufacturing

1 *Materials* Material costs per unit are estimated as follows:

| | Cost per shed | | |
|---|---|---|---|
| | Goliath (£) | General (£) | Gnome (£) |
| Wood: frame | 80 | 50 | 32 |
| door | 30 | 22 | 18 |
| Roofing | 40 | 30 | 26 |
| Glass | 10 | 8 | 6 |
| Handles, hinges, etc. | 12 | 10 | 10 |
| Total | 172 | 120 | 92 |

2 *Production labour* Estimated to total £48 096, as follows:
2 employees full-time at £240 per week each, plus 35% fringe costs (i.e. national insurance, pension costs, etc.) = 2 × £240 × 52 × 1.35 = £33 696.
4 temporary employees at £200 per week plus 20% fringe costs for 15 weeks = 4 × £200 × 15 × 1.20 = £14 400.

3 *Production overheads* Estimated at £34 000, as follows:

| | | |
|---|---|---|
| Equipment depreciation | = | £16 400 |
| Rent and rates | = | £13 000 |
| Utilities | = | £4 600 |

4 *Purchases* In addition to purchasing enough materials to meet sales requirements, it has been decided to increase the year-end stocks of materials by ten units of each shed type. (Finished sheds and work-in-progress amounts to remain at the same level as in the previous year.) Therefore, purchases will cost £130 120, as follows:

| | | |
|---|---|---|
| Goliath | (190 + 10) × £172 | = £34 400 |
| General | (320 + 10) × £120 | = £39 600 |
| Gnome | (600 + 10) × £92 | = £56 120 |

5 *Capital equipment* Machinery, equipment and tools costing £17 900 are to be bought in the year.

8.3.3 **Administration expenses**

These are estimated as follows, including finance charges:

| | |
|---|---|
| Sales manager £21 000 + 45% fringe costs | = £30 450 |
| Lease cost of company car | = £ 3 300 |
| Advertising costs | = £ 6 000 |
| Book-keeper £9000 + 35% fringe costs | = £12 150 |
| Auditing charges | = £ 1 600 |
| Interest payable on loan | = £ 6 500 |
| | £60 000 |

8.3.4 **Profit**

To determine the budgeted profit for the year ending 30 September 1993, Table 8.3 brings together the budgets for sales, manufacturing and administration. Tax is estimated at £10 500; and allowance is made for a net dividend of £15 000 to be paid during the year.

The profit before tax represents just over 10% of sales revenue. If Mr Green is unhappy with this budget, then he must find ways of increasing sales revenue (volumes and/or prices) and/or reducing expenses. Before management can accept the profit budget, it is also necessary to produce a budgeted balance sheet and a cash budget.

8.3.5 **Balance sheet**

Table 8.4 shows Green's balance sheet at 30 September 1992.
Now examine Case study 8.1.

Table 8.3 *Budgeted profit and loss account for Green's Garden Sheds Ltd for 1992/93*

| | | | (£) |
|---|---|---|---|
| Sales revenue | | | 301 200 |
| Cost of sales: | | | |
| Materials £172 × 190 | = | 32 680 | |
| £120 × 320 | = | 38 400 | |
| £ 92 × 600 | = | 55 200 | |
| | | 126 280 | |
| Production labour | | 48 096 | |
| Production overheads | | 34 000 | 208 376 |
| Gross profit | | | 92 824 |
| Administration and finance expense | | | 60 000 |
| Profit before tax | | | 32 824 |
| Taxation | | | 10 500 |
| Profit after tax | | | 22 324 |
| Dividend payable | | | 15 000 |
| Retained profit for the year | | | 7 324 |

Table 8.4 *Balance sheet for Green's Garden Sheds Ltd as at 30 September 1992*

|  | (£) | (£) |
|---|---|---|
| Fixed assets: | | |
| Machinery, equipment, tools, net | | 90 400 |
| Current assets: | | |
| Stock | 52 300 | |
| Debtors | 42 840 | |
| Cash | 7 580 | |
| | 102 720 | |
| Less: Current liabilities | | |
| Creditors | 32 320 | |
| Taxation | 10 000 | |
| Net working capital | | 60 400 |
| Total assets less current liabilities | | 150 800 |
| Less: Long-term liabilities | | |
| Long-term loans | 45 000 | |
| Warranty provisions | 20 000 | 65 000 |
| | | 85 800 |
| Share capital and reserves: | | |
| Called up ordinary share capital | | 60 000 |
| Accumulated retained profits | | 25 800 |
| | | 85 800 |

## Case study 8.1

### Problem

During the year to 30 September 1993, the following were
budgeted:

(i) Materials stock level to be increased by ten units of each
type of shed: 10 × (£172 + £120 + £92) = by 10 × £384 =
by £3840.
(ii) Debtors' level: 2 months (based on sales).
(iii) Creditors' level: 3 months (based on cost of purchases
£130 120, plus capital spending £17 900).
(iv) £5000 of the long-term loan would be repaid. Warranty
provisions would remain at £20 000.

### Question

On the basis of the information above, prepare (a) the budgeted
balance sheet at 30 September 1993, and (b) the cash budget,
showing all receipts and payments, for the year ending

30 September 1993, and ending with the correct cash balance as shown in the balance sheet.

*Solution*

(a) Green's balance sheet at 30 September 1993 (budgeted):

|  | (£) | (£) |
|---|---|---|
| Fixed assets ([£90 400 + £17 900] − £16 400) |  | 91 900 |
| Current assets: |  |  |
|   Stock (£52 300 + £3840) | 56 140 |  |
|   Debtors (2/12 × £301 200) | 50 200 |  |
|   Cash (see separate statement) | 2 389 |  |
|  | 108 729 |  |
| Less: Current liabilities: |  |  |
|   Creditors (3/12 × [£130 120 + £17 900]) | 37 005 |  |
|   Taxation | 10 500 |  |
| Net working capital |  | 61 224 |
| Total assets less current liabilities |  | 153 124 |
| Less: Long-term liabilities: |  |  |
|   Long-term loans (£45 000 − £5000) | 40 000 |  |
|   Warranty provisions | 20 000 | 60 000 |
|  |  | 93 124 |
|  |  |  |
| Share capital and reserves: |  |  |
|   Called up share capital |  | 60 000 |
|   Accumulated retained profits |  |  |
|   (£25 800 + £7324) |  | 33 124 |
|  |  | 93 124 |

(b) Green's cash budget for the year ending 30 September 1993:

| | |
|---|---|
| Receipts: | |
|   Owed by debtors at 30.9.92 | 42 840 |
|   + Sales for year ending 30.9.93 | 301 200 |
| | 344 040 |
|   − Debtors outstanding at 30.9.93 | 50 200 |
|   = Cash received from sales during year | 293 840 |
| Payments: | |
|   (i) Owed to creditors at 30.9.92 | 32 320 |
|   + Purchases for year (£130 120 + £17 900) | 148 020 |
| | 180 340 |
|   − Creditors outstanding at 30.9.93 | 37 005 |
|   = Paid out in respect of purchases during year | 143 335 |

|  | |
|---|---:|
| (ii) Production labour | 48 096 |
| (iii) Production overheads (£34 000 − £16 400) | 17 600 |
| (iv) Administration expenses | 60 000 |
| (v) Taxation paid in year (assumed) | 10 000 |
| (vi) Dividend paid in year | 15 000 |
| (vii) Long-term loan repaid in year | 5 000 |
| = Total payments during year | 299 031 |
| | |
| Cash balance at 30 September 1992 | 7 580 |
| Add cash receipts during year | 293 840 |
| Less cash payments during year | (299 031) |
| = Cash balance at 30 September 1993 | 2 389 |

Cash budgets need to be produced at least monthly to ensure that the business does not run out of cash during the year, and to provide a running standard against which to judge the actual cash position. If the cash balance is expected to go negative (or to fall too low), then the business will need to find other sources of cash, or otherwise modify the budget.

All three financial parts of the master budget (profit and loss account, balance sheet, and cash) should be divided up for control purposes into a number of budget periods (e.g. 12 one-month periods, or 13 four-week periods).

## 8.4 Using budgets

### 8.4.1 Time-lags

The pay-off from spending time and effort on budgeting comes not only from requiring managers to plan in adequate detail, but also from measuring actual performance against plan. For effective use of budgets, it is essential to report actual results as soon as possible after the budget period has ended. Delay in reporting actual results can delay the taking of corrective action. Also, long delays can reduce management motivation.

It is pointless producing and sending weekly reports if action is taken only once a month. On the other hand, timing may be important: small businesses, for example, may gain by being able to react quickly to changing events.

Many firms report 'flash' figures to management within a few days of the budget period just ended. These are rough numbers relating to the most essential aspects of business performance (e.g. sales revenue, sales volumes, production (or service) output, cash flows). The nature of the business will, to some extent, determine which flash figures are most suitable. The main report of actuals against budget should follow quickly, in no more than a week or two. Most business people much prefer rough figures soon to precise figures later.

## 8.4.2 **Appraising performance**

When appraising performance one needs a standard against which to judge actual results. If the budget is properly agreed, there should be no need to clutter up reports with last year's actual figures. The budget should take them into account, together with expected changes, in setting the current year's standard.

If conditions change, the budget figures may not represent a good estimate of the current year's results, nor any longer act as a meaningful commitment. Monthly reports may then include a latest estimate for the current year. This can help to show whether a variance in one month is merely a timing difference that will reverse itself next month, or the start of a trend resulting in large cumulative variances by the year end. Clearly, these could imply different management actions.

Flexible budgeting can allow for changes in business conditions: they often provide a useful standard for variable expenses when actual sales volume differs from budget (see section 9.3.1).

Major changes in business conditions during a year may make it desirable to revise budgets, despite the time and effort involved. Otherwise, managers may become demoralized if actual results are compared with budgets which have now become unattainable, or else complacent if budgets are now too easily achieved.

## 8.4.3 **Management action**

Budgets should help people manage better: they are not rigid targets which must be exactly achieved at all costs. If conditions have changed, deviation from budget may not be bad — nor exactly attaining budget good. Managers may not be able to control every item in their budgets, at least in the short run, but they are expected to react to changed conditions.

Budgetary control with monthly reporting may help managers to answer the following kinds of questions:

- What has performance been like recently? How does it differ from budget? Why?
- How, if at all, will these events cause latest estimates of current year results to differ from budget *if we take no action*?
- What, if anything, can be done to counter unfavourable variances from budgets, *or to increase favourable ones*? (Successful managers cash in on good luck!)
- How soon will such action be effective? How much difference will it make?
- After all proposed actions, what is now the latest estimate of current year's results?
- What about consequential effects on years beyond the current year?

## 8.4.4 **What can go wrong?**

If top management impose budgets, lower managers may feel little commitment to them. Budgets which are too hard to achieve switch managers off, even if arm-twisting obtains nominal agreement. But budgets which are too easy have little motive force. The most motivating budgets ('difficult but achievable') may often, in fact, not be fully achieved. Hence, small unfavourable variances may be a good sign, and making too much fuss about them could be a mistake. Too many budget reports use technical accounting jargon: it is much better to use terms, and physical measures, which the managers themselves understand.

If top managers make it clear they want subordinates to achieve budgets at all costs, there may be some undesirable consequences, such as the following:

1 All sorts of 'game-playing', to leave enough slack to give a better chance of achieving budgets.
2 A reluctance to 'over-perform' this year, however good the conditions, for fear of a much tougher budget target next year.
3 A feeling of resentment if people are held accountable for things largely outside their control, such as expense variances stemming from changes in output, in the absence of a flexible budget (see section 9.3.1).
4 'Short-termism'; for example, reducing discretionary expenditures too much for long-term health in order to improve the current year's bottom line.
5 Focusing only on financial numbers, even though intangibles, such as staff morale, matter too.

In highly uncertain conditions it may not be worth spending too much time on preparing budgets, since managers' commitment cannot be all that strong. When conditions change it may be tempting to revise the budgets. But this is very time-consuming, and ultimately amounts to adjusting the budget until it coincides with actual performance! If budgets are taken too lightly, however, **variances** may stem as much from sloppy budgeting as from poor actual performance.

There should be regular follow-up of actual-versus-budget reports, to seek reasons for variances and details of corrective action being taken. Otherwise, managers may come to regard budget preparation as merely an annual ritual which they can forget as soon as completed. There should also be a forecast of the latest results expected for the current year, otherwise people may over-react to temporary 'blips'. Without some kind of rolling budget, a business may be planning only a few months ahead, until next year's budget is agreed. Also, it may not be clear how the current year's budget fits into longer-term plans.

Some firms concentrate on profit and loss account budgets and tend to overlook the need for balance sheet budgets too. Such an approach risks ignoring the high cost of over-investment in assets such as stocks, debtors, or fixed assets.

## 8.5 Chapter summary

All but the smallest companies use budgets as a means of achieving the firm's objectives. They focus managers' attention on preparing, co-ordinating, and gaining commitment to, annual plans.

Many companies prepare an annual master budget for the profit and loss account, end-of-year balance sheet, and cash flows; and often split them into a number of shorter periods for control purposes. Different levels of management often negotiate targets which all accept as difficult but achievable. Zero-base budgeting provides a less frequent but more rigorous challenge to the cost/benefit rationale for all activities and their level of spend.

Sales volume is normally the foundation of the budget process. It provides the basis for operating expenses such as materials purchases and direct labour costs; for purchases of capital equipment; and affects working capital items such as stocks and debtors.

Prompt reporting of actual performance against budget can help management act quickly, either to mitigate adverse performance or to 'cash in' on good luck. Flexible budgets which allow for changes in sales volume can provide a useful standard for variable expenses. Only major unforeseen changes in business conditions are likely to make it worth the time and effort to revise the budget completely during the year.

## 8.6 Review questions

1 What are budgets?
2 How does a budget differ from a neutral forecast?
3 What benefits derive from budgetary control?
4 What steps are involved in developing a master budget?
5 What is a rolling budget?
6 Why may it be necessary to produce a number of draft budgets before establishing the master budget?
7 Why is there often an element of 'negotiation' in agreeing a budget commitment?
8 How does 'zero-base budgeting' compare with 'normal' annual budgeting?
9 Which is most important to business managers: eventual provision of precise actual results reported against budget, or prompt provision of approximate figures reported against budget? Why?
10 What are 'flash figures'?
11 What is flexible budgeting?
12 Can there be good reasons for failing to achieve an agreed budget? Give examples.
13 Why may top management *expect* subordinate managers to fail to achieve an agreed budget?
14 Why are there dangers in judging a business unit's performance entirely on the basis of current year's profits?
15 Why may it be unsatisfactory to judge a manager's performance on the basis of the financial results of his business unit?

To maximize learning, please *write out* your answers on a separate sheet of paper. *Then* check with the answers in Appendix C, pp. 243–4.

## 8.7 **Problems**

**1** The Wardown Car Wash provides an automatic washing service for cars and small vans. In addition to the basic wash at £1.50 per vehicle, a 'wash 'n' wax' option is available for £2.50. The washing equipment, which cost £60 000 installed, has been in use now for one year. It is estimated to have a useful life of five years or more.

Rent and rates for the forthcoming year amount to £2250 and will be paid half in April and half in October. In addition, annual operating costs (all paid in cash) are estimated as follows:

- washing solution          20p per vehicle
- wax (used only on
  wash 'n' wax)             45p per vehicle
- maintenance and repair    £50 per month.

During the forthcoming year, customer usage is expected to be as follows:

Vehicles per month

|           | Basic wash only | Wash 'n' wax |
|-----------|-----------------|--------------|
| April     | 1000            | 150          |
| May–Sept  | 1300            | 230          |
| Oct       | 1200            | 220          |
| Nov       | 1050            | 210          |
| Dec       | 900             | 205          |
| Jan       | 850             | 200          |
| Feb       | 500             | 80           |
| March     | 700             | 130          |

*Questions*

(a) Construct a profit and loss budget for the forthcoming year.
(b) How much is the budgeted profit for February? How much is it for May?
(c) Construct a monthly cash budget. In which month is the cash flow greatest? Which month is the worst for cash flow?

(See solution in Appendix C, pp. 244–5.)

**2** The Gherkin Delight Company buys and then bottles (pickled) gherkins. A standard costing system is used, labour cost being the basis for absorbing production overheads.

The following data is to be used in establishing the 1993 budget:

| Production data: | |
|---|---|
| Production volume | 1 200 000 bottles |
| Variable production overhead | £540 000 |
| Fixed production overhead (excluding depreciation) | £720 000 |
| Standard material cost | £0.27 per bottle |
| Standard labour cost | £0.50 per bottle |
| Selling and administrative data: | |
| Sales volume | 1 200 000 bottles |
| Fixed administrative and selling expenses | £150 000 |
| Variable administrative and selling expenses | £0.32 per bottle |
| Investment data: | |
| Plant and equipment depreciation expense for 1993 | £440 000 |
| Tools etc., depreciation expense for 1993 | £70 000 |

*Question*
Compute the selling price if the desired gross profit is 33⅓% of sales.

(See solution in Appendix C, p. 246.)

**3** Refer back to the data given in Problem 2 above.

*Question*
Construct the budgeted profit and loss account (before tax) for 1993 for the Gherkin Delight Company.

**4** The balance sheet for the Gherkin Delight Company as at 31.12.92 is as follows:

| Fixed assets | (£'000s) | (£'000s) |
|---|---|---|
| Plant and equipment | | |
| at cost | 2600 | |
| Less accum. | | |
| depreciation | 340 | |
| Net book value | | 2260 |
| Tools etc. at cost | 175 | |
| Less accum. | | |
| depreciation | 80 | |
| Net book value | | 95 |
| | | 2355 |
| | | |
| Current assets | | |
| Stocks | 595 | |
| Debtors | 395 | |
| Cash | 40 | 1030 |
| Less current liabilities | | |
| Creditors | 76 | |
| Corporation tax | 220 | |
| Dividend | 84 | |
| | | (380) |
| Total assets less | | |
| current liabilities | | 3005 |
| Shareholders' funds | | |
| Share capital: | | |
| ordinary £1 shares | | 1200 |
| Share premium | | |
| account | | 550 |
| Profit and loss | | |
| account | | 1255 |
| | | 3005 |

Additional investment for 1993 is estimated at £450 000 (£370 000 for plant and equipment and £80 000 for tooling etc.).

The stock level at the end of 1993 is planned to be £665 000.

By the end of 1993, it is planned to pay trade creditors (material suppliers) about two months in arrears. Other creditors are estimated to be about £8000 at that stage.

Customers are to be given one month's credit.

The accounts department advise that a tax charge of £185 000 is likely for the year of 1993. Tax is paid nine months after the accounting year end.

The managing director wishes to pay a final dividend of £100 000 in respect of 1993. No interim dividends are paid.

It is planned to raise £200 000 net (of share issue costs) by a one-for-ten rights issue.

*Question*
Using any necessary information from Problem 2 above, construct a budgeted balance sheet as at 31.12.93.

**5** Hackney Roof Racks Ltd produces roof racks for cars and small vans. Two types are produced, designated as Economy and Super. Three materials are used, designated as A, B and C. There are two producing departments — Stamping and Assembly. The following budget estimates have been made for the year 1993.

Sales forecast (units):

| | Cars | Vans |
|---|---|---|
| Economy | 20 000 | 4 000 |
| Super | 30 000 | 10 000 |

Unit sales prices to retailers:

| | |
|---|---|
| Economy | £15.00 |
| Super | £20.00 |

Stocks:

| | 31 December 1992 | | 31 December 1993 | |
|---|---|---|---|---|
| Direct material | Units | Unit cost | Units | Unit cost |
| A | 3 000 | £1.25 | 4 000 | £1.25 |
| B | 10 000 | £0.50 | 10 000 | £0.50 |
| C | 4 500 | £0.40 | 4 000 | £0.40 |
| Work-in-progress | Nil | | Nil | |
| Finished goods | | | | |
| Economy | 2 000 | £9.00 | 2 000 | £8.90 |
| Super | 4 000 | £12.50 | 3 000 | £11.99 |

Direct material requirements per unit:

Economy   Two units of material B and two units of material C.

Super     One unit of material A and two units of material B.

1993 estimated purchase prices per unit of material:

| | |
|---|---|
| Material A | £1.25 |
| Material B | £0.50 |
| Material C | £0.40 |

Estimated direct labour cost per unit:

| | Stamping department | Assembly department |
|---|---|---|
| Economy | £0.75 | £2.50 |
| Super | £1.00 | £3.50 |

Factory overhead budgets developed for 1993 indicate the following per unit overhead cost:

| | Stamping department | Assembly department |
|---|---|---|
| Economy | £2.25 | £1.60 |
| Super | £3.00 | £2.24 |

Other estimated costs:

| | |
|---|---|
| Distribution expense | £150 000 |
| Administrative expense | £70 000 |
| Corporation tax | 33% of profit before tax |

*Questions*

Utilizing the above information, prepare the following budget schedules for 1993:

(a) A summary of budgeted sales.
(b) A production (volume) budget.
(c) An estimate of direct material requirements.
(d) A purchases budget.
(e) A summary of estimated direct labour costs.
(f) A summary of factory overhead costs.
(g) A statement of estimated cost of goods sold.
(h) An estimated profit and loss account.

6  Rand Chemicals developed products and processes for itself and other firms in the chemical industry. Research spending of about £8 million amounted to about 3% of sales. The research division was important to Rand; and in 1992, top management was reviewing research effectiveness and control over research spending.

The directors set policy and exercised general control. A committee of the board, including the research director, closely monitored the research programme's conduct and results, guiding the research division on the following points:

• What specific fields of research might pay off in the long run.
• Whether to emphasize developing new products or improving existing ones.
• When to drop products with poor prospects, and when to intensify efforts.
• How to appraise the sales potential of new products.
• When to turn new items over to other divisions to start production.

Rand employed over 200 research personnel. The research division's managers included a director, a controller and department heads for each of eight different kinds of research. Each department head prepared annual budget estimates by project and by type of expense for spending on projects already in progress or due to start during the year. A department head could start a new project only if he could show that there was enough time to allow adequate research progress. The director of research had to approve all changes in personnel numbers, all salary increases, and any purchase of materials costing over £1000.

Rand used a number of reports in trying to control research costs. Each department head received a monthly report showing expenses by project for the month, for the year to date, and for the project's life. A detailed breakdown showed the time each research worker spent on each project. The research committee received a quarterly report of actual versus budgeted expenses. The research director's written review explained major variances, described progress to date, and appraised each project's future prospects. This helped the committee decide for each project whether to drop, continue, or modify it. In addition, the research controller prepared interim reports for department heads when a particular project's expenses had reached the budgeted limit, or when it seemed likely that a project might exceed its budget. The controller also prepared annual summary reports of expenses.

Rand's directors believed it was possible to allocate some research costs to products or to operating divisions (for example, product development or pilot plant costs). Until now, however, the company had not done so since management feared that division heads might oppose, on short-term grounds, research spending that in the long run could prove to be very worthwhile for the company as a whole. Instead, the accounts showed research as a separate expense item. The research director was keen to avoid any change that might upset operating division heads.

Nevertheless, the board was concerned about the overall profitability of Rand's research programme. Some board members felt it would improve the research programme's effectiveness if each product was made to bear its share of allocable research costs. But because of the significance of research to Rand's profitability and progress, the board was nervous about taking any action that might jeopardize the effectiveness of the company's research.

*Questions*

(a) Does Rand Chemicals control its research programme effectively?
(b) Should Rand allocate some or all research costs to products and/or divisions?
(c) In what respects is research spending different from other forms of spending?

(The solutions to Problems 3–6 will be provided in the *Instructors' Manual*.)

CHAPTER **9** *Variance analysis*

9.1 **The benefits of variance analysis**

Variance analysis is one of the most important practical financial control procedures. It involves comparing actual results with the budget; and finding out the reasons why differences (variances) have arisen. It helps reveal which factors have affected performance and how much; and alerts managers to take suitable action in good time. It can be easy for managers to jump to the wrong conclusion. By analysing variances and seeking to explain them, possibly after discussions between many different people, management is more likely to find out what is really happening.

**Example 9.1**
Company A's actual profit turns out to be lower than budgeted, despite sales revenue being higher. One might suppose that Company A has problems in controlling costs. But it may have increased sales revenue by selling a higher volume at lower prices. The higher sales volume, involving increased output, may well have caused higher total production costs. In this instance, the basic cause of lower profit might be one or more of the following:

 (i) Cutting prices in order to increase volume.
 (ii) Following competitors' price reductions.
(iii) Poor quality, resulting in price discounts.
(iv) Change in product sales mix.
 (v) Lack of cost control.

Calculating variances is only the first stage in improving business performance. They direct management's attention to questions that need looking at, rather than themselves providing the answers. To achieve superior performance normally requires a motivated, trained and experienced workforce. Managers may often be aware of deviations from budget before they see the management accounting report giving the details. Indeed, they may already have taken suitable action before the variances are even reported.

Sometimes variances turn out to be favourable. The temptation is to feel grateful and then pass on; but glossing over them too quickly may mean missing an opportunity. Something has gone better than expected. Why? Have there been changes in market conditions or in production processes? Could *further* improvements be possible if we accentuate the positive? Suppose a rival's plant has suffered a strike. Some of their customers may be looking to buy elsewhere, perhaps from us, at least for the time being. A chance may exist to boost sales and profit above budget; and perhaps to win some new permanent customers.

Budgets are an agreed plan for people to aim at. They need not be a straitjacket preventing managers from cashing in on improved conditions. In fact, taking action to maximize positive variances may pay off better than trying to minimize negative ones, some of which may be outside management's control.

Many accounts departments produce comprehensive monthly management accounts. This is fine for reconciling the financial accounts with the budget, but may not help managers trying to run a business. Most busy managers prefer a brief summary report highlighting the main variances from budget, together with an explanation of the key causes. They can then focus on deciding what action (if any) they need to take, rather than wading through pages of accounting data. Variance analysis should avoid spurious detail: for instance, not quoting variances to the nearest penny. Reporting to the nearest hundred or thousand pounds is probably quite adequate for most businesses.

Managers who are not getting the sort of information they think they need should ask their accounts department for it. The variances in this chapter are not a complete list. It may sometimes be useful to calculate extra ones or to modify some of the variance formulae. A balance must be struck between calculating every conceivable variance, resulting in a more complex analysis, and providing information that business managers can understand and use.

## 9.2 Sales variances

Sales variances occur when: sales *volumes*; selling *prices*; or the *mix* of products differ from budget.

### 9.2.1 Volume variances

Sales volume variances arise when the actual physical volume of sales differs from that budgeted. The amount is calculated as follows:
(actual volume − budgeted volume) × budgeted price per unit.

**Example 9.2**
Suppose Arsenal football club expect to sell 20 000 programmes for their match with Liverpool. The club prices programmes at £1 each. What is the sales volume variance if Arsenal sell only 17 200 programmes?

(Actual − budgeted volume) × budgeted price per unit
= (17 200 − 20 000) × £1.00
= −£2800 (i.e. an unfavourable variance of £2800).

When actual sales volume exceeds budget, the variance is positive (favourable). If actual sales volume is less than budget, the variance is negative (unfavourable).

**9.2.2 Price variances**

Sales price variances result when actual selling prices differ from those budgeted. The amount is calculated as follows:
(actual price per unit − budgeted price per unit) × actual units sold.

**Example 9.3**
Manning Farm Produce budgeted to sell 100 000 kilograms of potatoes during 1991 at 25 pence per kilogram. However, prices were lower than expected and, although 100 000 kg. were sold, the average price for the year was only 20 pence per kg. What was the sales price variance?
(Actual − budgeted price per kg.) × actual kgs sold = (20p − 25p) × 100 000
= −£5000 (i.e. an unfavourable variance of £5000).

In this example only the selling price varied, the volume sold remaining unchanged. The previous example (see section 9.2.1) dealt with a volume change only, the selling price remaining unchanged. But what happens when both the volume and the price turn out to be different from budget?

**9.2.3 Combined volume and price variances**

**Example 9.4**
The UK Oil Company budgeted to sell six million barrels of oil at $20 per barrel during May 1991. The company actually sold only five million barrels at $18.00 per barrel. Determine the price and volume variances. Figure 9.1 illustrates the budgeted and actual volumes and prices.
The variances are calculated as follows:

Budgeted sales = 6 million barrels at $20/barrel = $120 million.
Actual sales = 5 million barrels at $18/barrel = $90 million.
So sales volume variance + sales price variance = ($90 − $120) million
 = −$30 million.
Sales volume variance = (actual − budgeted volume) × budgeted price per unit
 = (5m − 6m barrels) × $20 per barrel = −$20m.
Sales price variance = (actual − budgeted price per unit) × actual units sold
 = ($18 − $20 per barrel) × 5m barrels = −$10m.

Figure 9.2 shows how these two variances combined amount to the difference between actual sales revenue and budgeted sales revenue.

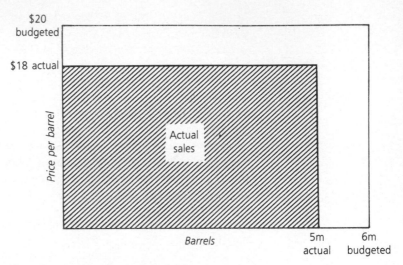

Figure 9.1 *Actual versus budgeted sales*

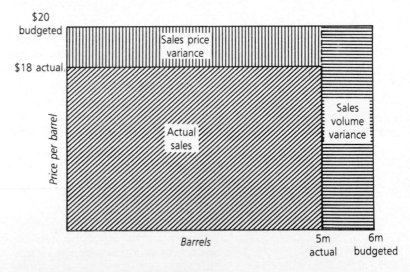

Figure 9.2 *Sales — price and volume variances*

Note that we have used the budgeted price when calculating the volume variance and the actual units sold for the price variance. This is the normal convention when splitting variances into their volume and price components. It recognizes that managers are often more able to control volume than price.

9.2.4 **Mix variances**

In multi-product businesses total sales revenue can vary from budget even if the total volume, and selling prices of the individual products, remain unchanged. This can happen when the actual mix of products or services is different from that budgeted.

**Example 9.5**

The actual and budgeted sales of the Modern Milk Company for June 1992 are shown in Table 9.1. This table indicates that actual sales revenue exceeded budget by £30 000 (£2.25m − £2.22m), even though the actual prices of each of the different flavours and the actual total volume (2.2m litres) were as budgeted. The favourable £30 000 mix variance arose by shifting 200 000 litres of sales towards higher-priced chocolate and strawberry flavours and away from banana flavour, as follows:

|  |  | (£'000s) |
|---|---|---|
| Shift from banana to chocolate = 100 000 litres × 10p per litre (higher price) | | = 10 |
| Shift from banana to strawberry = 100 000 litres × 20p per litre (higher price) | | = 20 |
| Total sales mix variance | | = 30 |

Table 9.1 *Modern Milk Company's sales for June 1992*

|  | Product | Budgeted | Actual |
|---|---|---|---|
| *Volume* ('000 litres) | Banana flavour | 600 | 400 |
|  | Chocolate flavour | 800 | 900 |
|  | Strawberry flavour | 800 | 900 |
|  | Total | 2 200 | 2 200 |
| *Price (per litre)* | Banana flavour | £0.90 | £0.90 |
|  | Chocolate flavour | £1.00 | £1.00 |
|  | Strawberry flavour | £1.10 | £1.10 |
| *Sales revenue* | Banana flavour | £540 000 | £360 000 |
|  | Chocolate flavour | £800 000 | £900 000 |
|  | Strawberry flavour | £880 000 | £990 000 |
| *Total sales revenue* | | £2 220 000 | £2 250 000 |

It may be easy to calculate mix variances when the individual prices and total sales volume remain unchanged. But it becomes more complex when volumes, prices and product mix all vary from budget. The way to split the total variance is to calculate volume variance and price variance as if the actual product mix was the same as that budgeted. The mix variance is then the remaining difference between the total sales variance and the (combined) volume and price variances.

Where there are only a few products, it may be simpler to calculate the price and volume variances for each product and add them together to give a total price variance and a total volume variance. This avoids the need to calculate a mix variance.

When seeking to explain differences between actual and budgeted profit, it is often more useful to calculate the change in contribution resulting from changes in sales volume (see section 9.3.1). Because changes in selling price (unlike changes in sales volume) affect equally the sales revenue, contribution and profit, price variance is the same whether calculating the effect on revenue or on profit.

## 9.3 Operating expense variances

Operating expenses include wages and salaries, cost of bought-out materials and services, and overhead costs. Manufacturing companies generally budget for direct labour, direct materials, manufacturing overhead and non-manufacturing costs. They calculate variances for each item and, where significant, investigate further.

### 9.3.1 Flexible budgets

Comparing actual costs against budget must allow for the actual level of output. Suppose a lengthy strike reduces a brewery's output to only 80% of budget. Should we applaud the brewery manager for just meeting his budget for materials, labour and overhead costs? Clearly not. If output volume falls to 80% of budget, we would expect variable costs to be only about 80% of budget too. To show this, we need to flex the budget in line with actual output. Flexible budgets thus provide a logical basis for looking at expense variances where costs vary with output.

### Example 9.6

Radio Aerials Ltd have budgeted as follows for the month (all totals in thousands): sales revenue £100 (25 units at £4.00 each); variable expenses £2.40 per unit (= £60 total); and fixed expenses £24. Actual results were: sales revenue £84 (20 units at £4.20); variable expenses £56; and fixed expenses £22. Table 9.2 uses a flexible budget format to analyse the £10 difference between budgeted profit of £16 and actual profit of £6.

The total −£10 variance between the original budget profit (£16) and the actual profit (£6) is split into two parts: (a) £16 − £8 = −£8; and (b) £8 − £6 = −£2, as follows:

(a) The variance of −£8 in contribution (and therefore in profit) between the original budget (£40) and the flexible budget (£32) is due to the decline in sales volume:

Table 9.2 *Flexing a budget for variance analysis*

| ('000 units) | Original budget (25) | | Flexible budget (20) | | Actual (20) |
|---|---|---|---|---|---|
| | (£'000) | | (£'000) | | (£'000) |
| Sales revenue | 100 | | 80 | | 84 |
| Variable expenses | 60 | | 48 | | 56 |
| Contribution | 40 | | 32 | | 28 |
| Fixed expenses | 24 | | 24 | | 22 |
| Profit | 16 | (a) | 8 | (b) | 6 |

| | | | | | |
|---|---|---|---|---|---|
| Sales revenue | −5 | × | £4.00 | = | −£20 |
| Variable expenses | −5 | × | £2.40 | = | +£12 |
| Contribution | −5 | × | £1.60 | = | −£8 |

The change in contribution due to volume variance:

= (actual volume − budget volume) × budget contribution per unit
= (20 − 25) × £1.60 = −£8

(b) The variance of −£2 in profit between the flexible budget and actual is due to three different factors:

| | Flexible budget | Actual | Variance |
|---|---|---|---|
| Sales price | £80 | £84 | +£4 (+£0.20 × 20) |
| Variable expenses | £48 | £56 | −£8 (−£0.40 × 20) |
| Fixed expenses | £24 | £22 | +£2 |
| Profit | £8 | £6 | −£2 |

Flexible budgets analyse variances step by step. They distinguish between variances due to a change in sales volume, and those due to expenses being different from expected at the actual sales volume. In practice, this is helpful because different managers are likely to be responsible.

In the example, it is essential to split the apparent +£4 variance on variable expenses (£60 − £56) between: +£12 variance due to the decline in sales volume; and −£8 variance due to spending too much at the actual sales volume. The variance on variable expenses (+£12) due to reduced sales volume forms part of the (−£8 = £32 − £40) contribution variance (see Table 9.2): it has little practical meaning on its own, and need not be calculated separately. In contrast, the manager(s) controlling variable

Table 9.3 *Names of operating cost variances*

|  | Price | Quantity |
|---|---|---|
| Material | *Price* | *Usage* |
| Labour | *Rate* | *Efficiency* |

expenses need(s) to calculate separately and use the ($-£8 = £48 - £56$) variance on variable expenses between the flexible budget and actual.

### 9.3.2 **Price variances**

Even with flexible budgets, actual operating expenses may deviate from budget, due to either the price or the quantity of materials, or to labour being different from budget. Much of variance analysis involves identifying differences between budget and actual either in price or in quantity. In this section, we look at variances relating to material and labour prices and, in the next section, we consider quantity variances.

Unfortunately, the terminology used for price variances and for quantity variances differs as between material and labour, as Table 9.3 shows. Input-cost variances are calculated as follows:
(budgeted cost per unit of input − actual cost) × actual units of input.

**Example 9.7**
Anne Teak Furniture Company produce high-quality household furniture. They have budgeted to produce 120 teak tables a month using 10 kilograms of wood

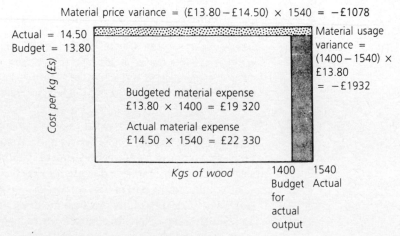

Figure 9.3 *Material — price and usage variances*

costing £13.80 per kg. Because of increased demand, they produce 140 tables in September 1992, using 11 kg. of wood per table. The price of teak wood has risen to £14.50 per kg. The material price variance is as follows:

= (budgeted price per kg. − actual price per kg.) × kg. of wood used
= (£13.8 − £14.5) × (140 × 11)
= −(£0.7 × 1540)
= −£1078 (i.e. an unfavourable price variance of £1078 − see Figure 9.3)

Note that we use the cost of wood per kg., not per table. The latter is affected not only by the price of wood per kg., but also by the amount of wood used to produce each table.

We can use a similar approach to calculate the direct labour rate variance.

### Example 9.8

Using the following information for Anne Teak Furniture Company, determine the direct labour rate variance for September 1992:

|  | Budget | Actual |
|---|---|---|
| Number of tables produced | 120 | 140 |
| Direct labour hours per table | 6.0 | 5.6 |
| Direct labour rate per hour | £6.50 | £7.00 |

= (budgeted direct labour rate per hour − actual rate) × actual direct labour hours used
= (£6.50 − £7.00) × (140 × 5.6)
= −(£0.50 × 784)
= −£392 (i.e. an unfavourable rate variance of £392 − see Figure 9.4)

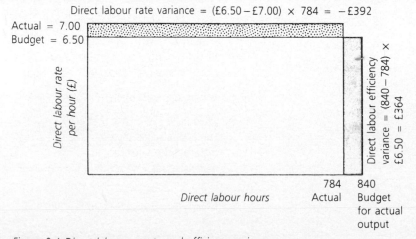

Figure 9.4 *Direct labour — rate and efficiency variances*

9.3.3 **Quantity variances**

Actual operating expenses can exceed budget not only because prices have risen, but also because the actual quantity of resources used (e.g. materials and labour) exceeds the budget. Usage variances are calculated as follows: (budgeted usage for actual output − actual usage) × budgeted cost per unit of input.

**Example 9.9**

Given the following budgeted and actual September 1992 figures for the Anne Teak Furniture Company, determine the material usage variance and the direct labour efficiency variance.

|  | Budget | Actual |
|---|---|---|
| No. of tables produced | 120 | 140 |
| Kgs of wood per table | 10 | 11 |
| Cost of wood per kg. | £13.80 | £14.50 |
| Direct labour hours per table | 6.0 | 5.6 |
| Direct labour rate per hour | £6.50 | £7.00 |

Material usage variance is as follows:

= (budgeted kgs of wood for actual output − actual kgs of wood) × budgeted cost per kg.
= [(10 × 140) − (11 × 140)] kgs × £13.80 per kg.
= −(140 kg. × £13.80 per kg.)
= −£1932 (i.e. an unfavourable variance due to more material being used than should have been for the actual level of output − see Figure 9.3)

Direct labour efficiency variance is as follows:

= (budgeted hours for actual output − actual hours) × budgeted rate per hour
= [(6.00 × 140) − (5.6 × 140)] hours × £6.50 per hour
= +(56 hours × £6.50 per hour)
= +£364 (i.e. a favourable variance due to more efficient use of direct labour than budgeted − see Figure 9.4)

We can now reconcile the material variances as follows:

| | | |
|---|---|---|
| Budgeted material expense (£13.80 × 1400) | | = £19 320 |
| Plus: unfavourable variances: | | |
| material price variance | £1078 | |
| material usage variance | £1932 | |
| | | £3 010 |
| Actual material expense (£14.50 × 1540) | | = £22 330 |

Likewise, we can reconcile the direct labour variances as follows:

Budgeted direct labour expense for actual output
   (£6.50 × 840)                                                    =   £5 460
Plus unfavourable direct labour rate variance                            392
Less favourable direct labour efficiency variance                       (364)
Actual direct labour expense (£7.00 × 784)                          =   £5 488

Now consider Case study 9.1.

---

### Case study 9.1

*Problem*
Anne Teak Furniture Company have produced the following budget for October 1992:

| | |
|---|---|
| No. of tables produced | 130 |
| Kgs of wood per table | 10 |
| Cost of wood per kg. | £14.50 |
| Direct labour hours per table | 6.0 |
| Direct labour rate per hour | £6.50 |

During October 1992, 148 tables were produced, requiring 1600 kg. of wood and 810 hours of direct labour. The cost of wood was £15.00 per kg. and the direct labour rate was £7.00 per hour.

*Questions*
Determine the following:

1 Material price variance.
2 Material usage variance.
3 Direct labour rate variance.
4 Direct labour efficiency variance.

*Solution*

1 Material price variance:

   = (budgeted price of wood per kg. − actual price of wood) × actual quantity of wood used.
   = (£14.50 − £15.00 per kg.) × 1600 kg.
   = − (£0.50 per kg. × 1600 kg.)
   = − £800

2 Material usage variance:

   = (budgeted kgs of wood for actual output − actual kgs of wood used) × budgeted price per kg.

= [(10 × 148) − 1600] kg. × £14.50 per kg.

= (1480 − 1600) kg. × £14.50 per kg.

= −(120 kg. × £14.50 per kg.)

= −£1740

These two material variances combined (−£2540) identify why the £24 000 actual cost of wood (1600 kgs. at £15.00 per kg.) exceeds by £2540 the £21 460 budgeted cost (10 kg. per table × 148 tables × £14.50 per kg.).

**3** Direct labour rate variance:

= (budgeted direct labour rate − actual rate) × actual direct labour hours used.

= (£6.50 − £7.00) per hour × 810 hours

= −(£0.50 per hour × 810 hours)

= −£405

**4** Direct labour efficiency variance:

= (budgeted direct labour hours for actual output − actual hours used) × budgeted rate per hour.

= [(6.0 hours × 148 tables) − 810 hours] × £6.50 per hour

= (888 − 810) hours × £6.50 per hour

= +£507

These two labour variances combined (£507 − £405 = £102) identify why the £5670 actual labour costs (810 hours at £7.00 per hour) were £102 less than the £5772 budgeted costs (888 hours at £6.50 per hour).

9.3.4 **Overhead variances**   We need to split overhead variances between fixed and variable, as follows:

**1** Providing the actual level of output does not dramatically change from the budget (i.e. stays within the relevant range), then the amount of *fixed* overhead should not change. The only reason for a variance, therefore, is if the actual cost of fixed overhead differs from budget. The fixed overhead **expenditure variance** is negative (unfavourable) when the actual fixed overhead costs exceed the budget, and positive when the actual cost is less than budget. (We thus maintain the convention of a positive variance meaning increased profit.)

**2** By definition, we expect *variable* overhead to change in line with output. We calculate the variable overhead expenditure variance as follows: (budgeted variable overhead per unit × actual units of output) − actual variable overhead.

### Example 9.10

The Spot-On Watches budget for February 1993 included £40 000 variable overhead costs based on output of 20 000 watches. Budgeted variable overhead is therefore £2 per watch produced. Actual variable overhead was £47 000, and output was 22 000 watches.

Variable overhead expenditure variance is as follows:

= (budgeted variable overhead per unit × actual units of output) − actual variable overhead

= (£2 per watch × 22 000 watches) − £47 000

= £44 000 − £47 000

= −£3000 (unfavourable variance)

## 9.4 Profit variances

### 9.4.1 Marginal costing systems

### 9.4.2 Standard costing systems

Figure 9.5 shows how to combine the sales variances and operating expense variances to explain the profit (before tax) variance, while Table 9.4 lists the constituent parts of the profit variance formulae.

Standard costs include: material cost; labour cost; and overhead charge — for both variable and fixed overheads (see section 2.6.3).

Because total standard costs include fixed overheads, we need to make two changes to the profit variance formulae (for marginal costing systems)

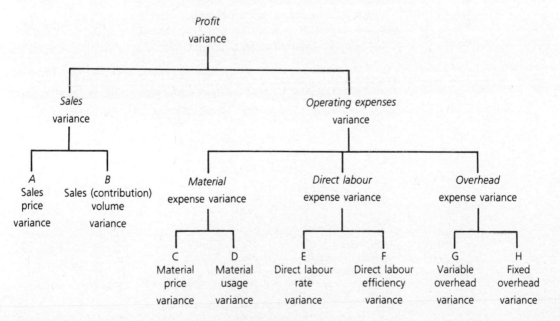

Figure 9.5 *Profit variance chart for marginal costing system*

Table 9.4 *Profit variance formulae for marginal costing system*

A. Sales price variance = (actual price per unit − budgeted price per unit) × actual units sold.

B. Sales (contribution) volume variance = (actual volume − budgeted volume) × budgeted contribution per unit.

C. Material price variance = (budgeted material price per unit − actual material price per unit) × actual units of material used.

D. Material usage variance = (budgeted material units *for actual output* − actual material units used) × budgeted material cost per unit.

E. Direct labour rate variance = (budgeted direct labour rate − actual direct labour rate) × actual direct labour hours used.

F. Direct labour efficiency variance = (budgeted direct labour hours *for actual output* − actual direct labour hours used) × budgeted direct labour rate per hour.

G. Variable overhead expenditure variance = (budgeted variable overhead per unit of output × actual units of output) − actual variable overhead.

H. Fixed overhead expenditure variance = budgeted fixed overhead − actual fixed overhead.

listed in Table 9.4. Firstly, the sales (standard profit) volume variance replaces the sales (contribution) volume variance (formula B); and secondly, we add a new variance, the fixed overhead volume variance. The formulae are as follows:

1 Sales (standard profit) volume variance = (actual volume − budgeted volume) × standard profit per unit.
2 Fixed overhead volume variance = (actual volume − budgeted volume) × standard fixed overhead rate.

### Example 9.11
The original monthly budget and actual results for Radio Aerials Ltd were shown in Table 9.2. Table 9.5 shows Radio Aerials' standard costs and standard profit per unit.

Table 9.5 *Standard profit for Radio Aerials Ltd*

|  | Per unit (£) | Total for 25 000 units (£'000) |
|---|---|---|
| Sales revenue | 4.00 | 100 |
| Variable expenses | 2.40[1] | 60 |
| Fixed expenses | 0.96[1] | 24 |
| Standard profit | 0.64 | 16 |

*Note:* [1]standard cost per unit = £2.40 + £0.96 = £3.36.

We can now calculate the two new variances as follows:

Sales (standard profit) volume variance
= (20 000 units − 25 000 units) × £0.64 per unit.
= −(5000 × £0.64)
= −£3200

This shows the reduction in total standard profit due to the lower sales volume.

Fixed overhead volume variance
= (20 000 units − 25 000 units) × £0.96
= −£4800

Because the budgeted fixed overhead was shared out over 25 000 (budgeted) units, a fall in actual volume to 20 000 units means that not all the fixed overhead is recovered. The technical term for this is **under-absorption**. Profit falls accordingly as the difference is written off in the period. Since we have assumed that production and sales are equal, these two variances combined (−£8000) equal the sales (contribution) volume variance in the marginal costing system. (To verify this, see section 9.3.1.)

Now examine Case study 9.2.

---

### Case study 9.2

#### Problem
Budget figures for Munchy Crunch Ltd, a small confectionery company, are shown below, together with the latest quarter's actual results.

### Budget

| | | (£'000s) |
|---|---|---|
| Sales: 500 tons @ £3000/ton | = | 1500 |
| Cost of sales: | | |
| Direct materials: | | |
| 600 tons @ £750/ton | = | 450 |
| Direct labour: | | |
| 500 hours @ (£6/hr × wks) | = | 150 |
| Mfg. overheads: variable | | 145 |
| fixed | | 180 |
| Other overheads: variable | | 55 |
| fixed | | 240 |
| Total costs | | 1220 |
| Profit (before tax) | | 280 |

|  | Actual |  |
|---|---|---|
|  |  | (£'000s) |
| Sales: 400 tons @ £3100/ton | = | 1426 |
| Cost of sales: |  |  |
| Direct materials: |  |  |
| 630 tons @ £800/ton | = | 504 |
| Direct labour: |  |  |
| 22 000 hrs @ £6.50/hr | = | 143 |
| Mfg. overheads: variable |  | 156 |
| fixed |  | 183 |
| Other overheads: variable |  | 57 |
| fixed |  | 244 |
| Total costs |  | 1287 |
| Profit (before tax) |  | 139 |

*Question*
Calculate and list the variances that explain the shortfall in Munchy Crunch's profit for the quarter, assuming that they operate a marginal costing system.

**Solution**
Profit variances for a marginal costing system:

(a) Sales price variance:

> = (actual price per unit − budgeted price per unit) × actual units sold
> = (£3100 − £3000) per ton × 460 tons
> = +£46 000

(b) Sales (contribution) volume variance:

> = (actual volume − budgeted volume) × volume variance budgeted contribution per unit
> = (460 − 500) tons × £1400 per ton[1]
> = −£56 000
> [1]£1500 (sales) − £150 (direct labour) − £450 (direct materials) − £200 (total variable overheads) = £700 000/500 tons = £1400 per ton budgeted contribution.

(c) Material price variance:

> = (budgeted material price per unit − actual price) × actual units of material used
> = (£750 − £800) per ton × 630 tons
> = −£31 500

(d) Material usage variance:

= (budgeted material units for actual output − actual material units used) × budgeted material cost per unit

= (460 × (600/500) − 630) tons × £750 per ton

= −£58 500

(e) Direct labour rate variance:

= (budgeted direct labour rate − actual rate) × actual direct labour hours used

= (£6 − £6.50) per hour × 22 000 hours

= −£11 000

(f) Direct labour efficiency variance:

= (budgeted direct labour hours for actual output − actual hours used) × budgeted rate

= ((50 hours/ton × 460 tons) − 22 000 hours) × £6/hour

= +£6 000

(g) Variable overhead expenditure variance:

= (budgeted variable overhead per unit × actual output) − actual variable overhead

= (£145 000 + £55 000) × 460/500 tons − (£156 000 + £57 000)

= £184 000 − £213 000

= −£29 000

(h) Fixed overhead expenditure variance:

= budgeted fixed overhead − actual fixed overhead

= (£180 000 + £240 000) − (£183 000 + £244 000)

= −£7 000

Total variances

= −£141 000

Total net unfavourable variances of −£141 000 account for the difference between £280 000 budgeted profit for the quarter and £139 000 actual profit.

Note that, for a standard costing system, the sales (contribution) volume variance (b) is replaced by the following two variances:

(b)(i) Sales (standard profit) volume variance:

= (actual volume − budgeted volume) × standard profit per unit

= (460 tons − 500 tons) × £280 000/500 tons

= −40 tons × £560 per ton

= −£22 400

(b)(ii) Fixed overhead volume variance:

$$= \text{(actual volume} - \text{budgeted volume)} \times \text{standard fixed overhead per unit}$$
$$= (460 \text{ tons} - 500 \text{ tons}) \times £420\,000/500 \text{ tons}$$
$$= -40 \text{ tons} \times £840 \text{ per ton}$$
$$= -£33\,600$$

Note that these two variances total *minus* £56 000, the same amount as for the sales (contribution) volume variance. This is always true when the levels of production and sales are equal.

## 9.5 Balance sheet variances

Variance analysis often focuses on profit and loss account items, but it is important not to ignore the balance sheet. Three current asset items in particular need close attention: stocks, debtors and cash. Stocks and debtors may rise rapidly because of falling sales and slow customer payments respectively; and the cash balance, of course, is the net result of thousands of separate cash receipts and payments. Stocks, debtors and cash depend very much on external influences. They can vary in the short term much more sharply than fixed assets, which usually require management to approve both purchases and disposals.

### 9.5.1 Stocks

Some managers may be tempted not to worry about excessive stocks. High levels of raw materials, bought-out items and work-in-progress can all reduce the risk of hold-ups in the production process. That means one less problem for production managers to worry about. In retail firms, on the other hand, high levels of goods ready for sale enable stores to meet customer demands instantly, without losing any sales due to stock-outs. So marketing people, too, may welcome high stocks.

The total cost of holding stock, however, can be much higher than one might think. The combined costs of storage space and handling, insurance, spoilage, pilfering, obsolescence, and other loss of value, together with financing costs, might easily amount to more than 25% per year of the aggregate cost of stocks held. Hence, there is a clear need to balance the benefits from holding stocks against the substantial costs.

Stocks need to be at a level that allows a satisfactory supply for production purposes, and provides an adequate customer service. But excessively high stock levels are very expensive, even if the costs do not all appear explicitly on the profit and loss account. The Japanese 'Just-In-Time' stock policy is famous; and many British managers have now recognized the high cost of a 'Just-In-Case' stock policy.

Large differences between actual and budgeted stock levels suggest a need for management action. Assuming we are using costs, the differences will represent quantity (not price) variances. Perhaps customer

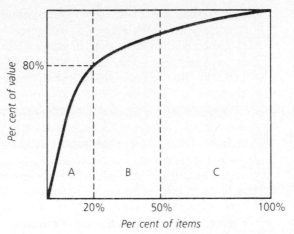

Figure 9.6 *ABC analysis*

needs are changing; or production problems may be leading to stock build-ups in raw materials, bought-out items or work-in-progress; or lack of co-ordination between sales and production may be causing shortages in some finished goods. Can we modify production quickly enough to match market changes? Or could we make a special promotion effort (or reduce prices) to clear excess stocks?

In many companies, it is probably worthwhile to review actual stocks and compare with budgets at least monthly. In managing stocks, as in many other areas of management, a useful device can be 'ABC analysis' (also known as the '80/20 rule'). This is based on the 'rule' that a small proportion (say 20%) of the total number of items will often account for a large proportion (say 80%) of the total value of all items. Figure 9.6 illustrates. The implication is obvious: rather than pay equal attention to all items, it makes better commercial sense to look first at the few items which account for the bulk of the investment in stocks, starting with Class A items, then Class B, and only afterwards considering the many small Class C items.

**9.5.2 Debtors**

Some business people believe that 'a sale is not a sale until the cash is in the bank'. As we know (see section 1.1.5), financial accounts normally recognize a sale (and the profit thereon) when goods pass to the customer or on rendering a service. With credit sales, this precedes the payment of cash. During the period between the customer receiving an invoice and making payment, the outstanding amount appears in the seller's records as a debtor (account receivable).

Failure to collect cash from debtors on time, in accordance with the credit terms, can be very costly. The seller's business could use the cash (for example, either to invest in profit-yielding assets, or else to reduce interest-bearing borrowing). And a customer whose financial soundness is suspect might not pay at all, or perhaps less than the full amount due. In any event, there may be a substantial delay. It is *overdue* debts, not bad debts, that represent the bulk of the *cost* arising from extending trade credit.

Variances between actual and budgeted debtors may require management action. Of course, if recent sales are different from budget, that is likely to affect the total amount of debtors. But expressing debtors as an average number of days' sales (based on actual sales) will allow for that. Without careful budgeting and variance analysis of the level of debtors, a firm might overlook important questions; for example: Are our credit terms appropriate? Are we being aggressive enough in collecting money from customers? Are there better ways to organize the collection process?

In addition to reviewing debtors in the aggregate (perhaps monthly), many firms also split debtors into age groups, depending on how long has elapsed since the date of the invoice. Attention can then focus on overdue invoices. Some firms even discuss outstanding invoices with their customers before the due date, just to make sure there are no problems to prevent or delay payment on time.

### 9.5.3 Cash

Cash balances are the result of all the various inflows and outflows of cash, which in nearly all businesses will involve a number of different managers. It is essential to budget cash carefully; to review actual cash balances and compute variances frequently; and to take appropriate action promptly. Running out of cash could well mean the end of the business, even if it appears to be profitable.

Some managers regard cash as the single most important aspect of the business to control. They argue that it can be reported very frequently and quickly, as a matter of routine, and that it is comprehensive, taking in virtually all aspects of the business. While its focus is short-term, they also regard cash as immune to the accounting distortions that can arise in accrual accounting; for example, from overhead absorption when stock levels change or from the impact of inflation. They also think it is much harder to manipulate cash amounts than accrual accounting numbers (for example, by adjusting accruals or other provisions).

### 9.5.4 Creditors

It can be useful to be aware of the level of total net working capital (that is, total current assets less total current liabilities). Even if some current assets are higher than budgeted, for example, creditors may be, too. This may be a matter for concern, since if a firm takes too much trade credit from suppliers, they may eventually decide to cut off supplies (or insist on cash on delivery). That can cause a good deal of trouble to a business, especially if it was not a calculated risk. In effect, one possible way to improve the cash balance (or the bank overdraft) might be to extend trade creditors beyond the normal budgeted level. Hence, focusing solely on the cash balance may not be adequate.

---

9.6 **Chapter summary**

Variance analysis involves comparing actual results with budget; and finding out where they differ and why. It will not always provide the reasons, but it can help to identify relevant questions.

Sales volumes, prices, or mix, may differ from budget. It is often useful to calculate how much a change in sales volume causes a change in contribution (and hence in profit).

Given actual sales volume, flexible budgets provide a sensible standard for operating expenses. Of course, their price or quantity may still vary even from a flexed budget.

To analyse the difference between actual profit and budget, one can combine price and quantity variances for sales, materials and labour, with overhead spending variances.

It is often useful also to set budgets for balance sheet items, such as stocks and debtors, and analyse variances.

---

## 9.7 **Review questions**

1 What is the benefit of variance analysis?

2 What are the two variances that comprise the sales variance? (Ignore the mix variance.)

3 What is a flexible budget? What is its purpose?

4 Why are volume variances calculated by using budgeted prices (rather than actual prices)?

5 What are the two variances that comprise:
   (a) material expense variances;
   (b) direct labour expense variance?

6 Why is there only one variance identified for:
   (a) fixed overhead (for marginal costing system);
   (b) variable overhead?

7 Why are there two fixed overhead variances for standard costing systems?

8 List the eight variances which together comprise the profit variance for a marginal costing system. How do these variances differ when analysing the profit variance for a standard costing system?

9 What variances, other than sales, operating expense and profit variances, might be worth calculating?

10 Does a thorough analysis of variances guarantee good business performance? If not, why not?

To maximize learning, please *write out* your answers on a separate sheet of paper. *Then* check with the answers in Appendix C, pp. 246–7.

## 9.8 **Problems**

**1**  Smith and Son Ltd budget to sell 6000 units during September at a price of £4.80 per unit. Actual sales revenue in September from selling 6400 units is £28 160.

*Questions*

(a)  What is the total sales variance for September?
(b)  Analyse the total sales variance between volume variance and price variance.

(See solution in Appendix C, p. 247.)

**2**  Monty and Winston Ltd budgeted sales revenue in 1992 at £1 800 000, variable expenses at £1 200 000 and operating profit at £175 000. Actual sales revenue was only £1 475 000 even though selling prices were 10% higher than budgeted.

*Questions*

(a)  Prepare a flexible budget for 1992.
(b)  Analyse the variances, as far as possible.
(c)  As the general manager, what use would you make of the calculated variances?

(See solution in Appendix C, pp. 247–8.)

**3**  Mr Horwood has a small workshop at the back of his house, where he employs three people making bedside cabinets. They each work for 40 hours a week, at a wage of £4.00 per hour. It takes four working hours to produce a cabinet, which sells for £32.00 and contains £5.60 worth of timber. Heating, rent, rates, etc., normally average £100 per week.

One weekend, one of the workers catches 'flu and is away for the whole of the next week. He receives no pay for that week. The other two workers work six hours overtime each, for which they are paid at 'time and a half'. They manage to produce 25 cabinets between them, but due to haste they use 10% more material than usual. Also, the timber price has risen by 20%. The weather is extremely cold that week, so the bill for overheads rises to £120 because of additional heating for longer hours.

*Questions*

(a)  Calculate the budgeted profit for the week.
(b)  Calculate the actual profit or loss for the week.
(c)  Prepare a statement explaining the difference between the actual financial result for the week and the budget. Distinguish between: (i) quantity differences; and (ii) price differences.

**4**  Karl Klem (Mainz) GmbH produces two models of cuckoo clock. The company's budget for 1992 was as follows:

|  | Bigbird | Sparrow | Total |
|---|---|---|---|
| Selling price each | DM 60 | DM 25 | |
| Sales quantities | 2000 | 8000 | |
|  | | (DM '000s) | |
| Sales revenue | 120 | 200 | 320 |
| Variable cost of sales | 60 | 160 | 220 |
| Contribution | 60 | 40 | 100 |

The actual figures for 1992 were as follows:

|  | Bigbird | Sparrow | Total |
|---|---|---|---|
| Sales quantities | 1800 | 9000 | |
|  | | (DM '000s) | |
| Sales revenue | 90 | 240 | 330 |
| Variable cost of sales | 50 | 185 | 235 |
| Contribution | 40 | 55 | 95 |

*Question*
Account for the drop in contribution between budget and actual.

**5**  Power Chain Ltd operates two small factories at Dudley and Wolverhampton in the West Midlands, each employing 100 people in production of bicycle chains. All employees work for 150 hours a month, at a wage rate of £8.00 per hour, each producing on average 10 chains per hour. Material costs amount to 60p per chain, and Power Chain normally sells 300 000 chains a month, for £2.40 each, mainly to bicycle manufacturers. Fixed costs are budgeted at £180 000 a month.

A dispute about working conditions closes the Dudley factory for the month of November, and all 100 Dudley production workers are laid off and receive no pay for that month. Fixed costs, however, fall by only £16 000. The 100 Wolverhampton workers are able to increase their productivity so that in November they actually produce 200 000 chains, all of which are sold at the usual price. They are rewarded by a productivity bonus amounting to 25% of their normal wages. Thanks to a nearby metal manufacturer going bankrupt, Power Chain Ltd is able to buy materials for the month at a discount of 20% off the normal cost.

*Questions*

(a) Calculate Power Chain's actual profit (or loss) for November.
(b) Prepare a table showing the difference between the actual result and the original budgeted contribution and profit for the month.
(c) Compare the actual result with a flexible budget, showing what the expenses 'should have been' at the actual volume of sales.
(d) Split the total labour cost variance for November between the difference due to efficiency (volume) and that due to rates of pay.
(e) Summarize all the variances to explain

the difference between the originally budgeted profit and actual profit.

**6** The budgeted and actual results of Leroy's Linoleum Ltd for the month of November 1992 are shown below:

|  | Budget (£'000s) | Actual (£'000s) |
|---|---|---|
| Sales | 400 | 414 |
| Cost of goods sold: |  |  |
| Labour | 100 | 109 |
| Material | 125 | 156 |
| Mfg. overhead | 80 | 82 |
|  | 305 | 347 |
| Gross profit | 95 | 67 |
| Selling and general overhead | 70 | 74 |
| Profit before tax | 25 | (7) |

The actual product sales mix was the same as budgeted, but actual selling prices were 10% below budget. Budgeted volume was 100 000 square metres. Labour rates remained as budgeted but material prices had increased by 4%.

Manufacturing overhead was reckoned to be 75% fixed and 25% variable. Actual fixed manufacturing overhead was £63 000.

Selling and general overhead was reckoned to be 90% fixed and 10% variable. Actual fixed selling and general overhead was £64 000.

*Question*
Calculate and list the variances which account for the difference between budgeted profit and actual profit. (You may show the variances *either* for a marginal costing system *or* for a full costing system.)

(The solutions to Problems 3–6 will be provided in the *Instructors' Manual*.)

CHAPTER **10** *Presenting reports*

---

10.1 **Introduction**

10.1.1 **A two-way process**

Once upon a time a business school teacher had to miss the last class session of term. In order not to deprive the students of his wisdom, he recorded a review lecture, in the course of which his tape-recorder solemnly uttered the assertion: 'Communication is a two-way process.' At any rate it ought to be; but too often (as on this occasion) it is not.

We have seen that meaningful budgets imply neither being imposed 'top-down' nor just emerging 'bottom-up'. Instead, there is normally a back-and-forth process of negotiation (see Figure 10.1). This is to encourage commitment from below, and acceptance of budget goals as adequate, from above. (Top management commitment to the budget process is perhaps most important of all.)

Management reports tell a story; but not everyone in the audience always understands the meaning. Rather like the oral epics of old, or children's favourite bedtime stories, they take place in a familiar framework. But, unlike them, the details of management reports change from month to month, from one 'telling' to the next; and they may contain a few surprises. It is common experience that children will sternly correct any incautious narrator who tries in the smallest particular to modify a favourite story!

Still, the stories in management reports should not unfold like detective novels in which it is only in the last chapter that the sleuth summons up what modesty or vanity he or she thinks suitable and explains to the survivors assembled in the library how to unravel the plot. The aim of management reports is to be clear, to make the story easy to follow, to allow readers to see the wood as well as the trees. Even repeating key points may be in order.

Readers should be keeping up with the story as it unfolds. The preparer of reports should be trying to anticipate a reader's reactions and questions, and answering them in the report itself; trying to help the readers in language they can follow, not bamboozle them with pseudo-scientific jargon. Acronyms, for example, should be used only with great care. They can save plenty of space, which is a definite advantage; but

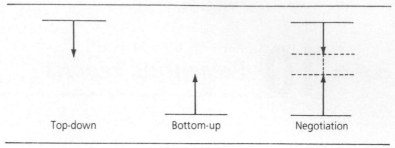

| Top-down | Bottom-up | Negotiation |

Figure 10.1 *Approaches to setting budgets*

if readers do not know what they stand for, that is rather a serious drawback!

Internal management reports are often regular and routine; for example, every month or once a quarter. Clearly, their formats should not change without good reason, and definitions of terms should be consistent over time. (Indeed, a glossary of key terms used, along with acronyms, once a year might be useful, to inform new readers and remind old ones.)

Laudable attempts to avoid over-complexity may risk leading to over-simplification instead. Sometimes a footnote may be useful to warn readers; for example, that last year contained 53, not 52, weeks. One of the problems in preparing internal reports can be that different readers may have very unequal levels of understanding. Thus, what is needless repetition to experts may constitute an easy-to-follow and helpful summary reminder for others.

In general, it is probably best to keep things as simple as possible, and not to assume too much expertise on the part of readers. A little repetition does not do much harm, whereas trying to build on a foundation of ignorance is always a mistake.

**10.1.2 Different approaches**

Sometimes management reports can simply use a few words: 'At the half-way stage, both income and spending are almost exactly in line with budget.' This brief sentence may, in fact, imply some quite complex facts: for example, that (as expected) less than half the year's budgeted income has been received in the first six months. If the budget is not formally phased over the year (as, in simpler cases, it may not be), it is possible for words to be more accurate in conveying meaning than 'precise' numbers could be.

In more complex cases, however, numbers may be very useful in reporting actual results against budget (possibly against a flexed budget — see section 9.3.1), in reporting percentage changes, and so on. Indeed, this is the normal way to produce management reports — in tables of numbers using a standard format, often comparing two sets of numbers. The usual profit and loss account, balance sheet and cash flow statement, too, consist of numerical amounts in standard formats.

Sometimes pictures can be helpful in giving a graphic impression, perhaps of trends over a period of time (maybe years, maybe months). Colours can also help: in some companies' annual reports the graphics are almost works of art! And often combining two methods can be even more effective; a picture with relevant numbers underneath, for example, or a table followed by a sentence summing up its key meaning.

Different people may find it easier to understand different kinds of communication — hence, variety may be useful. One finance textbook uses *four* different approaches: words, algebra, diagrams and numerical examples.

## 10.2 Tables

### 10.2.1 Degree of detail

It is common for internal reports to use excessive detail and to report numbers with far too many digits. This may also apply to external accounts: as recently as 1975, for example, General Motors Corporation, the largest manufacturing company in the world, published its annual accounts to the nearest dollar. (In 1951, R.J. Reynolds Tobacco's financial statements actually reported to the nearest cent!)

As a general rule, the first two significant digits of a number may matter, the rest will not. There may be a third digit to avoid needlessly crude rounding, or because reports may contain numbers of different magnitude. But more than three significant digits is probably too many.

There are two main reasons for avoiding excessive detail. The first is to avoid spurious accuracy — the pretence that the numbers are precisely accurate. General Motors' 1975 accounts were almost certainly not accurate to the nearest $1 million, let alone the nearest $1. With many balance-of-payments statistics, one is even unsure whether there was a surplus or a deficit, never mind any of the *numbers*.

The second reason is for ease of communication. Even if the figures were precisely accurate, it would not matter. Readers hardly ever require so much detail: instead, they need to take in quickly the rough order of magnitude, the key relationships, the essential trends. But this is much simpler with only two or three digits than with seven or eight. And simple mental arithmetic is much easier with only two or three digits than with more.

Table 10.1 portrays an internal management report with far too much detail. A British subsidiary of an American parent company was proud of this, as an example of *good* reporting (Cekal Ltd is a disguised name).

The report for Cekal Ltd contains 35 rows and 12 columns (6 money,

Table 10.1 Original income statement for Cekal Ltd

**Cekal Limited — Income Statement — Pounds Sterling**

| | Month of JUNE 1988 | | | | | | 9 Months to JUNE 1988 | | | | | |
| | Budget | | Actual | | | | Budget | | Actual | | | |
| | This year | % | This year | % | Last year | % | This year | % | This year | % | Last year | % |
|---|---|---|---|---|---|---|---|---|---|---|---|---|
| Total gross sales | 3 615 842 | | 4 193 632 | | 3 373 970 | | 35 843 052 | | 38 052 168 | | 29 308 975 | |
| Vol disc. | 39 842 | | 41 986 | | 45 400 | | 469 752 | | 479 735 | | 444 502 | |
| Gross sales | 3 576 000 | | 4 151 646 | | 3 328 570 | | 35 378 300 | | 37 572 433 | | 28 864 473 | |
| Less: Cash discount | 88 300 | | 109 889 | | 65 179 | | 700 900 | | 748 976 | | 544 060 | |
| Net sales | 3 487 700 | 100.0 | 4 041 757 | 100.0 | 3 263 391 | 100.0 | 34 677 400 | 100.0 | 36 823 457 | 100.0 | 28 320 413 | 100.0 |
| Less: Standard cost | 1 682 400 | 48.2 | 2 049 231 | 50.7 | 1 651 154 | 50.6 | 17 585 400 | 50.7 | 19 365 403 | 52.6 | 14 247 491 | 50.3 |
| Variances | 781 400 | 22.4 | 597 041 | 14.8 | 735 634 | 22.6 | 6 391 200 | 18.4 | 4 951 967 | 13.4 | 5 606 185 | 19.8 |
| Service labour | 68 700 | 1.9 | 74 351 | 1.8 | 55 735 | 1.7 | 468 000 | 1.4 | 473 493 | 1.3 | 373 129 | 1.3 |
| Free of charge | 38 400 | 1.1 | 32 779 | 0.8 | 54 999 | 1.7 | 209 600 | 0.6 | 183 708 | 0.5 | 187 378 | 0.6 |
| Other costs | 15 500 | 0.5 | 35 305 | 0.9 | 23 658 | 0.7 | 141 900 | 0.4 | 587 341 | 1.6 | 354 522 | 1.3 |
| Inter-co. contrib. | (351 000) | (10.0) | (227 088) | (5.6) | (285 581) | (8.8) | (2 865 000) | (8.3) | (2 260 950) | (6.1) | (2 828 234) | (10.0) |
| Total cost of sales | 2 235 400 | 64.1 | 2 561 629 | 63.4 | 2 235 599 | 68.5 | 21 931 100 | 63.2 | 23 300 962 | 63.3 | 17 940 471 | 63.3 |
| Manufacturing margin | 1 252 300 | 35.9 | 1 480 128 | 36.6 | 1 027 792 | 31.5 | 12 746 300 | 36.8 | 13 522 495 | 36.7 | 10 379 942 | 36.7 |
| Direct sales | 85 300 | 2.5 | 81 661 | 2.0 | 63 215 | 1.9 | 729 500 | 2.1 | 687 289 | 1.9 | 590 094 | 2.1 |
| Promotion | 141 100 | 4.1 | 241 122 | 6.0 | 141 959 | 4.4 | 1 849 300 | 5.3 | 1 999 408 | 5.4 | 1 287 941 | 4.5 |
| Service operations | 92 300 | 2.6 | 90 004 | 2.2 | 66 809 | 2.0 | 743 300 | 2.2 | 714 534 | 2.0 | 591 179 | 2.1 |
| Other marketing | 52 300 | 1.5 | 55 143 | 1.4 | 36 266 | 1.1 | 422 200 | 1.2 | 447 682 | 1.2 | 322 328 | 1.1 |
| Product distribution | 130 400 | 3.7 | 116 120 | 2.9 | 103 427 | 3.2 | 1 077 600 | 3.1 | 1 031 417 | 2.8 | 929 849 | 3.3 |
| Data processing | 60 200 | 1.7 | 57 193 | 1.4 | 47 553 | 1.5 | 511 400 | 1.5 | 484 857 | 1.3 | 455 452 | 1.6 |

Table 10.1 (continued)

**Cekal Limited** — Income Statement — Pounds Sterling

| | Budget | | Month of JUNE 1988 Actual | | Actual | | Budget | | 9 Months to JUNE 1988 Actual | | Actual | |
| --- | --- | --- | --- | --- | --- | --- | --- | --- | --- | --- | --- | --- |
| | This year | % | This year | % | Last year | % | This year | % | This year | % | Last year | % |
| Total selling expenses | 561 600 | 16.1 | 641 243 | 15.9 | 459 229 | 14.1 | 5 333 300 | 15.4 | 5 365 187 | 14.6 | 4 176 843 | 14.7 |
| Admin. and general | 273 700 | 7.8 | 438 457 | 10.8 | 239 710 | 7.3 | 2 228 800 | 6.4 | 2 402 034 | 6.5 | 2 042 701 | 7.2 |
| Develop. engineering | 88 900 | 2.6 | 79 147 | 1.9 | 74 155 | 2.3 | 760 400 | 2.2 | 690 227 | 1.9 | 641 418 | 2.3 |
| Parent service fee | 23 700 | 0.7 | 27 500 | 0.7 | 22 200 | 0.7 | 235 800 | 0.7 | 249 924 | 0.7 | 192 588 | 0.7 |
| Loan interest | 25 000 | 0.7 | (42 000) | (1.0) | 30 000 | 0.9 | 311 000 | 0.9 | 1 538 | — | 619 045 | 2.2 |
| Inter-co. contribution | 972 900 | 27.9 | 1 144 347 | 28.3 | 825 294 | 25.3 | 8 869 300 | 25.6 | 8 708 928 | 23.7 | 7 672 595 | 27.1 |
| | (149 700) | (4.3) | (174 532) | (4.3) | (125 201) | (3.8) | (1 279 400) | (3.7) | (1 125 346) | (3.1) | (1 281 159) | (4.5) |
| Total expenses | 823 200 | 23.6 | 969 815 | 24.0 | 700 093 | 21.5 | 7 589 900 | 21.9 | 7 583 582 | 20.6 | 6 391 436 | 22.6 |
| Operating income | 429 100 | 12.3 | 510 313 | 12.6 | 327 699 | 10.0 | 5 156 400 | 14.9 | 5 938 913 | 16.1 | 3 988 506 | 14.1 |
| I/Co. Gross margin | 68 700 | 2.0 | 208 697 | 5.1 | 176 155 | 5.4 | 1 313 600 | 3.8 | 1 476 671 | 4.0 | 1 370 820 | 4.8 |
| I/Co. Expenses | (149 700) | (4.3) | (174 532) | (4.3) | (125 201) | (3.8) | (1 279 400) | (3.7) | (1 125 346) | (3.1) | (1 281 159) | (4.5) |
| I/Co. Profit | (81 000) | (2.3) | 34 165 | 0.8 | 50 954 | 1.6 | 34 200 | 0.1 | 351 325 | 0.9 | 89 661 | 0.3 |
| Other income | 1 900 | — | 6 766 | 0.2 | (48 120) | (1.5) | 9 400 | — | 24 017 | 0.1 | 3 152 | — |
| Income before taxes | 350 000 | 10.0 | 551 244 | 13.6 | 330 533 | 10.1 | 5 200 000 | 15.0 | 6 314 255 | 17.1 | 4 081 319 | 14.4 |
| Less: Taxes on income | 185 500 | 5.3 | 272 100 | 6.7 | 175 000 | 5.3 | 2 756 000 | 8.0 | 3 159 912 | 8.6 | 2 163 205 | 7.6 |
| Net income | 164 500 | 4.7 | 279 144 | 6.9 | 155 533 | 4.8 | 2 444 000 | 7.0 | 3 144 343 | 8.5 | 1 918 114 | 6.8 |

6 percentages). The money columns contain up to 8 digits each; hence, Standard Costs, for example, contains 63 digits in a single row! This is surely too much for the eye to take in. This single page contains over 1300 money digits and over 400 percentage digits. (The original actually contained another 12 rows and about 350 more digits, dealing with the appropriation of net income.)

Table 10.2 sets out a revised version of Cekal Ltd's income statement, with only 14 rows and 8 columns. (It shows only three key items for 'last year', in a separate box.) No money column contains more than 3 digits. The result is to eliminate 90% of the money digits and 70% of the percentage digits. Even this revised report has a lot of detail. Might it somehow be possible to combine the inter-company rows? Do readers really need to see the rows for tax and net income after tax?

It might also be useful to append a sentence or two containing the key messages, for example:

Table 10.2 *Revised income statement for Cekal Ltd*

| Cekal Limited | | | Income Statement | | | | £ million |
|---|---|---|---|---|---|---|---|
| | Month of June 1988 | | | | 9 Months to June 1988 | | |
| | Budget | | Actual | | Budget | | Actual | |
| | (£m) | (%) | (£m) | (%) | (£m) | (%) | (£m) | (%) |
| Net sales | 3.49 | 100 | 4.04 | 100 | 34.7 | 100 | 36.8 | 100 |
| Standard cost | 1.68 | 48 | 2.05 | 51 | 17.6 | 50 | 19.4 | 53 |
| Variances | 0.78 | 22 | 0.60 | 15 | 6.4 | 18 | 5.0 | 13 |
| Other costs | 0.13 | 4 | 0.14 | 3 | 0.8 | 3 | 1.2 | 3 |
| (Inter-company) | (0.35) | (10) | (0.23) | (6) | (2.8) | (8) | (2.3) | (6) |
| Manufacturing margin | 1.25 | 36 | 1.48 | 37 | 12.7 | 37 | 13.5 | 37 |
| Selling expenses | 0.56 | 16 | 0.64 | 16 | 5.3 | 15 | 5.4 | 15 |
| Admin. and general, etc. | 0.41 | 12 | 0.50 | 12 | 3.5 | 10 | 3.3 | 9 |
| (Inter-company) | (0.15) | (4) | (0.17) | (4) | (1.3) | (3) | (1.1) | (3) |
| Operating income | 0.43 | 12 | 0.51 | 13 | 5.2 | 15 | 5.9 | 16 |
| Inter-company net | (0.08) | (2) | 0.04 | 1 | — | — | 0.4 | 1 |
| Income before tax | 0.35 | 10 | 0.55 | 14 | 5.2 | 15 | 6.3 | 17 |
| Tax | 0.19 | 5 | 0.27 | 7 | 2.8 | 8 | 3.2 | 9 |
| Net income | 0.16 | 5 | 0.28 | 7 | 2.4 | 7 | 3.1 | 8 |
| | | | Last year | | | | Last year | |
| Net sales | | | 3.26 | 100 | | | 28.3 | 100 |
| Manufacturing margin | | | 1.03 | 32 | | | 10.4 | 37 |
| Operating income | | | 0.33 | 10 | | | 4.0 | 14 |

In June, sales were 6% up on budget; profit margin improved slightly, so operating income was 19% up on budget. Over the 9 months to June, both sales and manufacturing margin were 6% up on budget; and both were 30% up on last year. Expenses fell slightly, so operating income was 14% up on budget (48% up on last year).

As well as comparing actual past performance with budget (and perhaps with last year, too), reports may usefully provide latest forecasts for the current year's outcome. If required, extra schedules can give more details, rather than trying to cram too much on to a single sheet. It is important for the links between reports at different levels of the business to be explicit. This enables managers to pursue items in more detail if they want, and avoids gaps in the system of responsibility accounting.

Budgets should be simple and easy to read, which implies not too much detail. Filling reports with trivial items obscures what really matters, and risks wasting the time of both preparers and users. Modern data-processing equipment can produce almost infinite facts about perform-ance; but control reports should focus on what is significant. In particular, this means not including in every monthly report items which 'might come in useful' once every five years. Signalling only important exceptions from an agreed standard can restrict needless detail, but requires judgement.

## 10.2.2 Layout

Tables often try to convey excessive information. As we have seen, they may contain too many rows, too many columns, too many digits. Also, the layout may not help the reader as much as it could.

For example, consider Table 10.3 comparing Allied and Axis air strength during World War Two (Kennedy, 1988). This table contains 287 digits. The text points out that the mere numbers considerably over-simplify the picture. The Allied superiority was even more marked when the

Table 10.3 *Aircraft production of the Allied and Axis powers, 1939–1945*

|                      | 1939   | 1940   | 1941   | 1942    | 1943    | 1944    | 1945   |
|----------------------|--------|--------|--------|---------|---------|---------|--------|
| United States        | 5 856  | 12 804 | 26 277 | 47 836  | 85 898  | 96 318  | 49 761 |
| USSR                 | 10 382 | 10 565 | 15 735 | 25 436  | 34 900  | 40 300  | 20 900 |
| Britain              | 7 940  | 15 049 | 20 094 | 23 672  | 26 263  | 26 461  | 12 070 |
| British Commonwealth | 250    | 1 100  | 2 600  | 4 575   | 4 700   | 4 575   | 2 075  |
| Total Allies         | 24 178 | 39 518 | 64 706 | 101 519 | 151 761 | 167 654 | 84 806 |
| Germany              | 8 295  | 10 247 | 11 776 | 15 409  | 24 807  | 39 807  | 7 540  |
| Japan                | 4 467  | 4 768  | 5 088  | 8 861   | 16 693  | 28 180  | 11 066 |
| Italy                | 1 800  | 1 800  | 2 400  | 2 400   | 1 600   | —       | —      |
| Total Axis           | 14 562 | 16 815 | 19 264 | 26 670  | 43 100  | 67 987  | 18 606 |

Table 10.4 *An alternative presentation for aircraft production, 1939–1945*

| '000 aircraft | US | USSR | UK | ** | **Total Allies** | Germany | Japan | Italy | **Total Axis** |
|---|---|---|---|---|---|---|---|---|---|
| 1939 | 6 | 10 | 8 | — | **24** | 8 | 4 | 2 | **14** |
| 1940 | 13 | 11 | 15 | 1 | **40** | 10 | 5 | 2 | **17** |
| 1941 | 26 | 16 | 20 | 3 | **65** | 12 | 5 | 2 | **19** |
| 1942 | 48 | 25 | 24 | 5 | **102** | 15 | 9 | 3 | **27** |
| 1943 | 86 | 35 | 26 | 5 | **152** | 25 | 17 | 1 | **43** |
| 1944 | 96 | 40 | 27 | 5 | **168** | 40 | 28 | — | **68** |
| 1945 | 50 | 21 | 12 | 2 | **85** | 8 | 11 | — | **19** |
| Annual average | 47 | 22 | 19 | 3 | **91** | 17 | 11 | 2 | **30** |

The Allies produced three times as many aircraft as the Axis

*Note:* ** Commonwealth production.

number of engines, or the structure weight of the aircraft, was compared with the Axis totals. Moreover, the Allies were producing many newer types of aircraft. So, reporting the numbers to the nearest single aircraft serves little point, especially since they are unlikely to be anything like that accurate.

Table 10.4 shows an alternative layout. Transposing columns and rows, rounding the numbers, adding averages for each column, and a sentence underneath the table — 'The Allies produced three times as many aircraft as the Axis' — all these help to communicate the message that the detail in the original table rather obscures. This effect is all too common in management accounting reports. Despite 16 extra digits for the 'average' row at the foot, the revised table contains 58% fewer digits, without losing any important meaning. Indeed, the new version is easier to understand.

Ehrenberg (1982) recommends a slight reduction in the size of tables containing mainly figures. He also suggests occasional regular gaps, perhaps every five lines, to help guide the eye — *not* gridlines (which, by the way, the original version of Table 10.1 contained in profusion).

## 10.3 Pictures

### 10.3.1 Types of picture

A picture is said to be worth a thousand words; but perhaps it is not worth quite so many numbers. Compared with tables, which can go into a good deal of detail, pictures can usually give only a general impression. Still, management reports may often use graphical presentation to convey messages effectively. Again, though, a few words of text may usefully support the picture.

There are three main types of picture, each with variants: pie-chart; bar-chart; and graph.

Pie-charts can give a general view of orders of magnitude, splitting

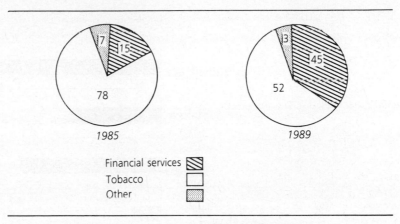

Figure 10.2 *BAT Industries: split of trading profit, 1985 and 1989*

a whole (e.g. annual sales revenue) into parts (e.g. areas of the world or product groups). Comparing two pie-charts over time can be very effective for periods as much as five or ten years apart, where there have been striking changes. To compare two or more pie-charts, the order of items needs to be the same, and any colour coding should be consistent. Opinions differ on whether the size of the pie should vary; but (subject to proper treatment of inflation's effects) we see no reason why not. It is probably better to see the full face of the pipe, rather than look at it obliquely (see Figure 10.2).

Bar-charts can be vertical (also called histograms) or horizontal. Expert opinion seems to be that horizontal bar-charts, though probably less common, are more effective. This may be because they are easier to label directly in a legible way. Segmented bar-charts can be hard to follow; and (as always) it can be tempting to try to convey too much information in a single bar-chart (see Figure 10.3).

Graphs are common, but again can give only a general impression. For instance, Figure 10.4 shows real interest rates between 1963 and 1989. The early norm seems to be just under 3% (a year); after some volatility, the interest rate becomes sharply negative in 1975; after which it climbs to around 6%, and stays around that level, with drops to 3% in 1980 and 1987. This is quite a lot of information to be conveyed by a single picture.

10.3.2 **Scales**

With vertical bar-charts, failure to start the vertical scale at zero can give a very misleading impression as Figure 10.5 illustrates. This chart, from Tesco's 1990 annual report, purports to show annual sales revenue (excluding VAT) per employee between 1986 and 1990. It combines two serious errors. First, the vertical scale starts at annual sales of £75 000

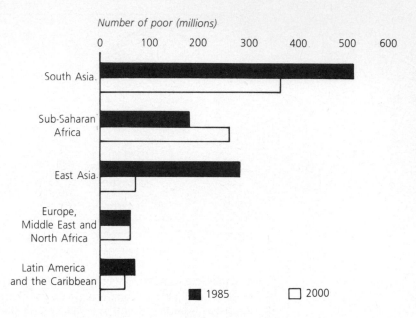

Figure 10.3 *Poverty in the developing world, 1985 and 2000*

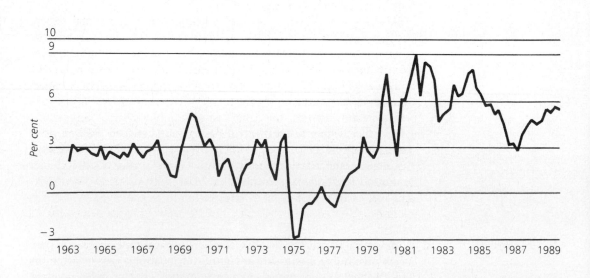

Figure 10.4 *Real interest rates, 1963–1989*

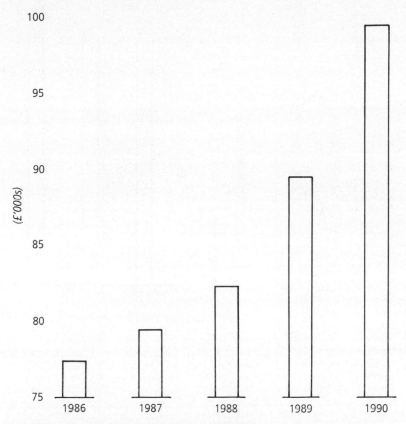

Figure 10.5 *Tesco: sales per employee (as published)*

per employee (rising to £100 000), instead of starting at zero. Thus, the increase between 1986 and 1990 from £77.2k to £99.4k (29%) *looks* like an increase from £2.2k to £24.4k (1000%). That is the general impression the eye receives from the chart.

Second, because the numbers are in money terms, they fail to allow for inflation of 22% over the period (about three-quarters of the increase). We are left with a *real* increase between 1986 and 1990 of just over 5% (average 1¼% a year), compared with the graphical impression of an increase of 1000% (average 80% a year).

A revised bar-chart (see Figure 10.6) is no doubt much less impressive, but much more truthful.

Figure 10.7 shows graphs portraying two demand curves (A) and (B). Which is more price-elastic? Answer: the demand curves shown in (A) and (B) are equally price-elastic, since they portray exactly the same position. But the scales are different, and potentially misleading to the eye. It will be evident that, unless one is very careful, it is possible for

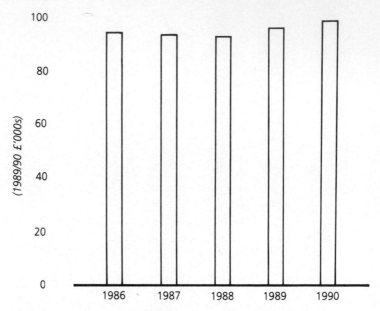

Figure 10.6 *Tesco: sales per employee (constant 1989/90 £s)*

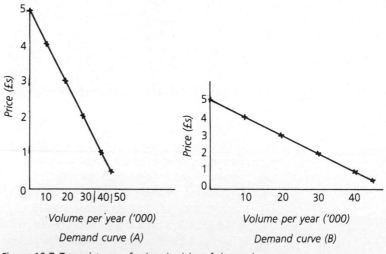

Figure 10.7 *Two pictures of price-elasticity of demand*

graphs to give a quite misleading impression, even if that is not intended (and sometimes, perhaps, it may be).

Log scales may be used when the rate of change is the point at issue; for instance, the fall in the purchasing power of the pound between 1965

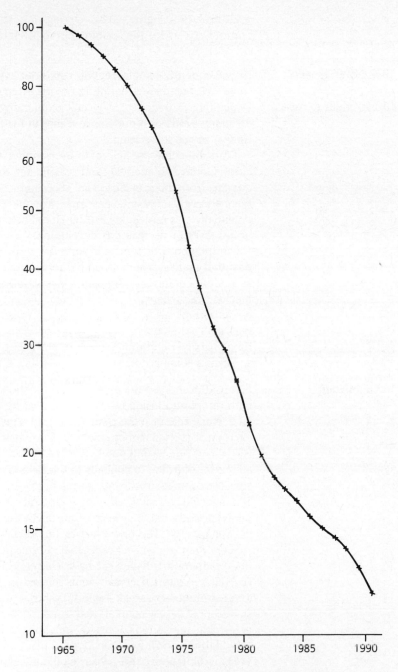

Figure 10.8 *The fall in the pound's purchasing power, 1965–1990*

and 1990 (see Figure 10.8). Or log–log scales may sometimes be appropriate, as for the learning curve in Figure 2.4 (p. 24).

## 10.4 Other aspects

### 10.4.1 Periods to cover

How frequently should reports come out? What period should they cover? Management accounting reports often come out once a month. Depending on their nature, weekly or quarterly may be appropriate but, for many kinds of report, once a month (or perhaps once every four weeks) seems to be usual.

It can sometimes be helpful to use running annual totals, adding the latest month (or quarter), and leaving off the equivalent month (or quarter) from the previous year. This can be especially valuable where there are regular seasonal patterns. (Irregular patterns, of course, could potentially give misleading results.) It can help pinpoint whether a trend of increases or decreases is developing.

The frequency of control reports depends on the importance of the data and management's potential for taking corrective or other action as a result. For instance, frequent news about sales and production levels may be vital; whereas rent or top management salaries (which may both be important also) need much less frequent attention. Swamping managers with too much information risks leaving them with not enough time to analyse and understand. In producing reports, it may be worth sacrificing some accuracy — often not that much — for speed.

### 10.4.2 Inflation

Figure 10.8 showed the extent of UK inflation between 1965 and 1990; with the pound losing 88% of its purchasing power in that period, at an average rate of more than 8% a year. This obviously has a serious effect on all sorts of money amounts. The easiest way to allow for inflation is constant purchasing power (CPP) accounting, which indexes money amounts according to changes in the Retail Prices Index. This permits sensible comparisons in real terms over a number of years, as Figure 10.6 showed. Usually, all money amounts are translated into end-of-period pounds; but, in principle, one might choose other base dates (such as January 1987, the base date for the Retail Prices Index).

Many management reports cover shorter periods; but even within a one-year period, inflation can have a big effect on conventional historical cost (HC) accounts. The main items affected are fixed assets, depreciation, and net monetary assets. Table 10.5 shows, on a CPP basis, the under-statement of depreciation of fixed assets in HC accounts where real assets are stable, at various rates of inflation and for various asset lives (Myddelton, 1984). For much typical plant and equipment, a life of 15 years and inflation of 8% a year, would mean understating depreciation by about 75%. For some companies this is significant: it would increase ICI's HC depreciation by over £400 million a year, for example, or more than half 1990's reported after-tax profits.

Table 10.5 *Understatement of historical cost depreciation, on a CPP basis*

| Life (years) | Inflation rate per year | | | | | |
| --- | --- | --- | --- | --- | --- | --- |
| | 2% | 5% | 8% | 10% | 12% | 15% |
| 5 | 6.1 | 15.5 | 25.2 | 31.9 | 38.7 | 49.2 |
| 10 | 11.3 | 29.5 | 49.0 | 62.7 | 77.0 | 99.3 |
| 15 | 16.7 | 44.5 | 75.2 | 97.2 | 120.2 | 156.5 |
| 20 | 22.3 | 60.5 | 103.7 | 134.9 | 167.8 | 219.5 |
| 25 | 28.1 | 77.4 | 134.2 | 175.4 | 218.8 | 286.8 |
| 30 | 34.0 | 95.2 | 166.5 | 218.2 | 272.4 | 356.9 |
| 40 | 46.2 | 133.1 | 235.4 | 309.0 | 385.2 | 502.2 |
| 50 | 59.1 | 173.9 | 308.7 | 404.3 | 502.1 | 651.4 |

The principle is similar for current cost accounting (CCA), another approach to adjusting HC accounts to allow for inflation. (Where CPP challenges the use of money as the unit of account, CCA challenges the use of historical costs.) But CCA uses specific indices for particular kinds of assets, whereas CPP uses the Retail Prices Index for all adjustments.

## 10.5 Chapter summary

Communication is a two-way process. A process of negotiation normally precedes agreement on an annual budget. The aim of management reports is to be clear, to make the story easy to follow. Different readers may not all have the same level of understanding. Combining two or more methods can be effective: words, tables, pictures.

As a rule, only the first two significant digits of a number are likely to matter. Two reasons for avoiding excessive detail are: to avoid spurious accuracy, and for ease of communication. Cutting out surplus digits, and reducing the number of separate items reported, can make tables much easier to read. It can also help to show averages for each column; and to add a sentence or two underneath a table to emphasize key messages.

Three main types of picture are: pie-charts, bar-charts and graphs. Horizontal bar-charts are easier to label directly. It is important for the scale to be both explicit and appropriate, otherwise (wittingly or not) pictures can mislead the eye, and hence the brain. Log scales may be suitable when portraying rates of change over time.

Many management reports appear once a month, though weekly or quarterly may be more suitable for different kinds of information. Cumulative annual totals can help pin-point movements in trends. Indexing for inflation can help produce sensible comparisons over long periods of time; but even within a year, constant purchasing power accounting (or current cost accounting) can make a big difference to fixed assets and depreciation.

## 10.6 **Review questions**

1 How can budgets get commitment from subordinate managers?
2 What is a major aim of management reports?
3 Name one advantage and one disadvantage of acronyms.
4 Why may repetition in reports sometimes be desirable?
5 What might be the purpose of circulating once a year a glossary of key terms and acronyms?
6 Name two reasons for avoiding excessive detail.
7 Why should the links between reports at different levels of an organization be explicit?

8 What two suggestions by Ehrenberg were noted dealing with the layout of tables?
9 Name three main types of picture.
10 Why do experts suggest that horizontal bar-charts may be more effective than vertical ones?
11 How can an inappropriate vertical scale mislead the eye?
12 When may log scales be suitable for charts?
13 What criteria are appropriate for deciding on the frequency of management reports?
14 How can inflation affect conventional historical cost accounts?
15 How does constant purchasing power accounting allow for inflation?

To maximize learning, please *write out* your answers on a separate sheet of paper. *Then* check with the answers in Appendix C, p. 248.

## Practical exercise
Try to find ways to improve the presentation of one or more of your own organization's management reports.

# *Abbreviations*

| | | | | |
|---|---|---|---|---|
| ABC | = Activity-based costing | | NPV | = Net present value |
| B/E | = Breakeven | | NRV | = Net realizable value |
| C/B | = Cost benefit (analysis) | | NTV | = Net terminal value |
| CCA | = Current cost accounting | | P & L | = Profit & loss (account) |
| COGS | = Cost of goods sold | | plc | = Public limited company |
| CPP | = Constant purchasing power | | RI | = Residual income |
| CV | = Current value | | RM | = Raw materials |
| DCF | = Discounted cash flow | | ROI | = Return on investment |
| EOY | = End of year | | RONA | = Return on net assets |
| FC | = Fixed costs | | RPI | = Retail Prices Index |
| FG | = Finished goods | | SL | = Straight line |
| FIFO | = First in first out | | SSAP | = Statement of Standard Accounting Practice |
| HC | = Historical cost | | | |
| IRR | = Internal rate of return | | VC | = Variable cost |
| LIFO | = Last in first out | | WACC | = Weighted average cost of capital |
| Ltd | = Limited (company) | | wda | = Writing-down allowance |
| NBV | = Net book value | | WIP | = Work-in-progress |

# Glossary

**Absorbed overhead** Overhead costs which, by means of overhead absorption, are included in product costs.

**Accounts** Profit and loss account for a period, balance sheet at the end of that period, and notes to the accounts, together with the auditors' report.

**Activity-based costing (ABC)** A costing method which relates overhead costs to products via 'cost-drivers' (or activities) which are reckoned to cause particular overhead costs.

**Agency theory** A theory of the relationship between an agent and a principal, particularly concerning how to give the agent incentives to achieve the principal's goals, and how to monitor the agent's actions.

**Amortization** Depreciation, usually of an intangible fixed asset, or a wasting asset such as a mine.

**Apportionment** Allotment to two or more cost centres of shares of indirect costs, on the basis of estimated benefit received.

**Asset** Valuable resource owned by a business, acquired at a measurable money cost.

**Audit** External examination of financial accounts (and records and systems) by independent professional accountants, to report whether accounts give a true and fair view.

**Average accounting rate of return** One of four popular capital investment appraisal methods, which divides average annual accounting profit by the amount invested.

**Average cost** (a) Total cost of a product or process divided by the number of units produced. (b) Method of valuing stock.

**Balance sheet** Classified statement of financial position of a business, showing assets, liabilities and shareholders' funds at a particular date.

**Breakeven chart** Chart plotting fixed and variable costs and sales turnover against volume, showing profit or loss at different volumes, within a limited (relevant) range.

**Breakeven point** Volume of output (x) at which sales turnover (Sx) exactly equals total costs. Breakeven point (x units) occurs where sales turnover (Sx) = variable costs (Vx) + fixed costs (F). In other words, the breakeven volume equals fixed costs divided by contribution $(S-V)$ per unit.

**Budget** Financial or quantitative statement, agreed in advance by those responsible, reflecting the policies to be pursued during a period.

**Budgetary control** System requiring managers to accept responsibility for achieving budget commitments.

**By-product** Low-value output produced incidentally in process of making main product.

**Capacity cost** Fixed cost of providing given productive capacity for a period.

**Capital allowance** Tax equivalent of depreciation of fixed assets, calculated according to Inland Revenue rules (= writing-down allowance).

**Capital expenditure** Expenditure which the balance sheet treats as an asset, in contrast to revenue expenditure which the profit and loss account treats as an expense.

**Capitalize** To record expenditure as an asset, in contrast to writing it off as an expense.

**Carrying cost** Cost of carrying inventory (e.g. interest, storage, insurance, etc.).

**Cash flow** Cash receipts less cash payments, for a period.

**Common costs** Costs of producing more than one product, needing to be apportioned between them.

**Consistency** Principle in accounting, and other

statistics, of treating similar items in the same way, to produce meaningful results and to allow comparisons over time.

**Consolidated accounts** (= group accounts) Accounts for a group of companies, consolidated by combining the separate assets and liabilities of all subsidiaries with those of the holding (parent) company.

**Continuous budget** (= rolling budget) Budget kept constantly up to date by adding new period at end when dropping most recent period.

**Contribution** (= variable profit) Sales turnover minus variable costs is the contribution to fixed costs and profit.

**Control** Process of managing the present and near future. Often consists of comparing actual performance with budget, finding reasons for any variance, and taking action to improve matters.

**Controllable** Cost reckoned to be under the control of responsible manager, the extent perhaps depending on time period involved.

**Cost** Amount given up in exchange for goods or services received, usually either cash or a promise to pay cash in future (but see also opportunity cost). Accounts may treat either as an asset or as an expense. Often carries some further qualifying adjective (e.g. variable cost, historical cost, marginal cost, etc.).

**Cost accounting** Method of measuring costs of parts of a business, specific products, and so on.

**Cost–benefit analysis** Process of trying to assess how worthwhile something is where either costs or benefits are hard to measure in financial terms.

**Cost centre** Unit or operation in respect of which costs are determined.

**Cost-driver** A measure of specific business activity which is proportional to its associated overhead cost.

**Cost of capital** Risk-adjusted weighted average cost of the (marginal) after-tax costs of ordinary share capital and debt. The criterion rate of return for capital investment projects.

**Cost of goods sold (COGS)** Costs identifiable with stocks (e.g. raw materials, components, direct labour, production overheads) but excluding selling and administrative expenses.

**Criterion rate** Required rate of return on capital investment projects. See: Cost of capital.

**Critical resource** (= limiting factor, key factor)

**Current asset** Cash or any asset expected to be converted into cash, or consumed in the normal

course of business, within twelve months from the date of the balance sheet (e.g. stocks, debtors).

**Current liabilities** Amounts owing to others, expected to be paid within twelve months from date of balance sheet (e.g. creditors, bank overdraft).

**Current value** Current replacement cost or net realizable value of asset. Often only a hypothetical estimate, unlike historical cost which is usually a definite known fact.

**Depreciation** Process of writing off as an expense the cost (or valuation) of fixed asset to spread total cost (or valuation) over its economic life.

**Differential cost** (= incremental cost)

**Direct cost** Cost that is directly identifiable with process or product.

**Direct labour** Labour cost directly identifiable with production.

**Direct labour hour rate** Estimated total overhead costs attributable to a cost centre divided by appropriate number of direct labour hours for a period (either expected or standard), forming the basis for absorbing overheads.

**Discounted cash flow (DCF)** A means of coping with the time value of money, whereby future cash flows are discounted back to their present value by means of a suitable discount rate.

**Discount factor** The factor which reduces future cash flows to their present value (see Appendix B).

**Discount rate** The interest rate used in calculating present value.

**Discretionary cost** (= non-variable cost) Cost which does not vary directly with production, but which is not necessarily fixed either. A discretionary cost changes at management's discretion (e.g. training, advertising, research).

**Disinvestment** The process of disposing of assets, either as going concerns or otherwise.

**Economic life** Of fixed assets. May differ from physical life.

**Economies of scale** Reductions in average costs per unit arising from increase in scale (e.g. due to greater technical efficiency of larger plant sizes, spreading of fixed costs over more units, etc.).

**Effectiveness** Achievement of purpose.

**Efficiency** Technical relationship between inputs and outputs.

**Efficiency variance** (= quantity variance) Standard price for a resource multiplied by difference between budgeted and actual quantity.

**Engineered cost** Any cost that has an explicit, specified physical relationship with a selected measure of activity.

**Equivalent units** Notional number of completed units (e.g. 200 units, 75% completed, might be reckoned as equivalent to 150 completed units).

**Exception reporting** System of reporting only exceptions to budget or standard.

**Expected value** Result of weighting the value of various possible future outcomes by the estimated chance of each happening.

**Expenditure** Amount spent, may be either revenue (expense) or capital (asset).

**Expenditure variance** (= spending variance) Usually a price variance related to overhead.

**Expense** Amount written off against profit in respect of goods or services consumed in a period.

**Factory cost** Cost of production, comprising materials, direct labour and production overheads.

**Feedback** Link between planning and control; modification of an activity as a result of comparing actual result with budget.

**Financial accounting** External accounting, leading to published accounts for shareholders and other outsiders.

**Financial year** The twelve-month period for which a firm prepares financial accounts.

**Finished goods** Stocks of completed manufactured products available for sale.

**First in first out (FIFO)** Method of valuing stock, assuming stock in hand at end of period consists of most recent purchases.

**Fixed asset** Resource, either tangible or intangible, held to use in producing goods or services, not for sale in the normal course of business.

**Fixed cost** (= period cost) Cost which is fixed for a given period (within the relevant range of output).

**Flexible budget** (= variable budget) System of flexing budget when actual sales volume differs from original budget, so that variable costs in flexed budget represent expected amount at actual sales volume.

**Forecast** (= future estimate) Neutral term, implying nothing about desirability of, or commitment to, the result.

**Fringe benefits** Costs of employment other than direct wages or salaries (e.g. cost of motor vehicles provided, low-rate loans, etc.). May exclude employer's social security contributions.

**Full costing** (= absorption costing) Costing method which allocates direct costs and apportions indirect costs (overheads) to products or cost centres.

**Funds-flow statement** Accounting statement showing, for larger companies, sources and uses (applications) of funds for a period.

**Goal congruence** Compatibility of individual goals with overall goals of organization.

**Group accounts** (= consolidated accounts)

**Horizon** Point in future beyond which financial calculations are not made explicitly (though including a terminal value in capital project evaluation makes them implicitly).

**Hurdle rate** (= criterion rate)

**Idle time** Unproductive time, due to circumstances beyond worker's control.

**Imputed cost** (= notional cost)

**Incremental cash flows** Cash flows which occur as a result of action (for example, investing in capital project), but not otherwise.

**Incremental cost** (= differential cost) Cost incurred if certain action is undertaken, but not otherwise.

**Indirect cost** (= overhead cost) Cost not directly identifiable with product or cost centre; full costing apportions on some reasonable basis, marginal costing not at all.

**Inflation** Rise in the general average level of money prices, usually measured by the annual rate of increase in the Retail Prices Index.

**Intangible asset** Long-life non-tangible asset owned by a business, acquired at a measurable money cost, and not yet written off either against reserves or against profit (e.g. patent rights, goodwill).

**Interest** Compensation for borrowing or lending (money) for a period of time, comprising (a) pure time-preference, (b) inflation premium, and (c) risk premium.

**Interim accounts** Financial accounts not subject to audit, covering a period less than twelve months.

**Internal rate of return (IRR)** That discount rate which, for a capital project, produces a net present value of zero.

**Inventory** (= stock)

**Investment centre** Business unit whose manager is responsible not only for costs and revenues, but also for investment in assets.

**Joint cost** Cost incurred before split-off point in producing joint products.

**Joint products** Two or more products, separated in the course of processing, each with sufficiently high saleable value to be worth treating as a main product (rather than one being a by-product).

**Key factor** (= limiting factor)

**Last in first out (LIFO)** Method of valuing stock, rare in the United Kingdom, which assumes that most recent purchases have been used up in the current period, leaving earlier purchases in stock at the end of the period.

**Lead time** Period elapsing between decision and start of operation; or from placing an order to receiving delivery.

**Learning curve** Phenomenon where labour-related costs of production may fall as producers learn through experience.

**Life-cycle costing** (= terotechnology) The inter-action of management, financial, engineering, and other disciplines, applied to physical assets in aiming to minimize economic life-cycle costs.

**Limited company** Form of business in which liability of owners is limited to the fully paid nominal amount of their shares. Abbreviated to 'Ltd'; in larger companies to 'plc' (public limited company).

**Limiting factor** (= critical resource) The specific input factor which, at a particular time, prevents a business from exceeding its current maximum output, often due to temporary shortage of supply (e.g. of labour, material, equipment, etc.).

**Long run** Period of time in which all fixed costs are reckoned to be variable.

**Long-run costs** Long-run costs mean total costs, where short-run costs are synonymous with variable costs.

**Loss** Negative profit, where expenses exceed sales turnover. Though not the aim, often the result of business.

**Machine hour rate** Method of apportioning over-head costs based on machine hours. Overheads attributable to one or more machines are divided by the number of machine hours expected to be worked.

**Management accounting** Accounting internally for management's own use, as opposed to external financial accounting for shareholders and other outsiders.

**Manufacturing costs** Material, direct labour and production overheads.

**Marginal cost** The change in cost incurred as a result of producing one more (or one less) unit. What costs are 'marginal' may depend on the decision being made.

**Marginal costing** Costing method which allocates

only variable costs, not fixed costs, to products. (Also, sometimes called 'direct costing'; but this may mislead, since a 'direct' cost may be fixed, or an indirect cost variable.)

**Master budget** Overall aggregation of various budgets for parts of a business into a single profit and loss account budget, balance sheet budget, and cash budget for the whole company.

**Matching principle** The balance sheet carries expenditures forward as assets only if the firm expects sales turnover in future periods against which to match them.

**Material cost** Cost of commodities other than fixed assets incorporated in manufactured products.

**Mix variance** Variance due to change in *mix* of products produced or sold.

**Net assets** (= capital employed) Total assets less current liabilities; that is, fixed assets plus working capital.

**Net book value (NBV)** Cost (or valuation) of fixed assets, less accumulated depreciation.

**Net current assets** (= working capital) Current assets less current liabilities.

**Net present value (NPV)** The net result of discounting future cash inflows and outflows at a pre-selected discount rate.

**Net realizable value (NRV)** Net amount for which an asset could currently be sold; if less than cost, the basis for valuing stock.

**Net terminal value (NTV)** The net result of compounding future cash flows to a terminal (horizon) date, using a pre-selected compound interest rate.

**Non-controllable** Applied to a cost, means not easily controllable by a manager, especially in the short-run.

**Non-variable cost** (= discretionary cost)

**Normal capacity** Productive capacity under normal conditions.

**Normal spoilage** Spoilage which is anticipated, and built into product costs.

**Normal volume** Standard long-run estimate of achievable volume.

**Notes to the accounts** Notes forming part of the financial statements, explaining many items in more detail than on the face of the accounts.

**Notional cost** Cost which does not represent actual out-of-pocket expenditure (e.g. interest on equity capital).

**Opportunity cost** The hypothetical benefit that might have been obtained by the next best alternative course of action, which was forgone in favour of the course actually taken.

**Out-of-pocket cost** (= cash payment)

**Over-absorption** Overhead absorbed by products in excess of overhead actually incurred. Happens when standard overhead recovery rate is applied to actual volume greater than budget.

**Overhead absorption** Apportionment of overhead costs to cost units by means of overhead recovery rates (often based on direct labour hours). Involves estimating overhead costs at normal volume, to set absorption rate, which is then applied to actual volume.

**Overhead cost** (= indirect cost) A cost not directly identifiable with a product or cost centre.

**Overhead recovery rate** Rate (perhaps per direct labour hour, or cost) at which overheads are recovered (absorbed) by products.

**Partnership** Form of enterprise with two or more partners (owners), each with unlimited personal liability to meet the firm's debts in full.

**Payback** One of four popular capital investment appraisal methods. The payback period is the time taken for a project's net cash inflows to equal (pay back) the amount invested.

**Period cost** Fixed cost, incurred in a period regardless of volume of output.

**Planning** Setting objectives and formulating policies to achieve them. Budgets are short-term plans, often for one year ahead, expressed in financial terms.

**Present value** Today's equivalent of a future sum of money (receipt or payment), when discounted at a suitable interest rate.

**Price variance** Variance due to difference between budget price and actual price, calculated using actual volume.

**Prime cost** Direct labour plus material cost.

**Product cost** Cost attributed to product, maybe equivalent to direct cost.

**Production cost** Direct labour plus material cost plus production overheads.

**Profit** Surplus of sales turnover over expenses for a period.

**Profit and loss account (P & L)** Accounting statement showing business result (profit or loss) for a period.

**Profit centre** Business unit with manager responsible for sales turnover as well as for expenses.

**Prudence** (= conservatism) Tendency of accountants to recognize sales (and therefore profit) only

when reasonable certainty exists, but to make provision for all known liabilities (losses and expenses) whether their amount is known with certainty or is a best estimate.

**Purchasing power** (= value of money) What money will buy in real terms, usually measured by the basket of goods and services comprising the constituent items in the Retail Prices Index.

**Qualified (audit report)** Audit report including a 'qualification', expressing uncertainty about or disagreement with some aspect of the financial accounts (for which a company's directors are responsible).

**Rate variance** Price variance relating to labour.

**Raw materials** Input to manufacturing process, held for a time as stocks.

**Realization** The accounting concept that recognizes sales revenue (and therefore profit) only when it is 'realized' in cash or in other assets, the ultimate cash realization of which can be assessed with reasonable certainty.

**Real terms** Amounts expressed in terms of constant purchasing power after adjustments to allow for inflation.

**Reinvestment rate** Assumption (explicit or implicit) about the rate of return a business can earn on cash inflows 're-invested' during a capital project's life.

**Relevant cost** Any cost relevant to a decision (that is, ignoring costs which it would not affect).

**Relevant range** Range of output within which fixed costs are not expected to change.

**Replacement cost** Amount for which it is estimated that an asset held could currently be replaced. Not the expected ultimate cost if the asset is actually replaced in the future.

**Reserves** Shareholders' funds other than called-up share capital, including: share premium, revaluation reserve and cumulative retained profits.

**Residual income (RI)** Profit less a capital charge representing interest on total capital (whether debt or equity). May be either before or after tax. Represents accounting profit less (notional) interest on equity capital.

**Residual value** Net realizable value of fixed asset at the end of its economic life.

**Retail Prices Index (RPI)** Monthly government statistic measuring the weighted average of money prices of a representative basket of goods and services. Based on January 1987 = 100. The year-on-year rate of increase in the RPI is usually regarded as 'the' rate of (general) inflation.

**Retained profits** (= retained earnings)  Amount of profits a company has earned (either for current period or cumulatively) and not yet paid out in dividends to shareholders. The link between the profit and loss account and the balance sheet.

**Retention money**  Proportion of price of goods supplied or work done withheld by purchaser for a period as security against possible failure by supplier to fulfil the contract.

**Return on investment (ROI)**  Profit divided by capital employed. In management accounts usually represents operating profit before interest and tax divided by operating assets employed. (In financial accounting, may represent profit after tax divided by shareholders' equity.)

**Return on net assets (RONA)**  Operating profit before interest and tax divided by net assets (= by capital employed). Apex of pyramid of ratios: = profit margin × net asset turnover.

**Revenue**  (a) Sales revenue, turnover. (b) Inland Revenue, the tax authorities. (c) Contrasted to capital, relating to the profit and loss account rather than to the balance sheet.

**Revenue centre**  Business unit whose manager is responsible for sales turnover (revenue), but not to any major extent for expenses.

**Revenue expenditure**  Expense, charged in profit and loss account, as opposed to capital expenditure which relates to assets in the balance sheet.

**Risk**  Chance of occurrence in future where the odds are known (e.g. as in roulette or throwing dice). Contrasts with uncertainty.

**Risk-free rate of return**  Rate of return available in market on securities regarded as having zero risk (usually government-guaranteed). A risk premium may be added separately.

**Rolling budget** (= continuous budget)  Budget which is continually updated by adding a new period at the end as the most recent past period is dropped.

**Safety stock**  Minimum stock level providing a cushion against fluctuations in maximum demand and in lead times.

**Sales mix**  Combination of quantities of various goods or services sold.

**Sales turnover** (= sales revenue)  A firm's trading income for a period from selling its products.

**Scrap**  Useless material resulting from production process.

**Semi-variable cost**  Cost which is partly fixed and partly variable.

**Sensitivity analysis**  Process of determining which variables matter most, and how much it affects outcome if each varies.

**Set-up cost**  Fixed cost necessary prior to production, often in respect of a single machine.

**Shareholders**  Usually refers to ordinary shareholders who own company in proportion to number of shares held; but legally may also refer to preference shareholders.

**Short run**  Period within which not all factors of production are variable (i.e. some are fixed).

**Short-run cost** (= variable cost (often))  Cost which may be changed within a 'short' time horizon.

**Shut-down cost**  Incremental cost incurred in ceasing production (e.g. redundancy payments).

**Single criterion fallacy**  Attempt to measure business success by reference to only one criterion. Ignores interrelationships between units, time periods, and so on, and qualitative aspects.

**Split-off point**  Point beyond which costs of joint products become separately identifiable.

**Spoilage cost**  Expected normal cost of spoilage as part of production process.

**Standard cost**  Pre-determined cost, perhaps per unit, that should be attainable.

**Standard performance**  Attainable level of performance.

**Standard volume**  Expected (normal) volume. May differ from budgeted volume in the short-term.

**Start-up cost**  Cost of initiating production, probably referring to larger scale process than set-up cost.

**Statement of Standard Accounting Practice (SSAP)**  Requirements regarding financial accounting treatment (e.g. SSAP 9 on stock valuation (see Appendix A)).

**Step-down method**  Allocation and apportionment of service department costs to other service departments as well as to production departments.

**Stock** (= inventory)  Holdings of goods, either as raw materials and components, work-in-progress or finished goods, with a view to sale (perhaps after further processing) in the ordinary course of business.

**Stock turnover**  Cost of goods sold in a period divided by value of stocks held.

**Straight-line depreciation**  Method of writing off cost of fixed asset in equal instalments over its estimated economic life. If life is $n$ years, annual depreciation expense is $1/n \times$ (cost − expected residual value).

**Sunk cost**  Cost already incurred, which cannot now be reversed.

**Target**  Outcome aimed for, but not necessarily expected, forecast or committed.

**Taxable profit**  Differs from 'profit before tax' in financial accounts (a) by deducting tax writing-down allowances instead of (book) depreciation, and (b) by taking account of any accounting expenses disallowed by the tax authorities, and of any timing differences.

**Taxation**  In company accounts, means UK corporation tax on taxable profits, plus any foreign tax on profits earned abroad. Excludes other taxes, such as social security, which are included in operating expenses.

**Terotechnology**  (− life-cycle costing).

**Total cost**  Implies fixed plus variable cost; direct plus indirect cost.

**Transfer price**  Internal price at which one part of a firm transfers goods or services to another part. Can be important in evaluating performance of profit centres.

**True and fair view**  Aim of financial accounting, implying consistent application of generally accepted accounting principles.

**Turnover**  Sales revenue, the 'turnover' of the products for a period.

**Unallocated cost**  Cost which cannot conveniently or usefully be allocated (e.g. because it would be unduly expensive or arbitrary).

**Uncertainty**  Chance of occurrence in future where (as is common in business) the odds are not known, hence have to be estimated subjectively (i.e. guessed).

**Under-absorption**  Balance of overhead cost not absorbed by products due to actual volume falling short of budget.

**Unit cost**  Cost of a unit produced.

**Usage method of depreciation**  Method of depreciating fixed asset by relating usage in a period to total expected usage over whole life. This basis makes depreciation a variable expense (rather than fixed).

**Usage variance**  Efficiency variance applied to materials.

**Value added**  Roughly = profit plus wages. Differ-ence between sales turnover and cost of bought-out materials and services.

**Value analysis**  A creative approach to examining products with a view to reducing cost and/or increasing value.

**Variable budget**  (= flexible budget)

**Variable cost**  Cost which varies in proportion to output (i.e. is constant per unit).

**Variance**  Difference between budget and actual amount. (Not to be confused with a statistical variance, which is a measure of dispersion around the mean (average) value of a group of data.)

**Virement**  The transfer of items from one financial account to another. In the context of budgeting, offsetting an over-run on one item against a shortfall in another.

**Volume variance**  Variance between budget and actual stemming from difference between budget and actual volume (both priced at budget price).

**Wages cost**  Cost of employees' remuneration; gross wages, possibly plus employers' social security contributions; possibly plus fringe benefits.

**Waste**  Normal loss of material in process of production.

**Weighted average cost of capital (WACC)**  Average of the after-tax marginal costs of various kinds of long-term capital (debt, equity, etc.), 'weighted' by their market value (or their book value).

**Working capital**  (= net current assets)  Excess of current assets over current liabilities.

**Work-in-progress (WIP)**  Partly-completed stocks in manufacturing process.

**Write off**  To charge an expenditure as an expense in the profit and loss account, as opposed to capitalizing it (i.e. recording it as an asset at cost on the balance sheet).

**Writing-down allowance (wda)**  = capital allowance.

**Zero-base budgeting**  Budgeting from the ground up, as though preparing the budget for the first time. Implication: nothing is justified except what can be explicitly defended. (In contrast, most actual budgets start from existing levels and, to a large extent, seek to justify only changes therefrom.)

# APPENDIX A

# *Statements of Standard Accounting Practice*

| SSAP | Subject |
|------|---------|
| 1 | Associated companies |
| 2 | Accounting policies |
| 3 | Earnings per share |
| 4 | Government grants |
| 5 | Value added tax |
| 6 | Extraordinary items and prior year adjustments |
| 8 | Taxation under the imputation system |
| 9 | Stocks and work-in-progress |
| 10 | Statements of source and application of funds |
| 12 | Depreciation |
| 13 | Research and development |
| 14 | Group accounts |
| 15 | Deferred taxation |
| 17 | Post-balance-sheet events |
| 18 | Contingencies |
| 19 | Investment properties |
| 20 | Foreign currency translation |
| 21 | Leases and hire-purchase contracts |
| 22 | Goodwill |
| 23 | Acquisitions and mergers |
| 24 | Pension costs |
| 25 | Segmental reporting |

As at 31 July 1991

# B *Present value tables*

Table B.1 *Present value of £1*

| Years hence | 1% | 2% | 4% | 6% | 8% | 10% | 12% | 14% | 15% | 16% | 18% | 20% | 22% | 24% | 25% | 26% | 28% | 30% | 35% | 40% | 45% | 50% |
|---|---|---|---|---|---|---|---|---|---|---|---|---|---|---|---|---|---|---|---|---|---|---|
| 1 | 0.990 | 0.980 | 0.962 | 0.943 | 0.926 | 0.909 | 0.893 | 0.877 | 0.870 | 0.862 | 0.847 | 0.833 | 0.820 | 0.806 | 0.800 | 0.794 | 0.781 | 0.769 | 0.741 | 0.714 | 0.690 | 0.667 |
| 2 | 0.980 | 0.961 | 0.925 | 0.890 | 0.857 | 0.826 | 0.797 | 0.769 | 0.756 | 0.743 | 0.718 | 0.694 | 0.672 | 0.650 | 0.640 | 0.630 | 0.610 | 0.592 | 0.549 | 0.510 | 0.476 | 0.444 |
| 3 | 0.971 | 0.942 | 0.889 | 0.840 | 0.794 | 0.751 | 0.712 | 0.675 | 0.658 | 0.641 | 0.609 | 0.579 | 0.551 | 0.524 | 0.512 | 0.500 | 0.477 | 0.455 | 0.406 | 0.364 | 0.328 | 0.296 |
| 4 | 0.961 | 0.924 | 0.855 | 0.792 | 0.735 | 0.683 | 0.636 | 0.592 | 0.572 | 0.552 | 0.516 | 0.482 | 0.451 | 0.423 | 0.410 | 0.397 | 0.373 | 0.350 | 0.301 | 0.260 | 0.226 | 0.198 |
| 5 | 0.951 | 0.906 | 0.822 | 0.747 | 0.681 | 0.621 | 0.567 | 0.519 | 0.497 | 0.476 | 0.437 | 0.402 | 0.370 | 0.341 | 0.328 | 0.315 | 0.291 | 0.269 | 0.223 | 0.186 | 0.156 | 0.132 |
| 6 | 0.942 | 0.888 | 0.790 | 0.705 | 0.630 | 0.564 | 0.507 | 0.456 | 0.432 | 0.410 | 0.370 | 0.335 | 0.303 | 0.275 | 0.262 | 0.250 | 0.227 | 0.207 | 0.165 | 0.133 | 0.108 | 0.088 |
| 7 | 0.933 | 0.871 | 0.760 | 0.665 | 0.583 | 0.513 | 0.452 | 0.400 | 0.376 | 0.354 | 0.314 | 0.279 | 0.249 | 0.222 | 0.210 | 0.198 | 0.178 | 0.159 | 0.122 | 0.095 | 0.074 | 0.059 |
| 8 | 0.923 | 0.853 | 0.731 | 0.627 | 0.540 | 0.467 | 0.404 | 0.351 | 0.327 | 0.305 | 0.266 | 0.233 | 0.204 | 0.179 | 0.168 | 0.157 | 0.139 | 0.123 | 0.091 | 0.068 | 0.051 | 0.039 |
| 9 | 0.914 | 0.837 | 0.703 | 0.592 | 0.500 | 0.424 | 0.361 | 0.308 | 0.284 | 0.263 | 0.225 | 0.194 | 0.167 | 0.144 | 0.134 | 0.125 | 0.108 | 0.094 | 0.067 | 0.048 | 0.035 | 0.026 |
| 10 | 0.905 | 0.820 | 0.676 | 0.558 | 0.463 | 0.386 | 0.322 | 0.270 | 0.247 | 0.227 | 0.191 | 0.162 | 0.137 | 0.116 | 0.107 | 0.099 | 0.085 | 0.073 | 0.050 | 0.035 | 0.024 | 0.017 |
| 11 | 0.896 | 0.804 | 0.650 | 0.527 | 0.429 | 0.350 | 0.287 | 0.237 | 0.215 | 0.195 | 0.162 | 0.135 | 0.112 | 0.094 | 0.086 | 0.079 | 0.066 | 0.056 | 0.037 | 0.025 | 0.017 | 0.012 |
| 12 | 0.887 | 0.788 | 0.625 | 0.497 | 0.397 | 0.319 | 0.257 | 0.208 | 0.187 | 0.168 | 0.137 | 0.112 | 0.092 | 0.076 | 0.069 | 0.062 | 0.052 | 0.043 | 0.027 | 0.018 | 0.012 | 0.008 |
| 13 | 0.879 | 0.773 | 0.601 | 0.469 | 0.368 | 0.290 | 0.229 | 0.182 | 0.163 | 0.145 | 0.116 | 0.093 | 0.075 | 0.061 | 0.055 | 0.050 | 0.040 | 0.033 | 0.020 | 0.013 | 0.008 | 0.005 |
| 14 | 0.870 | 0.758 | 0.577 | 0.442 | 0.340 | 0.263 | 0.205 | 0.160 | 0.141 | 0.125 | 0.099 | 0.078 | 0.062 | 0.049 | 0.044 | 0.039 | 0.032 | 0.025 | 0.015 | 0.009 | 0.006 | 0.003 |
| 15 | 0.861 | 0.743 | 0.555 | 0.417 | 0.315 | 0.239 | 0.183 | 0.140 | 0.123 | 0.108 | 0.084 | 0.065 | 0.051 | 0.040 | 0.035 | 0.031 | 0.025 | 0.020 | 0.011 | 0.006 | 0.004 | 0.002 |
| 16 | 0.853 | 0.728 | 0.534 | 0.394 | 0.292 | 0.218 | 0.163 | 0.123 | 0.107 | 0.093 | 0.071 | 0.054 | 0.042 | 0.032 | 0.028 | 0.025 | 0.019 | 0.015 | 0.008 | 0.005 | 0.003 | 0.002 |
| 17 | 0.844 | 0.714 | 0.513 | 0.371 | 0.270 | 0.198 | 0.146 | 0.108 | 0.093 | 0.080 | 0.060 | 0.045 | 0.034 | 0.026 | 0.023 | 0.020 | 0.015 | 0.012 | 0.006 | 0.003 | 0.002 | 0.001 |
| 18 | 0.836 | 0.700 | 0.494 | 0.350 | 0.250 | 0.180 | 0.130 | 0.095 | 0.081 | 0.069 | 0.051 | 0.038 | 0.028 | 0.021 | 0.018 | 0.016 | 0.012 | 0.009 | 0.005 | 0.002 | 0.001 | 0.001 |
| 19 | 0.828 | 0.686 | 0.475 | 0.331 | 0.232 | 0.164 | 0.116 | 0.083 | 0.070 | 0.060 | 0.043 | 0.031 | 0.023 | 0.017 | 0.014 | 0.012 | 0.009 | 0.007 | 0.005 | 0.002 | 0.001 | |
| 20 | 0.820 | 0.673 | 0.456 | 0.312 | 0.215 | 0.149 | 0.104 | 0.073 | 0.061 | 0.051 | 0.037 | 0.026 | 0.019 | 0.014 | 0.012 | 0.010 | 0.007 | 0.005 | 0.002 | 0.001 | 0.001 | |
| 21 | 0.811 | 0.660 | 0.439 | 0.294 | 0.199 | 0.135 | 0.093 | 0.064 | 0.053 | 0.044 | 0.031 | 0.022 | 0.015 | 0.011 | 0.009 | 0.008 | 0.006 | 0.004 | 0.002 | 0.001 | | |
| 22 | 0.803 | 0.647 | 0.422 | 0.278 | 0.184 | 0.123 | 0.083 | 0.056 | 0.046 | 0.038 | 0.026 | 0.018 | 0.013 | 0.009 | 0.007 | 0.006 | 0.004 | 0.003 | 0.002 | 0.001 | | |
| 23 | 0.795 | 0.634 | 0.406 | 0.262 | 0.170 | 0.112 | 0.074 | 0.049 | 0.040 | 0.033 | 0.022 | 0.015 | 0.010 | 0.007 | 0.006 | 0.005 | 0.003 | 0.002 | 0.001 | | | |
| 24 | 0.788 | 0.622 | 0.390 | 0.247 | 0.158 | 0.102 | 0.066 | 0.043 | 0.035 | 0.028 | 0.019 | 0.013 | 0.008 | 0.006 | 0.005 | 0.004 | 0.003 | 0.002 | 0.001 | | | |
| 25 | 0.780 | 0.610 | 0.375 | 0.233 | 0.146 | 0.092 | 0.059 | 0.038 | 0.030 | 0.024 | 0.016 | 0.010 | 0.007 | 0.005 | 0.004 | 0.003 | 0.002 | 0.001 | 0.001 | | | |
| 26 | 0.772 | 0.598 | 0.361 | 0.220 | 0.135 | 0.084 | 0.053 | 0.033 | 0.026 | 0.021 | 0.014 | 0.009 | 0.006 | 0.004 | 0.003 | 0.002 | 0.002 | 0.001 | | | | |
| 27 | 0.764 | 0.586 | 0.347 | 0.207 | 0.125 | 0.076 | 0.047 | 0.029 | 0.023 | 0.018 | 0.011 | 0.007 | 0.005 | 0.003 | 0.002 | 0.002 | 0.001 | 0.001 | | | | |
| 28 | 0.757 | 0.574 | 0.333 | 0.196 | 0.116 | 0.069 | 0.042 | 0.026 | 0.020 | 0.016 | 0.010 | 0.006 | 0.004 | 0.002 | 0.002 | 0.002 | 0.001 | 0.001 | | | | |
| 29 | 0.749 | 0.563 | 0.321 | 0.185 | 0.107 | 0.063 | 0.037 | 0.022 | 0.017 | 0.014 | 0.008 | 0.005 | 0.003 | 0.002 | 0.002 | 0.001 | 0.001 | 0.001 | | | | |
| 30 | 0.742 | 0.552 | 0.308 | 0.174 | 0.099 | 0.057 | 0.033 | 0.020 | 0.015 | 0.012 | 0.007 | 0.004 | 0.003 | 0.002 | 0.001 | 0.001 | 0.001 | | | | | |
| 40 | 0.672 | 0.453 | 0.208 | 0.097 | 0.046 | 0.022 | 0.011 | 0.005 | 0.004 | 0.003 | 0.001 | 0.001 | | | | | | | | | | |
| 50 | 0.608 | 0.372 | 0.141 | 0.054 | 0.021 | 0.009 | 0.003 | 0.001 | 0.001 | 0.001 | | | | | | | | | | | | |

Table B.2 *Present value of £1 received annually for N years*

| Years (N) | 1% | 2% | 4% | 6% | 8% | 10% | 12% | 14% | 15% | 16% | 18% | 20% | 22% | 24% | 25% | 26% | 28% | 30% | 35% | 40% | 45% | 50% |
|---|---|---|---|---|---|---|---|---|---|---|---|---|---|---|---|---|---|---|---|---|---|---|
| 1 | 0.990 | 0.980 | 0.962 | 0.943 | 0.926 | 0.909 | 0.893 | 0.877 | 0.870 | 0.862 | 0.847 | 0.833 | 0.820 | 0.806 | 0.800 | 0.794 | 0.781 | 0.769 | 0.741 | 0.714 | 0.690 | 0.667 |
| 2 | 1.970 | 1.942 | 1.886 | 1.833 | 1.783 | 1.736 | 1.690 | 1.647 | 1.626 | 1.605 | 1.566 | 1.528 | 1.492 | 1.457 | 1.440 | 1.424 | 1.392 | 1.361 | 1.289 | 1.224 | 1.165 | 1.111 |
| 3 | 2.941 | 2.884 | 2.775 | 2.673 | 2.577 | 2.487 | 2.402 | 2.322 | 2.283 | 2.246 | 2.174 | 2.106 | 2.042 | 1.981 | 1.952 | 1.923 | 1.868 | 1.816 | 1.695 | 1.589 | 1.493 | 1.407 |
| 4 | 3.902 | 3.808 | 3.630 | 3.465 | 3.312 | 3.170 | 3.037 | 2.914 | 2.855 | 2.798 | 2.690 | 2.589 | 2.494 | 2.404 | 2.362 | 2.320 | 2.241 | 2.166 | 1.997 | 1.849 | 1.720 | 1.605 |
| 5 | 4.853 | 4.713 | 4.452 | 4.212 | 3.993 | 3.791 | 3.605 | 3.433 | 3.352 | 3.274 | 3.127 | 2.991 | 2.864 | 2.745 | 2.689 | 2.635 | 2.532 | 2.436 | 2.220 | 2.035 | 1.876 | 1.737 |
| 6 | 5.795 | 5.601 | 5.242 | 4.917 | 4.623 | 4.355 | 4.111 | 3.889 | 3.784 | 3.685 | 3.498 | 3.326 | 3.167 | 3.020 | 2.951 | 2.885 | 2.759 | 2.643 | 2.385 | 2.168 | 1.983 | 1.824 |
| 7 | 6.728 | 6.472 | 6.002 | 5.582 | 5.206 | 4.868 | 4.564 | 4.288 | 4.160 | 4.039 | 3.812 | 3.605 | 3.416 | 3.242 | 3.161 | 3.083 | 2.937 | 2.802 | 2.508 | 2.263 | 2.057 | 1.883 |
| 8 | 7.652 | 7.325 | 6.733 | 6.210 | 5.747 | 5.335 | 4.968 | 4.639 | 4.487 | 4.344 | 4.078 | 3.837 | 3.619 | 3.421 | 3.329 | 3.241 | 3.076 | 2.925 | 2.598 | 2.331 | 2.108 | 1.922 |
| 9 | 8.566 | 8.162 | 7.435 | 6.802 | 6.247 | 5.759 | 5.328 | 4.946 | 4.772 | 4.607 | 4.303 | 4.031 | 3.786 | 3.566 | 3.463 | 3.366 | 3.184 | 3.019 | 2.665 | 2.379 | 2.144 | 1.948 |
| 10 | 9.471 | 8.983 | 8.111 | 7.360 | 6.710 | 6.145 | 5.650 | 5.216 | 5.019 | 4.833 | 4.494 | 4.192 | 3.923 | 3.682 | 3.571 | 3.465 | 3.269 | 3.092 | 2.715 | 2.414 | 2.168 | 1.965 |
| 11 | 10.368 | 9.787 | 8.760 | 7.887 | 7.139 | 6.495 | 5.937 | 5.453 | 5.234 | 5.029 | 4.656 | 4.327 | 4.035 | 3.776 | 3.656 | 3.544 | 3.335 | 3.147 | 2.752 | 2.438 | 2.185 | 1.977 |
| 12 | 11.255 | 10.575 | 9.385 | 8.384 | 7.536 | 6.814 | 6.194 | 5.660 | 5.421 | 5.197 | 4.793 | 4.439 | 4.127 | 3.851 | 3.725 | 3.606 | 3.387 | 3.190 | 2.779 | 2.456 | 2.196 | 1.985 |
| 13 | 12.134 | 11.343 | 9.986 | 8.853 | 7.904 | 7.103 | 6.424 | 5.842 | 5.583 | 5.342 | 4.910 | 4.533 | 4.203 | 3.912 | 3.780 | 3.656 | 3.427 | 3.223 | 2.799 | 2.468 | 2.204 | 1.990 |
| 14 | 13.004 | 12.016 | 10.563 | 9.295 | 8.244 | 7.367 | 6.628 | 6.002 | 5.724 | 5.468 | 5.008 | 4.611 | 4.265 | 3.962 | 3.824 | 3.695 | 3.459 | 3.249 | 2.814 | 2.477 | 2.210 | 1.993 |
| 15 | 13.865 | 12.849 | 11.118 | 9.712 | 8.559 | 7.606 | 6.811 | 6.142 | 5.847 | 5.575 | 5.092 | 4.675 | 4.315 | 4.001 | 3.859 | 3.726 | 3.483 | 3.268 | 2.825 | 2.484 | 2.214 | 1.995 |
| 16 | 14.718 | 13.578 | 11.652 | 10.106 | 8.851 | 7.824 | 6.974 | 6.265 | 5.954 | 5.669 | 5.162 | 4.730 | 4.357 | 4.033 | 3.887 | 3.751 | 3.503 | 3.283 | 2.834 | 2.489 | 2.216 | 1.997 |
| 17 | 15.562 | 14.292 | 12.166 | 10.477 | 9.122 | 8.022 | 7.120 | 6.373 | 6.047 | 5.749 | 5.222 | 4.775 | 4.391 | 4.059 | 3.910 | 3.771 | 3.518 | 3.295 | 2.840 | 2.492 | 2.218 | 1.998 |
| 18 | 16.398 | 14.992 | 12.659 | 10.828 | 9.372 | 8.201 | 7.250 | 6.467 | 6.128 | 5.818 | 5.273 | 4.812 | 4.419 | 4.080 | 3.928 | 3.786 | 3.529 | 3.304 | 2.844 | 2.494 | 2.219 | 1.999 |
| 19 | 17.226 | 15.678 | 13.134 | 11.158 | 9.604 | 8.365 | 7.366 | 6.550 | 6.198 | 5.877 | 5.316 | 4.844 | 4.442 | 4.097 | 3.942 | 3.799 | 3.539 | 3.311 | 2.848 | 2.496 | 2.220 | 1.999 |
| 20 | 18.046 | 16.351 | 13.590 | 11.470 | 9.818 | 8.514 | 7.469 | 6.623 | 6.259 | 5.929 | 5.353 | 4.870 | 4.460 | 4.110 | 3.954 | 3.808 | 3.546 | 3.316 | 2.850 | 2.497 | 2.221 | 1.999 |
| 21 | 18.857 | 17.011 | 14.029 | 11.764 | 10.017 | 8.649 | 7.562 | 6.687 | 6.312 | 5.973 | 5.384 | 4.891 | 4.476 | 4.121 | 3.963 | 3.816 | 3.551 | 3.320 | 2.852 | 2.498 | 2.221 | 2.000 |
| 22 | 19.660 | 17.658 | 14.451 | 12.042 | 10.201 | 8.772 | 7.645 | 6.743 | 6.359 | 6.011 | 5.410 | 4.909 | 4.488 | 4.130 | 3.970 | 3.822 | 3.556 | 3.323 | 2.853 | 2.498 | 2.222 | 2.000 |
| 23 | 20.456 | 18.292 | 14.857 | 12.303 | 10.371 | 8.883 | 7.718 | 6.792 | 6.399 | 6.044 | 5.432 | 4.925 | 4.499 | 4.137 | 3.976 | 3.827 | 3.559 | 3.325 | 2.854 | 2.499 | 2.222 | 2.000 |
| 24 | 21.243 | 18.914 | 15.247 | 12.550 | 10.529 | 8.985 | 7.784 | 6.835 | 6.434 | 6.073 | 5.451 | 4.937 | 4.507 | 4.143 | 3.981 | 3.831 | 3.562 | 3.327 | 2.855 | 2.499 | 2.222 | 2.000 |
| 25 | 22.023 | 19.523 | 15.622 | 12.783 | 10.675 | 9.077 | 7.843 | 6.873 | 6.464 | 6.097 | 5.467 | 4.948 | 4.514 | 4.147 | 3.985 | 3.834 | 3.564 | 3.329 | 2.856 | 2.499 | 2.222 | 2.000 |
| 26 | 22.795 | 20.121 | 15.983 | 13.003 | 10.810 | 9.161 | 7.896 | 6.906 | 6.491 | 6.118 | 5.480 | 4.956 | 4.520 | 4.151 | 3.988 | 3.837 | 3.566 | 3.330 | 2.856 | 2.500 | 2.222 | 2.000 |
| 27 | 23.560 | 20.707 | 16.330 | 13.211 | 10.935 | 9.237 | 7.943 | 6.935 | 6.514 | 6.136 | 5.492 | 4.964 | 4.524 | 4.154 | 3.990 | 3.839 | 3.567 | 3.331 | 2.856 | 2.500 | 2.222 | 2.000 |
| 28 | 24.316 | 21.281 | 16.663 | 13.406 | 11.051 | 9.307 | 7.984 | 6.961 | 6.534 | 6.152 | 5.502 | 4.970 | 4.528 | 4.157 | 3.992 | 3.840 | 3.568 | 3.331 | 2.857 | 2.500 | 2.222 | 2.000 |
| 29 | 25.066 | 21.844 | 16.984 | 13.591 | 11.158 | 9.370 | 8.022 | 6.983 | 6.551 | 6.166 | 5.510 | 4.975 | 4.531 | 4.159 | 3.994 | 3.841 | 3.569 | 3.332 | 2.857 | 2.500 | 2.222 | 2.000 |
| 30 | 25.808 | 22.396 | 17.292 | 13.765 | 11.258 | 9.427 | 8.055 | 7.003 | 6.566 | 6.177 | 5.517 | 4.979 | 4.534 | 4.160 | 3.995 | 3.842 | 3.569 | 3.332 | 2.857 | 2.500 | 2.222 | 2.000 |
| 40 | 32.835 | 27.355 | 19.793 | 15.046 | 11.925 | 9.779 | 8.244 | 7.105 | 6.642 | 6.234 | 5.548 | 4.997 | 4.544 | 4.166 | 3.999 | 3.846 | 3.571 | 3.333 | 2.857 | 2.500 | 2.222 | 2.000 |
| 50 | 39.196 | 31.424 | 21.482 | 15.762 | 12.234 | 9.915 | 8.304 | 7.133 | 6.661 | 6.246 | 5.554 | 4.999 | 4.545 | 4.167 | 4.000 | 3.846 | 3.571 | 3.333 | 2.857 | 2.500 | 2.222 | 2.000 |

# *Answers and solutions*

The answers to review questions and the solutions to the first two problems at the end of each chapter are given under the number of the chapter in which the questions and problems have been set.

**Chapter 1**

**Answers to review questions**

1 See Table 1.5 for main differences between financial accounting and management accounting.
2 Return on net assets = operating profit ÷ net assets.
3 Return on net assets = profit margin × asset turnover.

$$\frac{\text{Operating profit}}{\text{Net assets}} = \frac{\text{Operating profit}}{\text{Sales}} \times \frac{\text{Sales}}{\text{Net assets}}$$

4 Going concern, accruals, consistency and prudence.
5 To provide an adequate long-term financial return for their owners.
6 The owners may either change the top management team or sell out to new owners who will; or the business may go into liquidation.
7 Other aims might include:
  (a) prudence;
  (b) duty to the community;
  (c) high market share;
  (d) product (or service) leadership;
  (e) very good company image;
  (f) highly skilled, trained and motivated employees;
  (g) use of the latest technology.
8 Legislation relating to safety, environmental protection, minimum wages, redundancy and many others.
9 Three non-profit-seeking organizations:
  (a) hospitals aim to alleviate illness and suffering;
  (b) police aim to prevent and detect crime;
  (c) Ministry of Defence aim to protect the population against foreign invasion.
See also Table 1.6.

10 Management accounting can help achieve better value for money.
11 Important aspects include:
(a) company objectives;
(b) business definition;
(c) analysis of company's strengths and weaknesses;
(d) assessment of 'external' opportunities and threats;
(e) competitors;
(f) markets and products;
(g) financial, physical and human resources needed.
12 Depends on the business. Maybe as little as one or two years (e.g. for a fashion business), or as much as forty years (e.g. for a life assurance company).
13 The annual budgets for profit and loss account, balance sheet, and cash flow.
14 Programming, budgeting, reporting and appraisal.
15 See Table 1.8; for example:
(a) carrots motivate people more strongly than 'sticks';
(b) time-lags dilute incentives;
(c) motivation may flag where a goal is either 'too easy' or 'too hard';
(d) money may be less important than non-monetary rewards.

**Chapter 2**

**Answers to review questions**

1 Planning, controlling, decision making, reporting.
2 (a) A variable cost is a cost which varies directly in proportion to output, e.g. material costs in a manufacturing concern.
(b) A fixed cost is a cost which, within the 'relevant range' of output, is fixed for a given period, e.g. rates.
(c) A semi-variable cost is a cost which is partly fixed and partly variable, e.g. electricity costs.
(d) A discretionary cost is a cost which is neither fixed nor variable; it may change, but not necessarily in proportion to (or even in the same direction as) output; e.g. training, advertising, research.
3 A direct cost is directly *identifiable* with a particular process, product or other specified activity, while an indirect cost ( = overhead) is *not*.
4 Indirect costs are apportioned to products (or services) in order to determine the approximate total cost. The basis of apportionment is the common factor used in the process of sharing out indirect costs. Examples: floor space may be the basis of apportioning rent and rates; direct labour minutes may be the basis of apportioning indirect labour costs.
5 (a) Depreciation of equipment used on a single product.
(b) Factory rent (for a multi-product factory).
(c) Raw materials.
(d) Energy costs (for a multi-product organization).

6 Due to management decisions, inflation and specific price changes, many fixed costs change each year; moreover, fixed costs are fixed only within the 'relevant range' of output. If the actual range of activity extends beyond the 'relevant range', the fixed costs may change.

7 The extra cost incurred as a result of producing one more (or one less) unit of output.

8 None, unless the additional unit of output necessitates additional fixed costs, and providing the variable cost per unit remains constant.

9 No. At very high levels of output, marginal cost may be greater than average cost, due to overtime premiums etc.

10 No. While many direct costs are variable (e.g. materials), some direct costs are fixed (e.g. depreciation) and some variable costs are indirect (e.g. energy costs in a multi-product organization).

11 No. Many indirect costs are fixed (e.g. rates), but some indirect costs are variable (e.g. energy costs) and some fixed costs are direct (e.g. depreciation of equipment used on one product).

12 Labour costs in certain repetitive activities may be subject to a learning curve.

13 Labour productivity will be higher, therefore costs per unit lower, as one moves down the learning curve. Hence, there can be cost advantages in having a higher market share and producing more than competitors.

14 Economies of scale may exist because of initial fixed costs, such as design and research, because of specialization of labour and because of increased size of plant (capital costs rising less than in proportion to capacity) and specialization of plant.

15 The 'opportunity cost' of the course actually taken is the value of the 'next best' alternative forsaken. Because opportunity costs are hypothetical and subjective, and often difficult to quantify, they may be unsuitable for use in costing products.

**Solutions to problems**

1 (a)

| | £ | |
|---|---|---|
| | 6 000 | (depreciation: frying equipment) |
| | 1 500 | (depreciation: other equipment) |
| | 6 000 | (rent, rates and standing charges) |
| Fixed costs | 13 500 | |

| | £ | |
|---|---|---|
| Total expenses | 108 000 | |
| Less fixed costs | (13 500) | |
| advertising | (3 000) | |
| Variable costs | 91 500 | |

(b) Contribution           = Sales revenue − variable costs
                              = £135 000 − £91 500
                              = £43 500

$$\text{Contribution per £1 sales revenue} = \frac{£43\,500}{£135\,000} \times £1$$

$$= 32.2p$$

(c) Cost of fish uncooked

$$= \frac{£42\,000 \text{ expenses}}{£60\,000 \text{ sales}}$$

$$\times \quad £1.60 \text{ selling price} = £1.12$$

Varible frying costs:

| | £ |
|---|---|
| Frying oil and batter | 3 600 |
| Electricity and gas (£9 900 − £6 000) | 3 900 |
| | 7 500 |

Variable fried product costs:

| | £ |
|---|---|
| Fish | 42 000 |
| Potatoes | 9 000 |
| Other fried products | 9 000 |
| | 60 000 |

Frying costs

$$= \frac{£7\,500 \text{ frying costs}}{£60\,000 \text{ fried product costs}}$$

$$\times \quad £1.12 \text{ cost of uncooked fish} = 14p$$

Variable cost of fried fish    = £1.12 + 14p = £1.26

Contribution    = £1.60 − £1.26
                = 34p

(d)

| Direct costs | Indirect costs |
|---|---|
| Fish for frying | Frying oil and batter |
| Potatoes | Frying equipment: depreciation |
| Other fried products | Other equipment: depreciation |
| Fish sold uncooked | Rent, rates, gas and electricity |
| Other items | Advertising |

(e) Average cost per £1 sales:

$$= \frac{\text{Total costs}}{\text{Sales revenue}} = \frac{£108\ 000}{£135\ 000}$$

$$= \underline{80\text{p per }£1\text{ sales}}$$

2 (a) Fixed costs for the year:

| | £ |
|---|---|
| Ice-cream van depreciation | 3 000 |
| Vehicle licence, insurance, garaging and routine maintenance | 1 100 |
| Total fixed costs | 4 100 |

(b) Variable costs for the year:

| | £ |
|---|---|
| Cost of goods sold | 14 000 |
| Fuel, oil and vehicle repairs | 2 800 |
| Total variable costs | 16 800 |

(c) Contribution $\ =\ $ Sales revenue − variable costs

$$=\ £42\ 000 - £16\ 800$$

$$=\ £25\ 200$$

$$\text{Contribution per }£1\text{ sales} = \frac{\text{Contribution}}{\text{Sales revenue}}$$

$$= \frac{£25\ 200}{£42\ 000}$$

$$=\ \underline{60\text{p per }£1\text{ sales}}$$

(d) Direct cost of £6 000

sales of lollipops $\ =\ £6\ 000 \times \frac{1}{3}$

$$=\ \underline{£2\ 000}$$

(e) Total indirect costs for

the year $\ =\ £3\ 900 + £3\ 000$

$$=\ \underline{£6\ 900}$$

(f) Should Emilio buy two vans?

| | £ | £ |
|---|---|---|
| Additional sales revenue | | 31 500 |
| Less additional expenses: | | |
| cost of goods sold ($\frac{1}{3} \times £31\ 500$) | 10 500 | |
| driver-salesman | 12 000 | |
| ice-cream van: running costs[1] | 3 200 | |
| depreciation | 3 000 | |
| | | 28 700 |

Additional profit                                  <u>2 800</u>

$$^1 £1\ 100 \text{ fixed } + \left( \frac{31\ 500}{42\ 000} \times £2\ 800 \right) \text{ variable}$$

Emilio would make an additional £2 800 profit. But is this a satisfactory return considering the risk involved?

**Chapter 3**

**Answers to review questions**

1 Because indirect costs cannot be identified directly with products; they need to be apportioned to cost centres (on the most realistic and convenient basis that can be devised) and then absorbed by products on some reasonable basis.
2 Specific bases include:
(a) floor area (e.g. for rates);
(b) number of employees (e.g. for indirect labour);
(c) book value of assets (e.g. for insurance costs).
3 Absorption is the charging out ('recovery') of indirect costs apportioned to cost centres, to individual products that pass through that cost centre. Possible bases include:
(a) direct labour (either hours or costs);
(b) units of output;
(c) machine hours.
4 Activity-based costing is an approach for dealing with indirect costs which involves identifying an activity which appears to 'drive' indirect costs and apportioning specific indirect costs to products (or services) in proportion to the level of activity associated with that product.
5 Fixed costs profit is contribution (to fixed costs and profit, i.e. sales revenue less variable costs) *less fixed costs*.
6 (a) For each cost centre, allocate variable costs to the right product.
(b) For each product, total the variable costs from the various cost centres.
(c) For each product, deduct total variable costs from sales revenue, to give the product's contribution (to fixed costs and profit).
7 Advantages:
(a) easy to understand;
(b) simplifies budgeting and variance analysis.
Disadvantages:
(a) possible confusion of contribution with profit;
(b) encourages selling at below full cost.
8 Because the next best alternative may be no contribution at all.
9 A small positive contribution may still mean selling at below full cost. In the long term, the business cannot afford to sell all its products below full cost. In the short term, there may be no better alternatives.
10 (a) Past costs may have been unacceptable.

(b) Costs may since have changed, due to physical changes in usage (e.g. processes and/or materials).

(c) Costs may since have changed, due to changes in prices.

11 (a) Cost control, by comparing actual with standard.

(b) Setting selling prices.

(c) Valuing stock.

12 (a) Indicates total costs of a product or service.

(b) Identifies product profitability.

13 Service costs, unlike manufacturing costs, are often mostly fixed and contain little or no material costs.

14 (a) The effects of inflation over several years.

(b) Greater uncertainty due to unfamiliarity with non-repetitive work.

(c) Possible construction or installation activities in foreign countries.

(d) The longer-term exposure to currency fluctuations.

15 In a full costing system, product costs include fixed costs as well as variable costs. The fixed cost per unit is thus dependent upon the production volume. If part of the output for a period remains unsold at the end of it, then not all the fixed costs will be charged to the profit and loss account of the period in which they were incurred. (The balance will be carried forward in stock.) When sales volume exceeds production volume, then more fixed costs will be charged to the profit and loss account than were incurred in that period. The profit therefore depends upon both the volume of production and the volume of sales.

**Solutions to problems**

1 Easidig Garden Equipment Ltd

|  | Labour |  | Material |  | Total |  | No. units |  | Total cost |
|---|---|---|---|---|---|---|---|---|---|
| Fork | 0.90 | + | 2.90 | = | 3.80 | × | 8 000 | = | £30 400 |
| Spade | 0.90 | + | 2.40 | = | 3.30 | × | 7 000 | = | £23 100 |
| Shovel | 1.20 | + | 2.40 | = | 3.60 | × | 5 000 | = | £18 000 |
|  |  |  |  |  |  |  |  |  | £71 500 |

Manufacturing overheads of £39 000 thus amount to 54.5% of total labour and material costs. On that basis, total costs per unit are as follows:

|  | Fork £ | Spade £ | Shovel £ |
|---|---|---|---|
| Labour and material | 3.80 | 3.30 | 3.60 |
| Mfg overheads 54.5% | 2.07 | 1.80 | 1.96 |
|  | 5.87 | 5.10 | 5.56 |

The costs of the fork (£5.87) and shovel (£5.56) are quite a lot different from the total costs shown in the text of £5.60 and £6.00 respectively;

whereas the spade's total cost (£5.10) has remained exactly the same. This simply underlines that the basis of apportionment of overheads can make a big difference to the resulting total cost — and therefore that 'costs' are not precisely 'correct', but depend on the method of calculation and the underlying assumptions.

**2 Reynolds and Jukes Ltd**

(a) Materials 10 000 components $\times \dfrac{10 \text{ metres} \times £1.80}{100 \text{ components}} =$ £1 800.00

Labour: Turning $\dfrac{10\,000}{30 \times 60}$ = 5.56 hours @ £6.00 = 33.33

Milling $\dfrac{10\,000}{60 \times 60}$ = 2.78 hours @ £6.00 = 16.67 } 116.67

Grinding $\dfrac{10\,000}{15 \times 60}$ = 11.11 hours @ £6.00 = 66.67

Fixed overheads $\dfrac{10\,000}{100}$ × 90p     90.00

Variable overheads = 100% × direct labour costs     116.67

Standard cost     £2123.34

(b) Proposed selling price = standard cost + 10%
= £2 123.34 + £212.33
= £2 335.67 per 10 000 components
or £23.36 per 100

(c) (i) The advantage of the above method of determining product cost is that it uses known data, which is relatively easy to verify and update. The disadvantages are: an assumption has to be made about the 'normal' level of activity in order to spread fixed overheads; and the method used to allocate variable overheads (on the basis of direct labour costs) is arbitrary.

(ii) The 'cost-plus' method of setting selling prices has the advantage of being simple and easy to calculate. But its disadvantages are that it bears no explicit relationship to the capital employed and — more important — it ignores current market conditions (e.g. What do competitors charge? What would customers be prepared to pay?).

**Chapter 4**

**Answers to review questions**

1 A chart which graphically presents a firm's cost and sales revenue at different levels of sales volume and from which the volume of output needed to 'breakeven' can be (approximately) determined. The level of profit or loss at different levels of sales volume can also be approximated.

2 Fixed costs (total), variable costs (per unit) and sales revenue (per unit) for the firm's 'relevant range'.

3 (a) Single selling price per unit. (Selling price per unit may need to be reduced in order to achieve the desired level of sales.)

(b) An unchanging mix of products, if there is more than one product. (In multi-product firms, the sales mix is unlikely to be exactly the same as that predicted in constructing the breakeven chart.)

(c) A single unchanging variable cost per unit. (Variable cost per unit may change, for example, due to bulk buying (i.e. reduced variable cost) or overtime premiums (i.e. increased variable cost).)

(d) Fixed costs remain the same at all levels of output. (Actual maximum capacity may be different from 'theoretical' maximum capacity, thereby necessitating an increase in fixed costs within the ('theoretical') relevant range.)

(e) No changes in stock level. (It is unlikely that stock levels will be exactly the same at the end of the period considered as they were at the beginning.)

4 The excess of planned output above the breakeven level of output.

5 (a) Determine the greater of sales revenue and total costs for the maximum output level to be considered, and divide this number by the length of the vertical axis available.

(b) Identify the maximum output level to be considered and divide this number by the length of the horizontal axis available. The horizontal axis and the vertical axis should be of similar length.

6 Breakeven level of output:

$$(x) = \frac{F}{s - v}$$

where:  F is total fixed costs
s is the selling price per unit
v is the variable cost per unit

7 Total sales revenue less total fixed costs.

8 (a) When sales revenue equals fixed costs.

(b) Zero.

9 (a) Breakeven point will rise (assuming variable costs per unit are less than sales revenue per unit) because more units will need to be produced for the total contribution to equal total fixed costs.

(b) Breakeven point will fall because less total contribution is needed to equal the lower total fixed costs. Moreover, the percentage fall in breakeven will equal the percentage fall in fixed costs.

(c) No change, since actual volume does not affect breakeven volume.

(d) Breakeven point will rise because more units will need to be sold for total contribution to equal total fixed costs.

(e) Breakeven point will fall because contribution per unit increases.

10 Because the financial accounting rules (SSAP 9) require firms to attribute some fixed costs to the value of the closing stock level, any change in stock levels affects cost of goods sold, and hence profit. The fixed costs incurred during a period will therefore *not* equal the fixed costs charged in the period's profit and loss account.

11 (a) Overtime premiums or diminishing returns.
   (b) Bulk purchases at a discount.

12 Because fixed costs are not fixed for all levels of output, but increase in a 'step-function' as output increases.

13 (a) the benefits which customers receive;
   (b) competitors' prices;
   (c) the prices of possible substitute products;
   (d) the cost of making the product;
   (e) the firm's own pricing policy;
   (f) the desire to more fully utilize existing capacity.

14 Price-elasticity of demand is a measure of the relationship between prices and demand volumes. Such estimates will enable firms to estimate the price which will result in the highest level of profit.

15 Contribution. With a given level of fixed costs, this will maximize profit.

**Solutions to problems**

1 (a) Sales price = £18 per unit
   Variable costs = £240 000/40 000 units £6 per unit
   Contribution = £12 per unit

$$\text{Breakeven level of output} = \frac{\text{fixed costs}}{\text{contribution per unit}}$$

$$= \frac{£300\ 000 \text{ a year}}{£12 \text{ per unit}}$$

$$= 25\ 000 \text{ units per year}$$

(b) (i) $$\text{Breakeven level of output} = \frac{\text{fixed costs}}{\text{contribution per unit}}$$

$$= \frac{£400\ 000 \text{ a year}}{£12 \text{ per unit}}$$

$$= 33\ 333 \text{ units per year}$$

(ii) Sales price = £18 per unit
   Variable costs = £8 per unit
   Contribution = £10 per unit

$$\text{Breakeven level of output} = \frac{\text{fixed costs}}{\text{contribution per unit}}$$

$$= \frac{£300\ 000\ \text{a year}}{£10\ \text{per unit}}$$

$$= 30\ 000\ \text{units per year}$$

(iii)  Sales price      $=$ £16 per unit

Variable costs      $=$ £6 per unit

Contribution      $=$ £10 per unit

$$\text{Breakeven level of output} \;=\; \frac{£300\ 000\ \text{a year}}{£10\ \text{per unit}}$$

$$= 30\ 000\ \text{units per year}$$

**2** (a) 2A + 1B = 1 'unit', and let $x$ = breakeven no. of 'units'.
At breakeven level, sales revenue = total costs:

$$£34x = £300\ 000 + £14x$$
$$£20x = £300\ 000$$
$$x = 15\ 000\ \text{'units' a year}$$
$$(= 30\ 000A + 15\ 000B)$$

(b) For A: 
$$£12x = £160\ 000 + £4x$$
$$£8x = £160\ 000$$
$$x = 20\ 000\ \text{units a year}$$

For B: 
$$£10x = £140\ 000 + £6x$$
$$£4x = £140\ 000$$
$$x = 35\ 000\ \text{units a year}$$

(c) For A: 
$$£12x = y + £4x$$
$$£8x = y$$
$$x = y/8 \qquad \text{(i)}$$

For B: 
$$£10x = £(300 - y) + £6x$$
$$£4x = £(300 - y)$$
$$x = \tfrac{1}{4}(300 - y) \qquad \text{(ii)}$$

From (i) and (ii), $\dfrac{y}{8} = \dfrac{(300 - y)}{4}$

$$y = 600 - 2y$$
$$3y = 600$$
$$y = 200$$

Thus, fixed costs must be split: £200 000 to A, and £100 000 to B.
Check:

For A: 
$$£12x = £200\ 000 + £4x$$
$$£8x = £200\ 000$$
$$x = 25\ 000\ \text{units a year}$$

For B: 
$$£20x = £100\ 000 + £6x$$

$$£4x = £100\ 000$$
$$x = 25\ 000 \text{ units a year}$$

Alternatively, since the contribution for A (£8) is twice that of B (£4), the fixed costs need to be split in the ratio of 2:1.

**Chapter 5**

**Answers to review questions**

1 Independence, finance and attitude to risk.
2 Cost centres, revenue centres, profit centres and investment centres.
3 Any four from Table 5.2.
4 Any four from Table 5.3.
5 How to deal with:
  (a) depreciation;
  (b) interest payable;
  (c) tax;
  (d) inflation.
6 (a) Whether to use opening, average or closing investment.
  (b) Whether to use historical cost or revalued figures for fixed assets; and which method of stock valuation to use.
  (c) Whether to use gross fixed assets (at cost or revaluation) or just their net book value.
  (d) Whether to include actual cash and debtors.
  (e) Whether to use total assets as the investment figure, or to deduct (some or all) current liabilities.
  (f) Whether to include long-term liabilities (e.g. loans) and deferred tax liabilities as part of the capital employed.
7 (a) Return on investment (ROI).
  (b) Residual income (RI).
8 $\text{ROI} = \dfrac{\text{PBIT}}{\text{Net assets}}$.
9 RI = PBIT less capital charge (a predetermined percentage of net assets).
10 All divisions would undertake projects expected to give a return better than the group's minimum return. With ROI this would not be likely where the division's return is expected to be different (either higher or lower) from that of the group.
11 Goal congruence is the motivation of divisional managers towards improving their own division's results, also to act in the best interests of the company or group as a whole.
12 Any five from Table 5.6.
13 (a) Transfer goods at 'cost plus mark-up'.
  (b) Use different prices for buyer and seller.
  (c) Change from a profit centre organization.
14 It does not disguise fixed costs as 'variable' (from a buying division's

viewpoint), hence it avoids over-reliance on correctly estimating volume in advance.

15 How to induce the agent to achieve the principal's goals, and how to monitor his actions.

**Solutions to problems**

1 $\text{ROI} = \dfrac{\text{Profit before loan interest}}{\text{Net assets}} = \dfrac{1\ 132}{7\ 393}$

$$= \underline{\underline{15.3\%}}$$

$\text{RI} = \text{Profit before loan interest} - (18\% \times \text{net assets})$
$= \pounds 1\ 132\text{m} - (18\% \times \pounds 7\ 393\text{m})$
$= \pounds 1\ 132\text{m} - \pounds 1\ 331\text{m}$
$= \underline{\underline{-\pounds 199\text{m}}}$

The ICI Chairman cites the 'world economic decline' as a factor in the 1990 disappointing performance.

2 (a) Total transfer price $= [(20\% \times \pounds 2.15\text{m}) + (45\ 000 \times \pounds 36)]$
$= [\pounds 430\text{k} + \pounds 1\ 620\text{k}] \times 1.06$
$= \underline{\underline{\pounds 2\ 173\text{k}}}$

(b) Transfer price per barrel $= \pounds 2\ 173\text{k} \div 45\text{k barrels}$
$= \underline{\underline{\pounds 48.29}}$ (approx.)

(c) New average transfer price per barrel
$$= \frac{[(20\% \times \pounds 2.15\text{m}) + (49\ 500 \times \pounds 36)] \times 1.06}{49\ 500 \text{ barrels}}$$

$= \underline{\underline{\pounds 47.37}}$ (approx.), i.e. almost £1 a barrel cheaper.

**Chapter 6**

**Answers to review questions**

1 (a) Make-or-buy decisions.
   (b) Use-of-capacity decisions.
   (c) Capital investment decisions.
2 (a) Only *future* costs and revenues are relevant.
   (b) Only *incremental* costs and revenues must be considered.
   (c) *Cash flows* should be used rather than accounting profits, depreciation charges or accounting book values.
   (d) The *whole enterprise* should be considered, not just the section making the decision.
3 Cost and revenues which continue unchanged regardless of the decision can be ignored for the purpose of decision making.
4 If the Central Office overheads in total are unaffected by Division A's decision, then overhead savings should be ignored since they would merely be redistributed amongst other divisions. Savings of Central

Office overheads should be included to the extent that they are incremental to the decision.

5 (a) Whether adequate technical quality can be assured.
 (b) Whether delivery will be prompt and reliable.
 (c) Whether adequate volume can be assured.
 (d) Whether dual sourcing might be desirable.

6 Using the cash-flow approach is preferable to just estimating the effect on profits, because:
 (a) using cash flows allows us to take into account the time value of money;
 (b) most non-accountants find it easier to prepare; and
 (c) it avoids overemphasis on short-term book losses.
 However, it is advisable to be aware of the P & L account implications, especially if they are large.

7 Cost/benefit analysis involves the financial quantification of all the costs and benefits (financial and especially non-financial) relating to a specific business decision.

8 The term 'risk' is used for situations where the probability of each outcome is known. 'Uncertainty' exists in situations where the odds can only be estimated.

9 (a) Sensitivity analysis.
 (b) Subjective probabilities and expected values.

10 Sensitivity analysis is the technique whereby input variables (e.g. sales volume) are adjusted by a specific percentage and the effect upon the dependent result (e.g. profit) determined.

11 Because some 'most likely' figures (e.g. sales volume) are likely to vary by much more than 10%. Other 'most likely' figures may be relatively certain.

12 Subjective probabilities are more useful in estimating outcomes of occurrences that are likely to be repeated a number of times.

13 (a) People might believe that using subjective probabilities gives a scientifically correct decision.
 (b) Difficult to estimate the probabilities for each variable.
 (c) It may not be easy to identify the interrelationships between variables.
 (d) Likely to be time-consuming.
 (e) Not useful in assessing unique events.

14 The expected value is the sum of the probability multiplied by the outcome, for each possible outcome.

15 (a) (i) Produce goods only against firm orders, and (ii) arrange long-term supply contracts.
 (b) (i) Avoid over-dependence on a few customers, and (ii) arrange alternative sources of supply.
 (c) (i) Carry out extensive market research before developing new products, and (ii) stockpile raw materials.

**Solutions to problems**  1 (a) Additional profits of introducing late shift:

|  | £ per hour | £ per week (150 man-hours) |
|---|---|---|
| Extra sales revenue | 15.00 | 2250 |
| Extra labour costs | 9.50 | 1425 |
| Extra depreciation of equipment[1] | 1.67 | 250 |
| Floor space costs | — | — |
| Other overheads (⅓ variable) | 0.50 | 75 |
| Total costs | 11.67 | 1750 |
| Profit margin | 3.33 | 500 |
|  | 15.00 | 2250 |

[1]Since equipment will last only two-thirds of its current estimated life, depreciation charge will increase by 50% (per week).

Depreciation now = £2.00 per hour × 50 hours × 5 staff
= £500 per week

Extra depreciation is therefore £250 per week

$$= \frac{£250 \text{ per week}}{30 \times 5}$$

= £1.67 per hour.

By commencing a late-shift operation, Nippeys can expect an additional profit of £500 per week when this shift becomes fully utilized. The profit margin per hour is actually higher for the late shift than for the daytime shift. This appears to be a much more profitable alternative to the present arrangement of 'turning away' customers.

(b) Other alternatives that might be considered before making a final decision:
   (i) Extend the building and facilities to provide the necessary service on dayshift only.
   (ii) Increase prices to reduce unsatisfied demand, while increasing profits.
   (iii) Seek other alternatives which will allow more business to be handled with existing facilities.

2 (a) Effect on profit of away-supporters' ban:

|  | £m |
|---|---|
| Gate receipts | −0.10 |
| Programme sales | −0.05 |
| Policing costs | 0.14 |

| | |
|---|---|
| New system: equipment depreciation[1] | −0.07 |
| New system: running costs | −0.10 |
| Staffing costs on match days | 0.06 |
| Total effect on profit | −0.12 |

[1]£0.2m depreciated over three years.

In the first season, profit (before tax) is expected to be £0.12m lower as a result of the away-supporters' ban. In subsequent seasons, the adverse effect on profit might not be as large, particularly if more home-supporters attend and programme sales increase.

(b) In addition to the financial effects on the football club, the local community may be affected on match days as follows:
   (i) less violence and property damage;
   (ii) less traffic; and
   (iii) lower (perhaps higher?) retail sales of food, drink, etc.
If these effects are net benefits to the local community, the football club might consider the cost acceptable.

## Chapter 7

**Answers to review questions**

1 The generation of ideas; to take advantage of opportunities or provide solutions to problems.
2 To improve future capital investment decision making.
3 Payback period is the time taken for the net cash inflows from a project to equal the amount invested.
4 Cash flows after payback.
5 Average accounting profit per year divided by the amount invested.
6 It ignores the *timing* of profits by taking an average over time.
7 Today's equivalent of a future sum of money (receipt or payment). It is calculated by discounting the future cash flow at a predetermined discount rate.
8 The sum of the present values for both positive and negative cash flows.
9 A discount rate is the interest rate used in present value calculations, whereas the discount factor is the multiplying factor which reduces future cash flows to their present value. The discount factor is determined by the discount rate and when (number of years hence) the cash flow occurs.
10 That discount rate which, for a capital project, produces a net present value of zero.
11 A tax deductible expense which results in lower subsequent corporation tax payments.
12 This is a company's estimated cost of long-term finance, which depends upon the cost and mix of its equity and long-term debt.

13 (a)  A real discount rate.
   (b)  A money (or nominal) discount rate.
14 Options include:
   (a)  adjusting (up or down) the discount rate;
   (b)  shortening the project life for evaluation purposes;
   (c)  requiring a shorter payback;
   (d)  sensitivity analysis;
   (e)  using probability estimates for each variable;
   (f)  monte-carlo analysis.
15 A way of checking the effect on NPV (or any of the other project appraisal measures) of specific changes in the project's independent variables (e.g. selling price, volume, etc.).

**Solutions to problems**

**1 Toll road**

To determine the internal rate of return we need to discover what discount rate produces a net present value of zero. In this case it turns out that the answer lies between 4% and 6%.

| Year | Cash flow (£m) | | 4% (£m) | | 6% (£m) |
|---|---|---|---|---|---|
| EOY 0 | −800 | × 1.000 = | −800 | × 1.000 = | −800 |
| EOY 1–5 | −500 p.a. | × 4.452 = | −2 226 | × 4.212 = | −2 106 |
| EOY 6–30[1] | +300 p.a. | × 12.840[1] = | +3 852 | × 9.553[1] = | +2 866 |
| NPV | | | +826 | | −40 |

$$\text{IRR} = 6\% - \frac{40 \times 2}{(826 + 40)} = 6\% - \frac{80}{866} = 6\% - 0.09\% = 5.91\%$$

| [1] | EOY 1–30 | 17.292 | 13.765 |
|---|---|---|---|
| − | EOY 1–5 | −4.452 | −4.212 |
| = | EOY 6–30 | 12.840 | 9.553 |

**2 Chiltern Library**

| | Cash flow | | Discount | Present value | |
|---|---|---|---|---|---|
| Year | Conventional (£'000s) | Hi-tech (£'000s) | factor @ 4% | Conventional (£'000s) | Hi-tech (£'000s) |
| 0 | 1 400 | 1 600 | 1.000 | 1 400 | 1 600 |
| 1–50 | 60 p.a. | 49 p.a. | 21.482 | 1 289 | 1 053 |
| 50 | 10 | 10 | .141 | 1 | 1 |
| Present value of lifetime costs | | | | 2 690 | 2 654 |

The hi-tech building works out a little cheaper in the long run and, subject to other considerations, should be recommended. (Note that at a real discount rate of 6% the conventional building would be slightly cheaper.)

**Chapter 8**

**Answers to review questions**

1 Budgets are formal business plans comprising the following:
   (a) quantitative statements;
   (b) usually expressed in financial terms;
   (c) prepared and approved in advance;
   (d) covering a specific period of time;
   (e) for the whole or part of a firm's operations.
2 Managers accept a personal commitment to achieve their agreed budgets.
3 Budgetary control:
   (a) sets objectives;
   (b) co-ordinates activities;
   (c) motivates managers;
   (d) transmits information;
   (e) assesses performance of managers and business units; and
   (f) helps effective management action.
4 The master budget is the plan which the organization as a whole will work towards achieving. It comprises a budgeted profit and loss account, balance sheet and cash flow for the organization. The master budget involves:
   (a) stating basic assumptions and company objectives;
   (b) forecasting general economic and industry conditions;
   (c) preparing detailed sales budgets;
   (d) preparing detailed production budgets;
   (e) preparing capital expenditure budgets;
   (f) preparing cash budgets;
   (g) co-ordinating the various subsidiary budgets into the master budget.
5 A rolling budget is one in which figures for an extra budget period (e.g. one month) are added each time a budget period finishes. In this way, the budget always covers the next twelve months.
6 The first draft of the master budget frequently fails to satisfy completely all the interested parties. Therefore, it is often necessary to perform one or more iterations to achieve an acceptable master budget.
7 A budget has to be 'agreed' by a superior level of management as 'acceptable', as well as being 'agreed' as a *commitment* by a lower level manager. It is not surprising if there is sometimes, at first, a gap between what top management would like and what a lower level of management is prepared to commit itself to deliver.
8 Zero-base budgeting challenges the existence of all costs in a very thorough way, but less frequently (every 3–5 years). See Table 8.1 for more detail.
9 Business people nearly always prefer approximate figures soon to

precise figures later. In this way motivation is enhanced and necessary appropriate action may be taken sooner.

10 Flash figures are approximate financial figures, promptly reported, relating to the most essential aspects of business performance.

11 Flexible budgeting is the adjustment of budget figures to allow for actual volume achieved. Actual 'variable expenses' can then usefully be compared with the amounts shown by the 'flexed' budget.

12 Yes, there can be good reasons for failing to achieve an agreed budget. Apart from *over*-achievement, which is usually not to be discouraged, *under*-achievement might occur because of an unexpected recession in the economy.

13 Top management may deliberately negotiate a budget commitment from subordinate managers, for purposes of motivation, at a level somewhat beyond what they actually expect to be achieved.

14 Many elements of performance have longer-term implications. Thus, current year's profits may be affected by decisions taken several years ago; and by discretionary expenditure decisions (e.g. on research, training, advertising) which may affect several future periods. Too much emphasis on current year's profits might discourage 'investment' in such items.

15 Even if a business unit is performing badly, that does not necessarily mean that the manager's performance is poor.

**Solutions to problems**

1 (a) The Wardown Car Wash budgeted profit and loss account

| | £ | £ |
|---|---|---|
| Sales: | | |
| (12 700 × £1.50) + (2 345 × £2.50) | | 24 912 |
| Expenses: | | |
| Washing solution (15 045 × 20p) | 3 009 | |
| Wax (2 345 × 45p) | 1 055 | |
| Washing equipment: depreciation | | |
| (£60 000/5 years)[1] | 12 000 | |
| Maintenance and repair (£50 × 12) | 600 | |
| Rent and rates | 2 250 | |
| Budgeted profit | | 18 914 |

[1]Using conservative estimate of useful life and straight-line depreciation.

(b) Budgeted profit for February

| | £ | £ |
|---|---|---|
| Sales: | | |
| (500 × £1.50) + (80 × £2.50) | | 950 |

Expenses:

| | £ |
|---|---|
| Washing solution (580 × 20p) | 116 |
| Wax (80 × 45p) | 36 |
| Washing equipment: depreciation | 1 000 |
| Maintenance and repair | 50 |
| Rent and rates | 187 |
| | 1 389 |

Budgeted profit/(loss)  (439)

i.e. a loss of £439 is budgeted for February.

Budgeted profit for May

| | £ | £ |
|---|---|---|
| Sales: | | |
| (1 300 × £1.50) + (230 × £2.50) | | 2 525 |
| Expenses: | | |
| Washing solution (1 530 × 20p) | 306 | |
| Wax (230 × 45p) | 103 | |
| Washing equipment: depreciation | 1 000 | |
| Maintenance and repair | 50 | |
| Rent and rates | 187 | |
| | | 1 646 |
| Budgeted profit | | 879 |

(c) Monthly cash budget (£)

| | Apr Sept | May | Oct | Nov | Dec | Jan | Feb | Mar |
|---|---|---|---|---|---|---|---|---|
| Cash receipts | | | | | | | | |
| Basic wash | 1500 | 1950 | 1800 | 1575 | 1350 | 1275 | 750 | 1050 |
| Wash 'n' wax | 375 | 575 | 550 | 525 | 512 | 500 | 200 | 325 |
| Total receipts | 1875 | 2525 | 2350 | 2100 | 1862 | 1775 | 950 | 1375 |
| Cash payments | | | | | | | | |
| Washing solution | 230 | 306 | 284 | 252 | 221 | 210 | 116 | 166 |
| Wax | 67 | 103 | 99 | 94 | 92 | 90 | 36 | 58 |
| Maintenance & repair | 50 | 50 | 50 | 50 | 50 | 50 | 50 | 50 |
| Rent & rates | 1125 | — | 1125 | — | — | — | — | — |
| Total payments | 1472 | 459 | 1558 | 396 | 363 | 350 | 202 | 274 |
| Net cash flow | 403 | 2066 | 792 | 1704 | 1499 | 1425 | 748 | 1101 |

Cash flow is greatest in the period May–September.
Cash flow is worst (= lowest net cash inflow) in April.

**2** Standard cost per bottle

|  | £ |  |
|---|---|---|
| Material | 0.27 | |
| Labour | 0.50 | |
| Overhead: | | |
| Variable production overhead | 0.45 | (£540 000/1 200 000 bottles) |
| Fixed production overhead | 0.60 | (£720 000/1 200 000 bottles) |
| Plant and equipment: deprec. | 0.37 | (£440 000/1 200 000 bottles) |
| Tools, etc.: depreciation | 0.06 | (£70 000/1 200 000 bottles) |
| | 2.25 | |

To give gross profit margin of 33⅓% (on sales), selling price needs to be 1.5 × £2.25 = £3.37.

**Chapter 9**

**Answers to review questions**

**1** Variance analysis often provides additional insight into which factors have affected performance and to what extent.

**2** (a) Sales volume variance — when analysing the profit variance, this should be substituted by the sales (contribution) volume variance.
(b) Sales price variance.

**3** A flexible budget is one in which the budgeted variable costs are 'flexed' (increased or decreased) to represent the expected variable cost for the *actual* sales volume (as opposed to the budgeted sales volume). The purpose is to provide a more meaningful budget for costs which are expected to vary with output and sales.

**4** Prices are usually less controllable, by managers, than volumes. Volume variances are therefore isolated from price movements (actual v. budget) by using budgeted prices in order to focus management's attention on factors it can control.

**5** (a) Material price variance and material usage variance.
(b) Direct labour rate variance and direct labour efficiency variance.

**6** (a) Providing the actual level of output stays within the 'relevant range', the *amount* of fixed overhead should be unchanged. This being so, a fixed overhead expenditure variance should arise only if the *cost* of fixed overhead varies from budget.
(b) Variable overhead, by definition, changes in line with output. A variable overhead expenditure variance results from spending more (or less) on variable overhead than 'should' have been spent for the actual level of output.

**7** Apart from the fixed overhead expenditure variance (which is the same as for marginal costing systems), the fixed overhead volume variance identifies the loss in profit due to fixed overheads being under-recovered (unfavourable variance) or over-recovered (favourable variance). It arises when the actual output volume is different from that budgeted.

8 The eight variances in a marginal costing system are:
(a) sales price;
(b) sales (contribution) volume;
(c) material price;
(d) material usage;
(e) direct labour rate;
(f) direct labour efficiency;
(g) variable overhead expenditure;
(h) fixed overhead expenditure.
For a standard costing system:
(a) delete sales (contribution) volume variance; and add
(b) sales (standard profit) volume variance, and
(c) fixed overhead volume variance.

9 Balance sheet variances, particularly for stocks, debtors and cash.

10 Business performance is often improved by a thorough analysis of variances. Other factors such as a motivated, trained and experienced workforce are also necessary if superior performance is to be achieved.

**Solutions to problems**

**1 Smith & Son Ltd**

| | | | |
|---|---|---|---|
| Budgeted sales revenue | = 6 000 units × £4.80/unit | = | £28 800 |
| Actual sales revenue | = 6 400 units × £4.40/unit | = | £28 160 |
| (a) Total sales variance | = | (unfavourable) | £640 |

(b) Volume variance = increase in volume × budget price
= + 400 units × £4.80/unit = +£1 920

Price variance = fall in price × actual volume
= −£0.40/unit × 6 400 units = −£2 560

Total sales variance = −£640

**2 Monty and Winston Ltd**

| | Budget (£'000s) | Flexible budget (£'000s) | Actual (£'000s) |
|---|---|---|---|
| (a) Sales revenue | 1 800 | 1 341 | 1 475 |
| Variable expenses | 1 200 | 894 | |
| Contribution | 600 | 447 | |
| Fixed expenses | 425 | 425 | |
| Operating profit | 175 | 22 | |

(b) Sales price variance:
= (actual − budgeted price) × actual volume
= (1.10 − 1.00) × 1 341
= +134

Sales contribution variance:
= (actual − budget volume) × budgeted contribution
= (1 341 − 1 800) × ⅓
= −459 × ⅓
= −153

(c) The main problem on sales is evidently the drop in actual volume versus budget; and one might ask to what extent this stems from the 10% increase in selling price.

**Chapter 10**

**Answers to review questions**

1 By negotiation.
2 To be clear and to get across key messages.
3 Acronyms save space, but readers may not know what they all stand for.
4 To help remind readers who are not experts.
5 To remind old readers and to inform new ones.
6 To avoid spurious accuracy, and to help communication.
7 To support and maintain the system of responsibility accounting.
8 Make the numbers slightly smaller, and leave a gap every five lines.
9 Pie-charts; bar-charts; and graphs.
10 Perhaps because they are easier to label directly and legibly.
11 By implying a faster rate of increase than occurred, especially by not starting at zero.
12 When reporting rates of change.
13 The importance of the data, and management's potential for taking action.
14 Inflation means that HC accounts understate the 'cost' of fixed assets and depreciation thereon; and ignore losses/gains on net monetary assets/liabilities.
15 By indexing money amounts by the Retail Prices Index; and thus translating money amounts into 'real' terms, and allowing sensible comparisons over time.

# Bibliography

## Works cited

Chapman, L. (1979), *Your Disobedient Servant*, Penguin, p. 43.

Ehrenberg, A.S.C. (1982), *A Primer in Data Reduction*, Wiley, p. 227.

Ho, S.S.M. and Pike, R.H. (1991), 'Risk Analysis in Capital Budgeting Contexts: Simple or Sophisticated?', *Accounting and Business Research*, no. 83, Summer, pp. 227–38.

Hopwood, A.G. (1974), *Accounting and Human Behaviour*, Haymarket.

Jackson, D. (1982), *Introduction to Economics: Theory and data*, Macmillan, p. 304 [drawing on C.F. Pratten and other authors].

Kennedy, P. (1988), *The Rise and Fall of the Great Powers*, Unwin Hyman, p. 354.

Kerremans, M., Theunisse, H. and Overloop, G. van (1991), 'Impact of automation on cost accounting', *Accounting and Business Research*, no. 82, Spring.

Myddelton, D.R. (1984), *On a Cloth Untrue*, Woodhead-Faulkner, pp. 123–4.

Pike, R.H. and Wolfe, M. (1988), *Management Accounting*, October, pp. 28–30.

Tomkins, R. (1991), *Financial Times*, 21 June.

Vancil, R. (1979), *Decentralisation: Ambiguity by design*, Irwin.

## General

Amey, L.R. and Egginton, D.A. (1973), *Management Accounting: A conceptual approach*, Longman.

Anthony, R.N. (1988), *The Management Control Function*, Harvard Business School Press.

Anthony, R.N. and Young, W.W. (1988), *Management Control in Nonprofit Organisations*, Irwin, 4th edn.

Beer, S. (1971), *Brain of the Firm*, Penguin.

Benston, G.J. (ed.) (1977), *Contemporary Cost Accounting and Control*, Dickenson, 2nd edn.

Bruns, W.J. Jr and Kaplan, R.S. (eds) (1987), *Accounting and Management: Field study perspectives*, Harvard Business School.

Caplan, E.H. (1971), *Management Accounting and Behavioural Science*, Addison-Wesley.

Cyert, R.M. and March, J.G. (1963), *A Behavioural Theory of the Firm*, Prentice Hall.

Handy, C.B. (1976), *Understanding Organisations*, Penguin.

Johnson, H.T. and Kaplan, R.S. (1987), *Relevance Lost: The rise and fall of management accounting*, Harvard Business School.

McClelland, D.C. (1961), *The Achieving Society*, Van Nostrand.

McGregor, D. (1961), *The Human Side of Enterprise*, McGraw-Hill.

Maslow, A.H. (1954), *Motivation and Personality*, Harper & Row.

Mintzberg, H. (1973), *The Nature of Managerial Work*, Harper & Row.

Pendlebury, M.W. (ed.) (1989), *Management Accounting in the Public Sector*, Heinemann.

Pickering, J.F. and Cockerill, T.A.J. (eds) (1984), *The Economic Management of the Firm*, Philip Allan.

Pugh, D.S. (ed.) (1971), *Organisational Theory: Selected readings*, Penguin.

Scapens, R.W. (1991), *Management Accounting: A review of recent developments*, Macmillan, 2nd edn.

Scapens, R.W., Otley, D.T. and Lister, R.J. (1984), *Management Accounting, Organisational Theory and Capital Budgeting*, Macmillan.

Schiff, M. and Lewin, A.Y. (eds) (1974), *Behavioural Aspects of Accounting*, Prentice Hall.

Sizer, J. (ed.) (1980), *Readings in Management Accounting*, Penguin.

## 1. Accounting, planning and control

Anthony, R.N. (1965), *Planning and Control Systems: A framework for analysis*, Irwin.

Anthony, R.N., Dearden, J. and Bedford, N.M. (1989), *Management Control Systems*, Irwin, 6th edn.

Argenti, J. (1976), *Corporate Collapse: The causes and symptoms*, McGraw-Hill.

Emmanuel, C., Otley, D. and Merchant, K. (1990), *Accounting for Management Control*, Chapman & Hall, 2nd ed'.

Lowe, E.A. and Machin, J.L.F. (1983), *New Perspectives in Management Control*, Macmillan.

Reid, W. and Myddelton, D.R. (1988), *The Meaning of Company Accounts*, Gower, 4th edn.

## 2. The nature of costs

Buchanan, J.M. (1969), *Cost and Choice*, Chicago University Press.

Buchanan, J. and Thirlby, G.F. (eds) (1973), *LSE Essays on Cost*, Weidenfeld & Nicolson.

Coase, R.H. (1988), *The Firm, the Market and the Law*, Chicago University Press.

HMSO (1978), *A Review of Monopolies and Mergers Policy*, Annex C: 'Economies of scale and learning effects'.

Lewis, W.A. (1949), *Overhead Costs*, Unwin.

Pratten, C.F. (1971), *Economies of Scale in Manufacturing Industry*, Cambridge University Press.

## 3. Product costing

Anton, H.R. and Firmin, P.A. (eds) (1978), *Contemporary Issues in Cost and Managerial Accounting*, Houghton Miflin, 3rd edn.

Dearden, J. (1973), *Cost Accounting and Financial Control Systems*, Addison-Wesley.

Horngren, C.T. (1982), *Cost Accounting*, Prentice Hall, 5th edn.

Solomons, D. (ed.) (1968), *Studies in Cost Analysis*, Sweet & Maxwell, 2nd edn.

Taylor, W.B. (1980), *The Management of Assets: Terotechnology in the pursuit of economic life cycle costs*, ICMA.

## 4. Costs and revenues

Gabor, A. (1977), *Pricing, Principles and Practice*, Heinemann.

Hague, D.C. (1971), *Pricing in Business*, Unwin.

Townsend H. (ed.) (1971), *Price Theory*, Penguin, 2nd edn.

## 5. Decentralized management

Geneen, H.S. (1985), *Managing*, Granada.

Goold, M. and Campbell, A. (1987), *Strategies and Styles*, Blackwell.

Jay, A. (1967), *Management and Machiavelli*, Hodder & Stoughton.

Kotter, J.P. (1982), *The General Managers*, Free Press.

Marsh, P. (1990), *Short-termism on Trial*, International Fund Managers Association.

Solomons, D. (1965), *Divisional Performance: Measurement and control*, Irwin.

Tomkins, C. (1973), *Financial Planning in Divisionalised Companies*, Haymarket.

Vancil, R. (1979), *Decentralisation: Ambiguity by design*, Irwin.

Verlage, H.C. (1975), *Transfer Prices for Multinational Enterprises*, Rotterdam University Press.

Vroom, V.H. and Deci, E.L. (eds) (1970), *Management and Motivation*, Penguin.

## 6. Making decisions

Arnold, J. and Hope, T. (1990), *Accounting for Management Decisions*, Prentice Hall, 2nd edn.

Carsberg, B. (1975), *Economics of Business Decisions*, Penguin.

Loasby, B.J. (1976), *Choice, Competition and Ignorance*, Cambridge University Press.

Mishan, E.J. (1971), *Cost Benefit Analysis*, George Allen & Unwin.

Pettigrew, A.M. (1973), *The Politics of Organisational Decision-Making*, Tavistock.

Staubus, G.J. (1988), *Activity Costing for Decisions*, Garland.

## 7. Capital investment decisions

Bierman, H. and Schmidt, S.C. (1975), *The Capital Budgeting Decision*, Macmillan, 4th edn.

Bower, J.L. (1970), *Managing the Resource Allocation Process*, Irwin.

Bromwich, M. (1976), *The Economics of Capital Budgeting*, Penguin.

Clarke, G., Wilson, B., Daines, R.H. and Nadauld, S.D. (1988), *Strategic Financial Management*, Irwin.

Dean, J. (1951), *Capital Budgeting*, Columbia.
Tomkins, C. (1991), *Corporate Resource Allocation*, Blackwell.

## 8. Budgets

Berne, E. (1964), *Games People Play*, André Deutsch.
Chapman, L. (1978), *Your Disobedient Servant*, Penguin.
Hofstede, G.H. (1968), *The Game of Budget Control*, Tavistock.
Hopwood, A.G. (1974), *Accounting and Human Behaviour*, Haymarket.
Machin, J.L.J. (1980), *The Expectations Approach*, McGraw-Hill.
Stedry, A.C. (1960), *Budget Control and Cost Behaviour*, Prentice Hall.

Vatter, W.J. (1969), *Operating Budgets*, Wadsworth.
Wildavsky, Λ. (1975), *Budgeting: Λ comparative theory of the budgeting process*, Little Brown.

## 9. Variance analysis

Laidler, E. (1985), *Variance Analysis*, CIMA, Macmillan.

## 10. Presentation and communication

Ehrenberg, A.S.C. (1975), *Data Reduction*, Wiley.
Ehrenberg, A.S.C. (1982), *A Primer in Data Reduction*, Wiley.
Morgenstern, O. (1963), *On the Accuracy of Economic Observations*, Princeton, 2nd edn.

# Index